CATALOGUE OF GREEK COINS SICILY

CATALOGUE OF GREEK COINS SICILY

EDGAR THURSTON

GYAN

Published by

GYAN

Gyan Publishing House
5, Ansari Road
Daryaganj, New Delhi-110002
Phone: 011-47034999, 9811692060
E-mail: books@gyanbooks.com

Distribution Network
gyanbooks.com
India, USA, Canada, UK, Australia

ISBN: 978-93-3301-721-3 (PB)

First Published, 1896

2nd Impression 2026

Printed at: Gyan Press, Delhi.

CATALOGUE OF GREEK COINS SICILY
Author: EDGAR THURSTON

A CATALOGUE

OF

THE GREEK COINS

IN

THE BRITISH MUSEUM.

SICILY.

LONDON:
PRINTED BY ORDER OF THE TRUSTEES.
LONGMANS & CO., PATERNOSTER ROW;
B. M. PICKERING, 196, PICCADILLY; B. QUARITCH, 15, PICCADILLY; AND
A. ASHER & CO., 13, BEDFORD STREET, COVENT GARDEN, AND AT BERLIN.
PARIS: MM. C. ROLLIN & FEUARDENT, 4, PLACE LOUVOIS.

CATALOGUE OF GREEK COINS.

SICILY.

EDITED BY

REGINALD STUART POOLE.

SYRACUSE, BY BARCLAY V. HEAD.

THE OTHER CITIES OF SICILY, BY PERCY GARDNER, M.A.

SICULO-PUNIC CLASS AND LIPARA, BY THE EDITOR.

LONDON:

PRINTED BY ORDER OF THE TRUSTEES.

1876.

PREFACE.

In the following Catalogue, the coins of each city have been classified under the Periods to which they have appeared to belong, from various indications afforded by a comparison of their style of art with that of other Sicilian coins of which the dates have been ascertained.

It has, however, been thought unadvisable to furnish precise dates for the commencement and the termination of the several Periods, which have been accordingly specified in general terms as (i.) Of Archaic Art. (ii.) Of Transition. (iii.) Of Finest Art. (iv.) Of Decline; early. (v.) Of Decline; late. (vi.) Of Roman Dominion. Under each city, except Syracuse, the coins of the three metals are separately described; in many instances it has been, therefore, necessary to repeat the chronological arrangement.

The coins of Syracuse, on account of the extent and importance of the series, have been classified in a manner somewhat more elaborate than that which has been thought best in the case of the other cities. The order adopted by Mr. B. V. Head, in his "Chronological Sequence of the Coins of Syracuse," London, 8vo, 1874, has been here selected as being that which is now generally accepted by Numismatists, and references to Mr. Head's plates representing the Museum examples have been added to the descriptions of all such types as are not engraved in the present work.

Throughout the Syracusan Series the division into Periods as specified above has been retained, while at the same time a more precise method of classification according to dates has been found practicable; so that, in the case of Syracuse, the several Periods are made to coincide with the following dates:—

(i.) Period of Archaic Art, from the latter part of 6th cent.—B.C. 479.
(ii.) Period of Transition, from B.C. 479—412.
(iii.) Period of Finest Art, from B.C. 412—345.
(iv.) Period of Decline; early, from B.C. 345—275.
(v.) Period of Decline; late, from B.C. 275—212.
(vi.) Period of Roman Dominion, from B.C. 212.

These dates may doubtless be taken as indicating in a general manner the duration of the Periods of Art throughout the Island, with the single exception of that of the Roman Dominion, which over the greater part of Sicily began at an earlier date than at Syracuse.

For the attributions of several coins, among which may be mentioned those of Piacus, Mytistratus, &c., I am indebted to Dr. Imhoof-Blumer, of Winterthur, Switzerland.

In the Siculo-Punic class only such coins have been included as bear either the names or the types of Sicilian cities, the remainder being too closely connected with the purely Carthaginian series to be separated from it with advantage. In like manner the coins of the islands, those of Lipara and Sardinia excepted, have been relegated to the Punic Series.

In the case of Lipara it has been considered inexpedient to follow the same system of classification as has been adopted in Sicily, the coins of that island not affording sufficient indications of the epochs at which they were issued; they have, therefore, been simply divided into classes according to the types which they bear, the sequence of these classes being generally, though probably not in every case, chronological.

The metal of each coin and its size is stated in inches and tenths. The weight is given in English grains of all gold and silver coins, and of all copper coins bearing marks of value. Tables for converting grains into grammes, and inches into millimètres as well as into the measures of Mionnet's Scale, are placed at the end of the volume (pp. 290–292).

REGINALD STUART POOLE.

British Museum,
May, 1876.

CONTENTS.

SICILY.

No.	Wt.	Metal. Size.	Obverse.	Reverse.
			ABACAENUM.	
			SILVER.	
			Period of Transition.	
1	11·3	Æ ·5	ABAKA I Bearded male head r., hair in bunch behind: plain border.	ΛΟΝΛΙΛ (in ex) Boar r., r. fore-leg bent: border of dots.
2	12·	Æ ·55	Bearded male head r., bound with wreath, hair in bunch behind: border of dots.	ΛΙΑΚ ABA Boar standing r.; in front, acorn: plain border.
3	8·8	Æ ·5	A B Similar.	I A I Λ Similar; no acorn.
4	10·	Æ ·5	ABAK Similar.	AI Ν I Boar standing r.; above, barleycorn.
			Period of Finest Art.	
5	12·8	Æ ·45	Bearded head r., hair short: border of dots.	ABA Boar standing r.; in front, acorn.
6	9·3	Æ ·45	Head of water-nymph, three-quarter face l.: border of dots.	ABA Sow walking l.; at her feet, pig l.

No.	Wt.	Metal. Size.	Obverse.	Reverse.
7	9·9	AR ·45	Same. (Same die.)	Same. (Same die.)
8	12·7	AR ·45	Similar.	BA A Similar type r.

COPPER.

No.	Wt.	Metal. Size.	Obverse.	Reverse.
9		Æ ·8	Female head r., wearing ear-ring and sphendone; behind, barley-corn: border of dots.	ABAK NON Fore-part of man-headed bull swimming r.: border of dots.
10		Æ ·8	Similar.	Similar.
11		Æ ·7	Female head r., wearing ear-ring, necklace, and sphendone: border of dots.	ABAKA I NI NΩN Fore-part of bull butting l.: border of dots.
12		Æ ·55	Similar type l.: same border.	ABAKAINI N Similar.

Period of Decline; late.

No.	Wt.	Metal. Size.	Obverse.	Reverse.
13		Æ ·85	Head of Apollo? r., laur.	ABAKAJ N IN Bull walking r.: border of dots.

ACRAE.

COPPER.

Period of Decline; late.

No.	Wt.	Metal. Size.	Obverse.	Reverse.
1		Æ ·8	Head of Persephone r., hair rolled and bound with ears of barley: border of dots.	AKA IΩN Demeter l., veiled, wearing long chiton and peplos; holds torch and sceptre: border of dots.
2		Æ ·8	Same.	Same.

No.	Wt.	Metal. Size.	Obverse.	Reverse.

ADRANUM.

COPPER.

Period of Decline; early.

No.	Wt.	Metal. Size.	Obverse.	Reverse.
1		Æ ·9	Head of Apollo l., laur.: border of dots.	Α ΔΡΑΝ ΙΤΑΝ Lyre of seven strings: border of dots.
2		Æ 1·	Same.	Same.
3		Æ ·85	Head of young river-god l., with short horns, wearing tainia: border of dots.	IИ AϤΔA TAN Bull butting r.: border of dots.

ADRANUM?

COPPER.

Period of Decline; early.

No.	Wt.	Metal. Size.	Obverse.	Reverse.
1		Æ 1·25	Head of Apollo l., laur.; beneath neck, ΑΠΟΛ: plain border.	Lyre of seven strings: plain border.
2		Æ 1·3	Similar.	Similar.

(The above two coins are restruck on coins of Syracuse: Obv., Head of Pallas. Rev., Star-fish between dolphins.)

No.	Wt.	Metal. Size.	Obverse.	Reverse.
3		Æ ·8	Head of Apollo l., laur., hair short.	Lyre of seven strings: border of dots.

(Restruck on a coin of Morgantia: Obv., Head of Helios. Rev., Tripod.)

No.	Wt.	Metal. Size.	Obverse.	Reverse.
4		Æ1·25	Head of Sikelia ? l., wearing myrtle-wreath and sphendone.	Lyre.

(Restruck on a coin of Syracuse: Obv., Head of Pallas. Rev., Star-fish between dolphins.)

AETNA.

COPPER.

Period of Decline; late.

With marks of value.

Trias.

No.	Wt.	Metal. Size.	Obverse.	Reverse.
1	68·	Æ ·8	Bust of Apollo r., radiate, and wearing chlamys: border of dots.	ΑΙΤΝΑΙ ΩΝ Warrior facing, head l., wearing helmet and tunic; holds spear and shield; in field l., ⁝ : plain border.
2	95·	Æ ·7	Similar.	ΑΙΤΝ ΑΙΩΝ Similar, but warrior looks r.
3	90·	Æ ·8	Similar.	Similar.
4	69·	Æ ·85	Similar.	Similar.
5	82·	Æ ·8	Similar.	ΑΙΤΝΑΙ ΩΝ Similar type and same border; marks of value in field r.
6	46·	Æ ·7	Similar.	ΑΙΤΝ ΑΙΩΝ Similar.

No.	Wt.	Metal. Size.	Obverse.	Reverse.
			Hexas.	
7	39·	Æ ·6	Head of Persephone r., wearing wreath of barley: border of dots.	AIT N AIΩN Cornucopiæ, filleted; in field l., ⁚.
8	46·	Æ ·6	Similar.	AITNA ΩN Similar type; in field r., marks of value: plain border.
9	44·	Æ ·55	Similar type.	N AIΩN Similar type.

[For coins of the earlier Aetna see under Catana, p. 43.]

AGRIGENTUM.

GOLD.

Period of Finest Art.

With marks of value.

No.	Wt.	Metal. Size.	Obverse.	Reverse.
1	20·4	AV ·4	AKP Eagle, with wings closed, standing l. on rocks, devouring serpent which he holds in his talons; beneath, ●●: plain border.	Crab; beneath, ƸIΛA ƸOVV: plain border.
2	19·5	AV ·4	Same. (Same die.)	Same. (Same die.)

SILVER.

Period of Archaic Art.

No.	Wt.	Metal. Size.	Obverse.	Reverse.
3	129·5	AR ·95	AKRAC ƸOTVVA Eagle, with wings closed, standing l.	Crab.

No.	Wt.	Metal. Size.	Obverse.	Reverse.
4	133·1	Æ ·95	Similar.	Similar.
5	136·9	Æ ·95	AKRAC ANTOS Similar type: plain border.	Similar.
6	131·3	Æ ·8	AKRA CANT Similar type.	Similar.
7	129·6	Æ ·95	ƎOTИA ƆAЯꓘA Similar type.	Similar.
8	130·4	Æ ·85	Similar.	Similar.
9	136·	Æ ·9	[ƎOT]VA ƆAЯꓘA (*sic.*) Similar type.	Similar.
10	125·1	Æ ·9	Same. (Same die.)	Same. (Same die.)
11	130·1	Æ ·75	AKRA Eagle, with closed wings, standing l.	Crab.
12	129·5	Æ ·7	Similar.	Similar.
13	134·	Æ ·8	AKRA Similar.	Crab.
14	138·4	Æ ·8	AKRA Similar.	Similar.
15	135·3	Æ ·8	Similar.	Similar type; beneath, E V.
16	135·4	Æ ·85	Similar.	Similar.
17	135·5	Æ ·85	AK RA Similar.	Crab.
18	128·2	Æ ·8	Similar.	Similar.
19	132·9	Æ ·75	Same inscr. Eagle, with closed wings, standing r.	Similar.
20	131·7	Æ ·8	AK AЯ Similar.	Similar.
21	136·5	Æ ·8	AKRA ƎAƆ Similar type l.	Similar.
22	132·4	Æ ·8	AЯꓘA AƎ Similar type r.	Similar.

No.	Wt.	Metal. Size.	Obverse.	Reverse.
23	130·4	Æ ·7	AЯKA ꟽA) Similar type l.	Similar.
24	129·9	Æ ·8	AKRA CAN Similar.	Similar.
25	136·3	Æ ·8	AKRACA ƐOTꟽ Similar.	Similar type; beneath, A+Ǝ.
26	131·3	Æ ·8	AKRA Similar type.	Similar type; beneath, barley-corn.
27	129·9	Æ ·8	AK RA Similar type r.	Similar.
28	117·2	Æ ·75	Similar type l.; in place of inscr., an illegible *graffito*.	Similar type; beneath, eagle l.
29	132·5	Æ ·75	AK RA Similar.	Similar type; beneath, young male head r.
30	134·1	Æ ·8	ЯK A A Eagle, with closed wings, standing r.: plain border.	Similar.
31	131·2	Æ ·7	No inscr. visible. Similar type l.	Similar; beneath, Corinthian helmet without crest l.
32	133·6	Æ ·8	AK R A Eagle, with closed wings, standing r. on rock.	Similar; beneath, A.
33	133·5	Æ ·75	AK RA Eagle, with closed wings, standing l.	CAΣ Crab.
34	128·3	Æ ·85	AK AЯ Similar type r.	Similar.
35	134·1	Æ ·8	ЯK A A Similar type: plain border. (Same die as no. 30.)	Similar. (Same die as last but one.)
36	132·5	Æ ·85	AK RA Similar type.	CA Σ Crab; beneath, young male head r., diademed.

No.	Wt.	Metal. Size.	Obverse.	Reverse.
			Period of Transition.	
37	258·1	Æ 1·05	ΑΚRΑϹ ΑΝΤΟΣ Eagle, with closed wings, standing l.	Crab.
38	267·	Æ 1·	ΑΚRΑϹ ΣΟΤΝΑ Eagle, with closed wings, standing l. on line of dots.	Crab.

No.	Wt.	Metal. Size.	Obverse.	Reverse.
39	267·	Æ ·95	Similar.	Similar.
40	271·9	Æ ·9	Similar.	Crab; beneath, barleycorn.
41	267·9	Æ 1·	Similar.	Similar; beneath, dolphin r., inverted.
42	269·3	Æ ·95	Similar.	Similar; beneath, rose, on either side of which, spray.
43	268·2	Æ ·95	ΑΚRΑϹ ΑΝ ΤΟΣ Similar.	Similar.
44	251·3	Æ ·9	ΑΚRΑϹ ΣΟΤΝΑ Eagle, with closed wings, standing l. on capital of Ionic column (meta).	Crab.
45	265·7	Æ ·95	ΑΚΡΑ ΣΟΤΝΑϽ Similar type: border of dots.	Crab; above, Φ; beneath, rose having two sprays on either side.
46	268·7	Æ 1·	ΑΚRΑϹ ΣΟΤΝΑ Similar type.	Crab; beneath, spray in the shape of two volutes, one curled upwards, the other downwards.

No.	Wt.	Metal. Size.	Obverse.	Reverse.
47	65·6	Æ ·6	ΓΕΝ Eagle, with closed wings, standing l. on Corinthian capital: cable-border.	ΜΙΛ Crab.
48	13·6	Æ ·45	ΑΚ ΑЯ Eagle, with closed wings, standing l. on Corinthian capital: border of dots.	Crab; beneath, rose.
49	13·7	Æ ·45	Similar.	Similar.
50	12·1	Æ ·35	Similar.	Similar type; beneath, Λ Ι.
51	7·9	Æ ·4	Similar.	Similar.
52	8·7	Æ ·4	Similar.	Similar type; beneath, ΊΛΙ ?
			Period of Finest Art.	
53	258·6	Æ 1·05	Α TINON Two eagles standing r. on supine hare, which lies on rocks; the farther, with spread wings, about to tear the prey; the nearer, with closed wings, raising its head and screaming.	Quadriga r., driven by youth holding reins in both hands and goad in r.; horses in high action, the rein of the farthest broken and hanging down; above, Nike flying l., crowning charioteer; below, ΜΥ[Ρ]; in ex., Skylla r., her l. hand raised.
54	267·4	Æ 1·05	ΑΚΡΑΓΑΝΤΙΝΟΝ Similar type; in field l., fly.	Same. (Same die.)

No.	Wt.	Metal. Size.	Obverse.	Reverse.
55	266·1	AR 1·1	Similar type; in field l. ƐΙΛΑ.	ΑΚΡΑΓ ИΙΤИΑ on tablet fixed up by nail; to l. (end of inscr.) ΛΟ. Quadriga l., driven by Nike, who holds goad in r. and reins in l.; horses in high action, the rein of the farthest broken and hanging down; in ex., club l.: border of dots.

56	225·1	AR 1· plated?	Similar type; in field l., lion's head l., mouth open.	Similar.
57	271·2	AR 1·1	Ч ΩЧ ΙΤЧΑ ˥ Similar type.	Quadriga r., driven by draped female? figure, holding reins in both hands; above, Nike flying l., crowning charioteer; in ex., crab upside-down: border of dots.

No.	Wt.	Metal. Size.	Obverse.	Reverse.
58	267·8	AR 1·1	Similar type l.; above, ΣΤΡΑΤΩΝ; behind, horned head of young river-god r.	ΑΚΡΑΓΑΝΤΙ ΝΟΝ (in ex.) Quadriga l., driven by Nike, who holds reins in both hands and goad in l.; above, vine-branch, with leaves and fruit: border of dots.

59	269·6	AR 1·1	ΑΚΡΑΓ ΑΝΤΙΝ Ο Ν Eagle, with wings spread, standing l. on supine hare and devouring it; supporting the hare, a rock, on which, barleycorn? and scallop-shell: border of dots.	Crab, and broad sea-fish l., with open mouth and spines along its back; on either side of crab, scallop-shell and conch?

60	238·7	AR 1·1	Same. (Same die.)	Same. (Same die.)

No.	Wt.	Metal. Size.	Obverse.	Reverse.
61	266·7	Ʀ 1·	ΑΓΑ Two eagles standing r. on supine hare; the farther, with spread wings, about to tear the prey; the nearer, with closed wings, raising its head and screaming: border of dots.	ΑΚΡΑ ΝΤ ΙΝΟΝ Crab, and Skylla l., her r. hand to her head, the l. round neck of one of the dogs.

62	62·9	Ʀ ·8	Similar type l.: border of dots between two plain borders.	ΑΚΡ ΓΑΝ Crab, the shell of which presents the form of a human face, and cray-fish r.; on either side of crab, barleycorn and cicada r. upwards.

63	30·9	Ʀ ·6	Eagle standing r., with spread wings, on supine hare, about to tear it; behind eagle, barleycorn. (Double-struck.)	Α Ν Crab, and pistrix l., holding fish in its mouth.
64	30·8	Ʀ ·65	Eagle standing as above on supine colt; behind eagle, barleycorn: border of dots.	Α Ρ Α Similar types, but pistrix r.

No.	Wt.	Metal. Size.	Obverse.	Reverse.
65	29·8	Æ ·65	Eagle standing as above l. on supine hare: same border.	A K A R Crab, and tunny-fish l.
66	30·6	Æ ·7	AK RA Similar.	Similar types.
67	33·1	Æ ·65	RA Similar type: plain? border.	A A R Similar.
68	32·6	Æ ·65	No inscr. Similar type: border of dots.	A ЯꓘA Crab, and tunny-fish r.
69	30·9	Æ ·6	Similar.	KRA Similar.
70	31·9	Æ ·65	Similar type r.: same border.	ꓘA Similar.
71	32·4	Æ ·7	Similar.	AKRA Similar.
72	11·	Æ ·5	AKPA Eagle standing l., with closed wings, on rocks, attacking with its beak serpent which it holds in its talons: plain border.	Crab; beneath, A: plain border.
73	10·9	Æ ·5	AKPAΓANTINON Two eagles standing r. on supine hare; the farther, with spread wings, about to tear the prey; the nearer, with closed wings, raising its head and screaming: plain border.	A Crab, and broad sea-fish r., with open mouth and row of spines along its back: plain border.
74	11·4	Æ ·5	Same. (Same die.)	Same. (Same die.)

Period of Decline; early.

No.	Wt.	Metal. Size.	Obverse.	Reverse.
75	32·4	Æ ·55	Free horse, cantering, r.	Crab; beneath, pellet.
76	25·5	Æ ·55	Similar type; above, star.	Similar type; above, M.
77	18·7	Æ ·45	Head of Zeus, laur., l.; behind, Δ.	AKPAΓA NTINΩN Eagle, with spread wings, standing r.

No.	Wt.	Metal. Size.	Obverse.	Reverse.
78	13·4	AR ·45	Similar type; beneath, **Μ**.	Similar.

No.	Wt.	Metal. Size.	Obverse.	Reverse.
79	10·5	AR ·4	Bearded head of river-god r. (Hypsas or Akragas), with short horn, wearing wreath of reeds.	**ΑΚΡΑΓΑΝΤ Ι ΝΩΝ** Eagle, with spread wings, standing r. and looking back.
80	8·3	AR ·45	Similar type; beneath, **Μ**.	Similar. (Much defaced.)

Period of Decline; late.

No.	Wt.	Metal. Size.	Obverse.	Reverse.
81	56·	AR ·75	Head of Zeus r., laur.: border of dots.	**ΑΚΡΑΓ ΑΝΤΙΝ** Eagle, with spread wings, standing r.; in field r., **Α**: plain border.
82	53·3	AR ·7	Similar.	**ΑΚΡΑΓΑΝ ΤΙΝΩΝ** Similar type and same border; in field r., **Ε**.
83	50·	AR ·75	Similar.	Similar; in field r., **Σ**.

No.	Wt.	Metal. Size.	Obverse.	Reverse.
84	57·7	AR ·8	Similar; behind head, **ΦΙ**.	**ΑΚΡΑΓΑΝΤΙ ΝΩΝ** Similar type l.; in field l., **Τ Φ Ι**: plain border.
85	25·8	AR ·6	Similar type and same border.	**ΑΚΡΑΓΑ Ν Τ ΙΝΩΝ** Similar type r.; in field r., **Α**: plain border.

COPPER.

Period of Finest Art.

With marks of value.

Hemilitron.

No.	Wt.	Metal. Size.	Obverse.	Reverse.
86	341·	Æ1·1	ΑΚ ΡΑΓΑΝ ΙΝΟΝ Eagle, with wings spread, r., holding in its claws tunny-fish, and throwing back its head and screaming: border of dots.	Crab, holding in l. claw eel; beneath, conch and cuttle-fish; around, ●●●●●●.
87	320·	Æ1·1	Similar.	Same. (Same die.)
88	277·	Æ1·05	ΑΚ? Eagle, with spread wings, r.; holds in its claws hare? which it attacks with its beak.	Crab, holding in l. claw eel; beneath, cuttle-fish and conch; around, marks of value (five visible).
89	359·	Æ1·1	Eagle, with spread wings, r.; holds in its claws supine hare l., and throws back its head and screams; in field r., cicada: plain border.	Crab; beneath, Triton r., holding conch with both hands and blowing into it; around, marks of value.
90	316·	Æ1·05	Similar type l.; in field l., cicada.	Similar (three marks of value visible).
91	344·	Æ1·05	Α Κ ΡΑΓΑΝ ΤΙΝΟΝ Eagle, with spread wings, r.; holds in its claws tunny-fish, and throws back its head and screams: border of dots.	Similar (five marks of value visible).
92	301·	Æ1·15	No inscr. Eagle, with wings spread, r.; holds in its claws a supine hare, which it attacks with its beak: plain border.	Crab; beneath, pistrix r.; on either side, ●●●●●●.
93	233·	Æ1·1	Similar type.	Similar type; beneath, sea-horse r. (four marks of value visible).

No.	Wt.	Metal. Size.	Obverse.	Reverse.
94	272·	Æ1·1	Similar type l.: border of dots.	Crab, holding in l. claw eel? beneath, sea-horse l.; marks of value doubtful.
95	209·	Æ1·05	Similar type r.: same border.	Similar types; above and below, ●●● ●●●.
96	342·	Æ1·25	Similar type: same border.	Crab; beneath, cray-fish l. and scallop-shell; around, ●●●●●●.
97	255·	Æ1·05	Similar type: same border.	Crab; beneath, scallop and another shell and cray-fish l.; around crab, marks of value (four visible).
98	216·	Æ1·1	A ꓶAЯꓘ Eagle, with wings spread, r.; holds in its claws inverted fish, and raises its head: plain border.	Crab; beneath, cray-fish l.; above, conch; around, marks of value (two visible).
99	272·	Æ1·1	AK PA Eagle, with wings spread, r.; holds in its claws supine hare, which it attacks with its beak: plain border.	Crab; beneath, cray-fish l.; above, marks of value (five visible).
100	294·	Æ1·25	Similar type: border of dots.	Similar types; above, fig-leaf; on either side, marks of value.
101	205·	Æ1·	Eagle, with wings spread, r.; holds in its claws tunny-fish, and raises its head and screams.	Similar types; same symbol; around, marks of value (five visible).

(Some of the above coins may be of a lower denomination, the marks of value usually being obscure.)

Trias.

No.	Wt.	Metal. Size.	Obverse.	Reverse.
102	161·	Æ ·85	AK PA Eagle, with spread wings, r., holding supine hare in its claws, and attacking it with its beak: border of dots.	Crab; beneath, cray-fish l.; between the two, ●●●.

No.	Wt.	Metal. Size.	Obverse.	Reverse.
103	93·	Æ ·8	Similar type.	Similar.
104	60·	Æ ·8	AKPA Similar type: plain border.	Similar.
105	140·	Æ ·8	A ꟼKA Similar type.	Similar.
106	165·	Æ ·8	Similar type: plain border.	Crab; beneath, cray-fish l.; above, fig-leaf; in field r., shell; around, ● ● ●.
			Hexas.	
107	132·	Æ ·75	A P Eagle, with wings spread, r., holding in its claws inverted bird, which it attacks with its beak: plain border.	Crab; beneath, two tunny-fishes l.; on either side, ● [●].
108	117·	Æ ·75	Similar; but eagle holds supine pig.	Crab; beneath, two tunny-fishes r.; on either side, mark of value.
109	111·	Æ ·7	Eagle, with wings spread, r., holding in its claws tunny-fish, which it attacks with its beak: border of dots.	Similar.
110	103·	Æ ·7	A Similar.	Crab; beneath, two tunny-fishes r. and l., passing; on either side, ● [●].
111	113·	Æ ·8	AK Similar type: plain border.	Crab; beneath, perch l.; between the two, ● ●.
			Uncia.	
112	53·	Æ ·7	AK PA Eagle, with wings closed, standing r. on tunny-fish, looking back: plain border.	Crab; beneath, perch r.; above, ●.
113	64·	Æ ·6	Similar, but eagle l.	Similar types; beneath, ●.
114	59·	Æ ·7	Similar.	Similar types; between them, on r., mark of value.

No.	Wt.	Metal. Size.	Obverse.	Reverse.
			Without marks of value.	
115		Æ ·5	Eagle's head, without neck, r.: plain border.	[monogram] Crab: border of dots.
116		Æ ·5	Similar.	Similar.
			Coins of the above class, restruck.	
117		Æ 1·2	Head of young Herakles r., wearing lion's skin, in incuse circle.	Plain.
			(Restruck on a coin resembling no. 94.)	
118		Æ 1·15	Similar.	Same.
			(Restruck on a coin resembling no. 86.)	
119		Æ 1·1	Similar.	Same.
			(Restruck on a coin resembling no. 96; but with fig-leaf above crab.)	
120		Æ 1·15	Similar.	Same.
			(Previous devices defaced.)	
121		Æ ·85	Similar.	ΜΙΚΙΟΝΟΣ in incised letters.
			(Restruck on a coin resembling no. 102.)	
122		Æ 1·05	Head of young river-god r., diademed; behind, barley-corn? plain border: all in incuse circle: behind, in a smaller incuse circle, scallop-shell.	Plain.
			(Previous devices defaced.)	
123		Æ 1·2	Female head r., diademed: plain border: in incuse circle.	Head of young Herakles r., wearing lion's skin? in incuse circle.
			(Restruck on coin resembling no. 90, obv.)	

No.	Wt.	Metal. Size.	Obverse.	Reverse.

Period of Decline; early.

With marks of value.

Hemilitron.

No.	Wt.	Metal. Size.	Obverse.	Reverse.
124	281·	Æ 1·	ΑΚΡΑΓΑΣ Head of young river-god (Akragas or Hypsas) l., diademed, and with short horns: border of dots.	Eagle, standing l. on the capital of an Ionic column (meta) and looking back; in field l., crab; in field r., ●●● ●●●: plain border.
125	279·	Æ ·95	Similar.	Similar.

No.	Wt.	Metal. Size.	Obverse.	Reverse.
126	257·	Æ 1·	Similar.	Similar.
127	257·	Æ 1·	Similar.	Similar. (Marks of value differently arranged, three being visible.)

Without marks of value.

No.	Wt.	Metal. Size.	Obverse.	Reverse.
128		Æ ·75	ΑΚΡΑ ΓΑ Head of Zeus l., laur.: border of dots.	Eagle, with spread wings, l., holding in its claws supine hare, which it attacks with its beak; behind, Δ.
129		Æ ·65	ΑΚΡΑΓΑΣ Similar.	Similar type.
130		Æ ·55	Similar type r.: border of dots.	ΑΚΡΑΓΑΝ ΤΙΝΩΝ Winged thunderbolt: plain border.

No.	Wt.	Metal. Size.	Obverse.	Reverse.
			Phintias tyrant, B.C. cir. 287–279.	
131		Æ ·8	ΑΚΡΑΓΑΝΤΟΣ Head of Apollo l., laur.	ΦΙ Two eagles, standing l. on supine hare, the farther with wings spread, attacking the prey, the nearer throwing back its head and screaming.
132		Æ ·7	Similar type.	Same.
133		Æ ·55	Traces of inscr. Head of Apollo l., laur.: border of dots.	Eagle, standing r., and looking back; above, ΦΙ.

No.	Wt.	Metal. Size.	Obverse.	Reverse.
134		Æ ·55	ΑΚΡΑΓΑΝΤΙ Similar.	Similar.
135		Æ ·8	Head of Persephone l., crowned with barley; behind, ΝΕ: border of dots.	ΒΑΣΙΛΕΟΣ ΦΙΝΤΙΑ Boar, standing at bay, l.
136		Æ ·8	Similar type: same border.	Similar: plain border.
137		Æ ·8	Similar.	Similar.
138		Æ ·8	Head of Artemis l., wearing earring and necklace, hair in a knot behind; behind shoulder, quiver: border of dots.	Similar.
139		Æ ·9	ΣΩΤΕΙΡΑ Similar.	ΦΙΝΤΙΑ ΒΑΣΙΛΕΟΣ Similar.
			Period of Decline; late.	
140		Æ ·8	Head of Apollo r., laur.: border of dots.	Two eagles, standing l. on supine hare, the farther with wings spread, attacking the prey, the nearer throwing back its head and screaming; above, traces of monogram?

No.	Wt.	Metal. Size.	Obverse.	Reverse.
141		Æ ·85	Same.	Similar type; above, HDI: plain border.
142		Æ ·85	Similar type, but crawling over head, serpent; on either side, Λ and A: border of dots.	Similar type: same border.
143		Æ ·95	Similar.	Similar type; above, caduceus: same border.
144		Æ ·85	Similar type, without serpent; behind, Δ.	Similar type; above, A: same border.
145		Æ ·85	Similar type; behind, K: border of dots.	Similar type r.: same border.
146		Æ ·85	ΑΚΡΑΓΑΝΤΙΝΩΝ Young male head r., diademed (Zeus Soter); behind, bunch of grapes: border of dots.	ΔΙΟΣ ΣΩΤΗΡΟΣ Eagle, with closed wings, standing r. on thunderbolt and looking back: border of dots.

147		Æ ·85	Similar.	Similar.
148		Æ ·85	Head of Apollo r., laur.: border of dots.	ΑΚΡΑΓΑΝ ΤΙΝΩΝ Tripod-lebes with neck and three handles: border of dots.
149		Æ ·95	Similar.	Similar.
150		Æ ·95	Similar.	ΑΚΡΑΓΑΝ ΤΙΝΩΝ Naked warrior r., having chlamys wrapped round l. arm, and thrusting with spear: border of dots.
151		Æ ·95	Similar.	Similar.

No.	Wt.	Metal. Size.	Obverse.	Reverse.
152		Æ ·95	Similar.	ΑΓΑΝ ΤΙΝ ΩΝ Similar.
153		Æ ·85	Head of Persephone r., crowned with barley; behind, ΒΩCΙΟC.	ΑΚΡΑΓΑΝ ΤΙ ΝΩΝ Asklepios, facing, clad in himation, extending r. hand.
154		Æ ·85	Similar type; in front, ΑCΚΛΑΠΙΟC; behind, Æ.	Similar.
155		Æ ·9	Head of Zeus r., laur.: border of dots.	ΑΚΡΑΓΑΝΤΙ ΝΩΝ Eagle, with spread wings, facing, head r., on thunderbolt: border of dots.
156		Æ ·95	Similar.	ΑΚΡΑΓΑΝΤΙΝΩΝ Similar.
157		Æ ·75	Head of Asklepios r., laur.: border of dots.	ΑΚΡΑΓΑΝ ΤΙΝΩΝ Serpent twined round staff: border of dots.
158		Æ ·7	Female head r., wearing sakkos? border of dots.	ΑΚΡΑ ΓΑΝΤΙΝΩΝ Tripod-lebes with neck and three handles: plain border.
159		Æ ·7	Similar.	Similar.

Imperial Coinage.

AUGUSTUS.

No.	Wt.	Metal. Size.	Obverse.	Reverse.
160		Æ ·85	AVGVS PP AGRIGETIN (*sic.*) Head of Augustus r., bare: border of dots.	SALASSO COMITIÆ · SEX · REO · IIVR · around; in field, L · CLODIO RVFO PRO · COS

No.	Wt.	Metal. Size.	Obverse.	Reverse.
.61		Æ ·9	AVGVS TO · P·P · AGRI- GENTI Similar type.	Similar; countermarked with boar, r.
162		Æ ·8	Similar.	Similar. (Same countermark.)
163		Æ ·9	Similar.	Similar; countermarked with plough, l.
164		Æ ·8	Similar.	Similar; not countermarked.
165		Æ ·8	INΩN AKPAΓAN Head of Augustus r., bare.	TINΩN AKPAΓAN Head of Agrippa ? r., bare.

Coin-Weights ?

Tetras.

No.	Wt.	Metal. Size.	Description
1	236·	Æ ·65	Piece of metal in the shape of a tooth, with flat base; on one side, eagle l.; on the other, crab, beneath which, A; on base, ⁘.

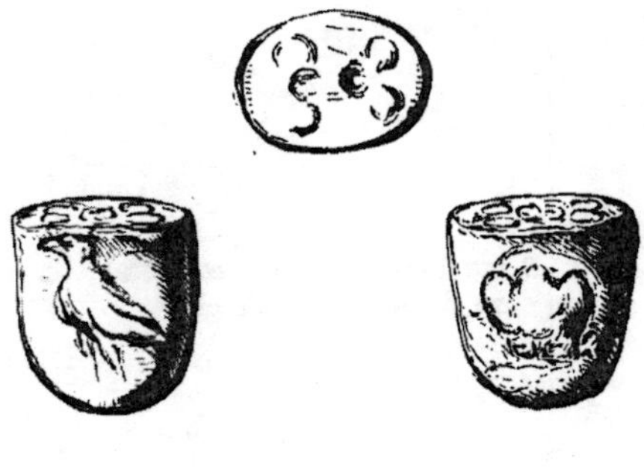

No.	Wt.	Metal. Size.	Description
2	225·	Æ ·7	Similar.

No.	Wt.	Metal. Size.	Obverse.	Reverse.
			Trias.	
3	189·	Æ ·7	Piece of metal of similar shape, but base in the form of a sector of a circle, and so three unequal sides: on the two smaller sides, eagles' heads and necks back to back; beneath the l. hand one, A: on the larger side, crab: on the base, ● ● ●.	

4	188·	Æ ·7	Similar.	
			Hexas.	
5	105·	Æ ·6	Piece of metal in the shape of a tooth, with flat base; on one side, eagle l.; on the other, crab? on base, ● ●.	
			Uncia?	
6	74·	Æ ·7	Almond-shaped piece of metal; on one side, eagle's head l.; on the other, crab's claw.	
			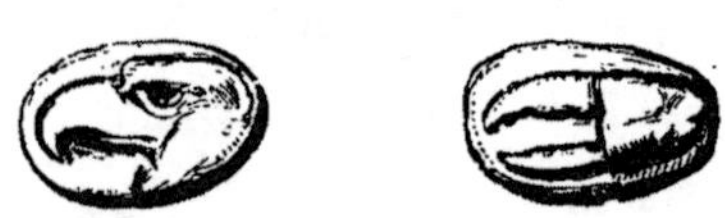	

No.	Wt.	Metal. Size.	Obverse.	Reverse.
			AGYRIUM.	
			COPPER.	
			Period of Finest Art.	
1		Æ ·9	Eagle, with closed wings, r.; behind, spray of olive: border of dots.	ΑΊ ΥΡ ΙΝ ΑΙ Wheel of four spokes, between which, letters of inscr.
2		Æ ·9	Similar.	ΑΓ ΥΡ ΙΝ ΑΙ Similar type.
3		Æ ·7	ΙΝΑΙΟΝ Young male head r., with short hair: (Iolaös?) plain border.	ΠΑΛ ΑΓΚΑΙΟΣ Fore-part of man-headed bull, swimming r.: border of dots.
			Period of Decline; early.	
4		Æ 1·2	Traces of inscr. Head of young Herakles r., wearing lion's skin: plain border.	Fore-part of man-headed bull r.: plain border.
5		Æ 1·2	Fore-part of man-headed bull r.	Man-headed bull r.; above, star of eight rays.
			(These two pieces are restruck on coins of Syracuse. Obv. Head of Pallas; Rev. Dolphins and star-fish.)	
6		Æ 1·1	Head of young Herakles, or Iolaös, r., wearing tainia tied in front, and lion's skin tied round his throat, and falling back on his neck like a hood.	ΑΓΥΡΙΝΑΙΩΝ (in ex.) Leopard r., devouring hare, which lies l.

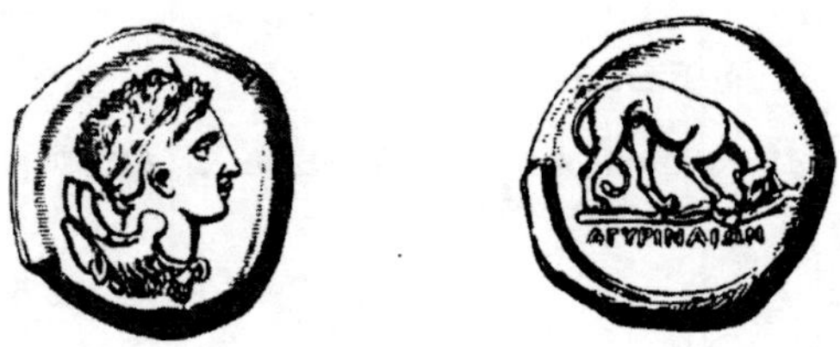

No.	Wt.	Metal. Size.	Obverse.	Reverse.
7		Æ 1·	Head of young river-god r., with short horns, diademed.	ΑΓΥΡΙΝ (in ex.) Bridled horse, trotting r.
8		Æ ·7	Head of Apollo r., laur.; behind shoulder, strung bow.	ΑΓΥΡΙΝΑΙΩΝ (in ex.) Hound r., on the scent.
9		Æ 1·	ΕΥΞΕΛ ΕΥ ΘΕΡΙΟΞ Head of Zeus Eleutherios r., laur.; hair short: plain border.	ΓΥΡΙ ΝΑΙ Thunderbolt erect; in field r., eagle r.: plain border.

No.	Wt.	Metal. Size.	Obverse.	Reverse.
10		Æ 1·	Head of Pallas r., wearing crested helmet.	ΡΙΝΑ Strung bow and club?: plain border.

(Restruck on coin like the preceding or the corresponding coinage of Syracuse.)

Period of Decline; late.

No.	Wt.	Metal. Size.	Obverse.	Reverse.
11		Æ ·85	ΕΠΙ ΣΩΠΑΤΡΟΥ Head of Zeus r., laur.; in front, [monogram]: border of dots.	ΝΑΙΩΝ Male figure l. (Iolaös), wearing short chiton and endromides; holding horn and pedum? behind, Nike, flying l., crowning him; at his feet, hound l., looking up: plain border.
12		Æ ·9	Similar.	ΑΓΥΡΙ ΝΑΙΩΝ Similar.
13		Æ ·75	Head of bearded Herakles r.: border of dots.	ΑΓΥΡΙΝΑΙ ΩΝ Iolaös? r., naked, burning with an iron the necks of the hydra: plain border.

No.	Wt.	Metal. Size.	Obverse.	Reverse.
			ALAESA.	
			COPPER.	
			Period of Decline; early.	
1		Æ ·9	Head of Sikelia? r., wearing myrtle-wreath: border of dots.	ΙΣ ИΩИ Lyre of seven strings: border of dots.
			Period of Decline; late.	
2		Æ ·85	Head of Zeus l., laur.: border of dots.	ΑΛΑΙΣΑΣ ΑΡΧ Eagle, standing l., wings spread; in field l., bucranium: border of dots.
3		Æ ·85	Similar type; behind, ΧΡ: same border.	Similar; in field l., tripod-lebes.
4		Æ ·9	Head of Apollo l., laur.; behind, Χ.	ΣΑΣ ΑΡΧ Clasped right hands; above, ear of barley r.; beneath, caduceus r.
5		Æ ·85	Similar type; behind, strung bow: border of dots.	ΑΛΑΙ ΣΑΣ Apollo, standing l., holding in r. wreath, his l. resting on lyre; in field l., Χ: border of dots.
6		Æ ·8	Similar type: same border.	Similar.
7		Æ ·75	Similar type r.: same border.	Similar.
8		Æ ·8	Similar (rude).	Similar.
9		Æ ·65	Head of Apollo l., laur.: border of dots.	ΑΛΑΙΣΑΣ ΑΡΧ Lyre; in field r., helmet?: border of dots.
10		Æ ·55	Similar.	ΑΛΑΙ ΣΑΣ Χ Tripod-lebes with neck and three handles: border of dots.

No.	Wt.	Metal. Size.	Obverse.	Reverse.
11		Æ ·5	Head of young Dionysos r., crowned with ivy: border of dots.	ΑΛΑΙΣΑΣ ΑΡΧ Male figure l., naked, resting on spear; in field l., cornucopiæ: border of dots.
12		Æ ·5	Similar type l.: same border.	Same inscr. Cuirass; in field l., cornucopiæ: border of dots.
13		Æ ·5	Head of Artemis? l.: border of dots.	Same inscr. Quiver, to l. of which, strung bow; in field r., bucranium: border of dots.
14		Æ ·5	Similar.	Same inscr. Quiver, to r. of which, strung bow; in field l., cornucopiæ.
			Roman Coinage.	
15		Æ ·8	HA– ARC Head of Artemis? l., wearing stephane.	Inscr. illegible. Tripod-lebes: border of dots.
16		Æ ·85	HA·' AR Similar type r.: border of dots.	CÆC·R II VIR Lyre.
17		Æ ·9	HALAESA ARC.... Head of Apollo? l.	M CASSIVS M ANT Wreath.

ALAESA?

COPPER.

Coinage struck by Timoleon and his allies assembled to resist the Carthaginian invasion, B.C. circ. 340.

No.	Wt.	Metal. Size.	Obverse.	Reverse.
1		Æ 1·15	ΑΡΧΑΓΕΤΑΣ Head of Apollo l., laur.: border of dots.	ΣΥ ΜΜ Α Χ ΙΚ ΟΝ Lighted pine-torch fixed in the ground, between two stalks of barley: plain border.
2		Æ 1·25	Same. (Same die.)	Same. (Same die.)

(These coins are restruck on coins of Syracuse. Obv. Head of Pallas. Rev. Star-fish between dolphins.)

No.	Wt.	Metal. Size.	Obverse.	Reverse.
3		Æ 1·	Σ . K E Λ Head of Sikelia l., wearing earring, necklace, and sphendone adorned behind with star.	Similar.
4		Æ ·9	TAΣ Head of Apollo l., laur.	ΣY MMAX Thunderbolt erect; in field l., bunch of grapes.

No.	Wt.	Metal. Size.	Obverse.	Reverse.
5		Æ ·9	A Same type.	KON Same type and symbol: plain border.
6		Æ ·85	KAINON (in ex.) Horse prancing l., bridle loose: plain border.	Griffin, galloping l.

No.	Wt.	Metal. Size.	Obverse.	Reverse.
7		Æ ·85	Similar. (Inscr. not visible.)	Same type: plain border.
8		Æ ·9	Similar; above horse, star of eight rays.	Similar; beneath griffin, cicada l.

(These coins are usually attributed to Caena.)

ALUNTIUM.

COPPER.

Period of Finest Art.

No.	Wt.	Metal. Size.	Obverse.	Reverse.
1		Æ ·75	Head of Pallas l., wearing crested Athenian helmet: border of dots.	ΑΛΟΝΤΙΝΟΝ Cuttle-fish: plain border.

Period of Decline; late.

No.	Wt.	Metal. Size.	Obverse.	Reverse.
2		Æ 1·	Head of bearded Herakles r., bound with wreath.	ΑΛΟΝΤΙΝ ΩΝ Eagle, standing r., on part of a carcase, wings spread: plain border.

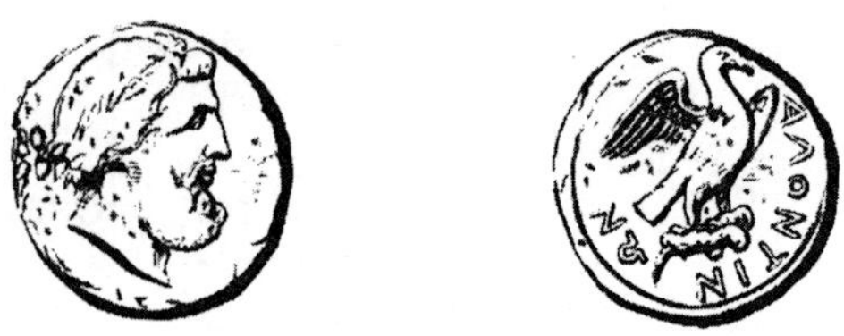

No.	Wt.	Metal. Size.	Obverse.	Reverse.
3		Æ ·85	Similar type.	ΑΛΟΝΤΙΝΩΝ Similar.
4		Æ ·85	Young male head l., (the traditional Trojan founder?) wearing Phrygian helmet, bound with wreath, and the apex ending in bird's head: border of dots.	ΑΛΟΝΤΙΝΩΝ Man-headed bull, standing l., a stream of water pouring from his mouth: plain border.
5		Æ ·75	Similar type.	Same inscr. Similar type; in ex., crab: same border.
6		Æ ·8	Similar.	ΑΛΟΝΤΙΝ ΩΝ Similar type: same border.
7		Æ ·6	Head of bearded Herakles r.: border of dots.	ΑΛΟΝΤΙ ΝΩΝ Bow and arrows in case, and club l.: plain border.

No.	Wt.	Metal. Size.	Obverse.	Reverse.
8		Æ ·5	Head of young Dionysos r., bound with ivy; hair long; behind, bunch of grapes: border of dots.	ΑΛΟΝ ΤΙΝΩΝ within a wreath of olive, tied above.

AMESTRATUS.

COPPER.

Period of Decline; late.

No.	Wt.	Metal. Size.	Obverse.	Reverse.
1		Æ ·65	Head of young Dionysos r., bound with ivy; hair long.	ΑΜΗΣΤΡΑ ΙΝΩΝ Horseman, armed with helmet and large round shield, galloping l., his spear at rest; above horse, ΛΕΥ.
2		Æ ·8	Bust of Artemis r., wearing stephane; behind shoulder, bow and quiver.	ΑΜΗΣΤΡ ΤΙΝ Apollo, facing, clad in chlamys, and playing on lyre.

ASSORUS.

COPPER.

Period of Roman Dominion.

No.	Wt.	Metal. Size.	Obverse.	Reverse.
1		Æ ·85	ASSORV Head of Apollo r., laur.	CRYSAS The river-god Chrysas, standing l., holding amphora and cornucopiæ; chlamys over left arm: border of dots.

No.	Wt.	Metal. Size.	Obverse.	Reverse.
2		Æ ·75	Female head r., wearing stephane and earring; hair in a knot behind.	ASSORV Yoke of oxen r.: border of dots.

CALACTE.

COPPER.

Period of Decline; late.

No.	Wt.	Metal. Size.	Obverse.	Reverse.
1		Æ ·8	Head of Pallas r., wearing crested Athenian helmet; behind, ear of barley: border of dots.	KA ΛA KTI NΩN Owl, standing r., on amphora r.: plain border.
2		Æ ·8	Similar type; behind, : same border.	Similar.
3		Æ ·65	Head of young Dionysos r., bound with ivy; over his shoulder, thyrsos; in field l., X · L.	KAΛA KTINΩN Bunch of grapes.
4		Æ ·6	Similar type: plain border.	Similar: plain border.
5		Æ ·6	Head of Apollo r., laur.: border of dots.	KAΛA KTINΩN Lyre.
6		Æ ·5	Head of Hermes r., wearing petasos.	KAΛA KTINΩN Caduceus r.: plain border.

No.	Wt.	Metal. Size.	Obverse.	Reverse.

CAMARINA.

SILVER.

Period of Archaic Art.

No.	Wt.	Metal. Size.	Obverse.	Reverse.
1	13·	AR ·45	IЯ A M AK Pallas standing l., wearing long chiton with diploïs, ægis, and crested helmet, and leaning on spear; behind her, shield: plain border.	Nike, flying l., wearing long chiton with diploïs; at her feet, swan l.: all within olive-wreath.
2	12·7	AR ·5	A M AK Similar.	Similar, but types r.
3	9·4	AR ·5	KAMARI NAION Pallas standing, as before, but shield in front: plain border.	Similar, but types l.

No.	Wt.	Metal. Size.	Obverse.	Reverse.
4	11·8	AR ·5	Similar.	Similar.
5	10·6	AR ·5	KAMARI NAOIN (*sic*) Similar.	Similar.
6	8·3	AR ·5	KAMA RINAION Similar.	Similar.

No.	Wt.	Metal. Size.	Obverse.	Reverse.
			Period of Transition.	
7	129·4	AR ·8	Corinthian helmet l., without crest, on round shield.	KAMA ЯI Dwarf fan-palm in fruit; on either side, greave: all in circular incuse.
			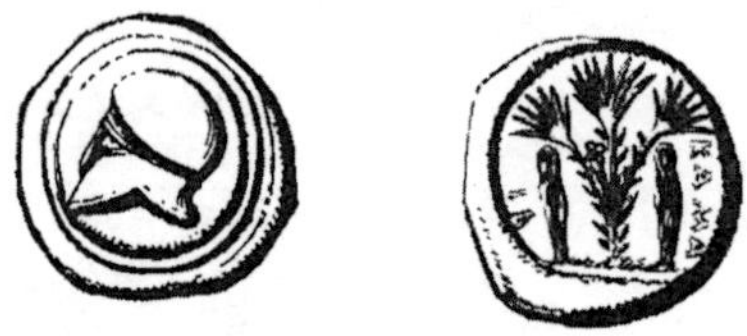	
			Period of Finest Art.	
8	233·6	AR 1· plated	KAMAPINAOIN (*sic*) Head of bearded Herakles l., wearing lion's skin.	Quadriga l., driven by Pallas, wearing helmet and long chiton, and holding reins in both hands; horses galloping in step; above, Nike, flying r., crowning charioteer: border of dots.

9	265·8	AR 1·	INAI O N Similar type.	Similar type; in ex., crane, flying l.: same border.
10	250·8	AR 1·1	ИOI AИIЯAMAK Similar type.	Similar.

No.	Wt.	Metal. Size.	Obverse.	Reverse.
11	266·	Æ 1·15	**KAMAPI** Similar type: plain border.	**И O I AИIꟼAMAꓘ** Similar type; Pallas wears helmet with tall plume, and ægis: same border.
			(Obverse double-struck.)	
12	261·	Æ 1·	No inscr. Similar type.	Same. (Same die.)
13	261·5	Æ 1·15	Head of young Herakles l., whiskered, wearing lion's skin, with the paws tied at the throat; in front, upper part of strung bow.	**KAM A PIИA** (in ex.) Quadriga r., driven by Pallas, wearing crested helmet and long chiton; she holds reins in both hands, goad in r.; horses galloping; above, Nike, flying l., crowning charioteer; in ex., dividing inscr., two amphoræ: plain border.

No.	Wt.	Metal. Size.	Obverse.	Reverse.
14	264·2	Æ 1·	**KAMAPINAION** Similar type, without whisker.	No inscr. Similar type and symbols; on line of ex., **ΕΞΑΚΕΣΤΙΔΑΣ.**

No.	Wt.	Metal. Size.	Obverse.	Reverse.
15	260·5	AR 1·1	KAMAPINAI ΩN Similar type, with whisker; in front, olive-spray, with leaf and fruit.	Quadriga r., driven by Pallas, wearing crested helmet and long chiton with diploïs; she holds goad and reins; horses rearing as the chariot turns; above, Nike, flying l., crowning charioteer; in ex., barley-corn: plain border.

16	122·8	AR ·9	Bust of river-god Hipparis, three-quarter-face, towards l.; having small horn on either side of the forehead, hair loose; on neck, EYAI?; on either side, a fish, downwards: all in circle of waves.	KAM A NA Nymph Kamarina, seated r., on the back of swan swimming l., with wings spread; the nymph looks l., her r. arm is round the swan's neck, her peplos falls over her knees, and she holds the upper part with both hands as a sail; beneath swan, waves, amid which, fish r.; in field r., fish, leaping: border of dots.

No.	Wt.	Metal. Size.	Obverse.	Reverse.
17	132·	Æ ·9	Ƹ IϘA Π Head of river-god Hipparis l., with small horns, hair loose; on either side, a fish, upwards: plain border.	A Ϻ I Ϙ A Nymph Kamarina, draped, seated on swan as before; no waves beneath swan, but around, three fishes, upwards: same border.

18	127·8	Æ ·9	KAMAPINAIO N Head of river-god Hipparis l., with small horns, hair short, diademed; beneath, VΛ: border of dots.	KAMAPINA between two lines. Nymph Kamarina, draped, seated r. on swan, swimming l., wings spread, her l. holding inflated peplos; beneath swan, waves, amid which, a fish, l.

19	131·9	Æ ·75	Same. (Same die.)	Same. (Same die.)
20	60·6	Æ ·7	Head of nymph Kamarina, three-quarter-face, towards l., hair loose, wearing ear-ring and necklace; on either side, rising from behind neck, a fish: border of dots.	KAM API Nike? flying l., clad in long chiton with diploïs, holding fillet and caduceus: border of dots.

No.	Wt.	Metal. Size.	Obverse.	Reverse.
21	10·1	Æ ·5	KAMA Head of nymph Kamarina l., wearing sphendone, broad in front and behind, earring and necklace: border of dots.	Traces of inscr. Similar type.

No.	Wt.	Metal. Size.	Obverse.	Reverse.
22	10·3	Æ ·4	Similar type r.	Nike? clad in long chiton with diploïs, flying r., her r. arm raised above head.
23	12·3	Æ ·5	A Head of Pallas l., wearing crested Athenian helmet.	Nike? flying l., wearing long chiton with diploïs, and carrying fillet and caduceus.

No.	Wt.	Metal. Size.	Obverse.	Reverse.
24	13·1	Æ ·5	ANIЯAMAꓘ Head of nymph Kamarina l., wearing sphendone, broad in front and behind and ornamented with star, earring, and necklace: border of dots.	Swan, flying l., over waves, with spread wings and head bent down; amid waves, a fish l.
25	10·3	Æ ·45	Same. (Same die.)	Similar.

No.	Wt.	Metal. Size.	Obverse.	Reverse.
				COPPER.
				Period of Transition.
				With marks of value.
				Hemilitron.
26	408·	Æ 1·1	Gorgon's head.	● ● ● ● ● ●; between lines, two obelisks.
27	400·	Æ 1·	Similar.	Same marks of value.
28	368·	Æ 1·	Similar.	Similar.
29	344·	Æ 1·2	Similar.	Similar.
30	230·	Æ ·9	Similar.	Similar.
				Pentuncia.
31	274·	Æ ·9	Similar type.	● ● ● ● ●
				Trias.
32	253·	Æ ·9	Similar type.	 in triangular incuse.
33	165·	Æ ·8	Similar.	● ● ●
				Period of Finest Art.
				Trias.
34	65·	Æ ·75	Gorgon's head, diademed.	ΚΑΜΑ Owl r., holding up with l. claw lizard; in ex., ● ● ●.
35	59·	Æ ·65	Similar type.	Similar; in field r., barley-corn.
			Similar type; hair serpentine.	Similar; in field r., Γ.

No.	Wt.	Metal. Size.	Obverse.	Reverse.
37	56·	Æ ·55	Similar.	ΚΑΜΑ Owl l., holding up with r. claw lizard; same marks of value.
38	53·	Æ ·55	Similar type, hair in tresses: border of dots.	Similar: plain border.
39	54·	Æ ·6	Head of Pallas l., wearing crested Athenian helmet, on the side of which, wing.	ΑΜΑΚ Similar type; same marks of value.
40	49·	Æ ·6	Similar type: border of dots.	ΚΑΜΑ Similar.
			Uncia.	
41	14·	Æ ·45	Gorgon's head.	ΚΑΜΑ Owl r., holding up with l. claw lizard; in field r., Α; in ex., ●.
42	20·	Æ ·5	Head of Pallas l., wearing crested Athenian helmet.	ΑΜΑΚ Similar type l.; same mark of value.
			Period of Decline; early.	
43		Æ ·6	ΚΑΜΑΡΙΝΑΙΩΝ Head of Pallas l., wearing crested Athenian helmet: border of dots.	Free horse prancing l.; in ex., ear of barley.
44		Æ ·6	ΚΑΜΑΡΙΝΑΙΩΝ Similar type r.: same border.	Similar type r.; same symbol: border of dots.

CATANA.

SILVER.

Period of Archaic Art.

No.	Wt.	Metal. Size.	Obverse.	Reverse.
1	251·7	Æ 1·05	Man-headed bull, kneeling r. on r. knee; above, branch of river-plant r.; beneath, river-fish r.: border of dots.	KAT AИE Nike, advancing l., wearing long chiton with diploïs, and bearing fillet in her outstretched r. hand: border of dots.

No.	Wt.	Metal. Size.	Obverse.	Reverse.
2	267·4	Æ 1·	Similar; branch larger.	Same. (Same die.)
3	266·8	Æ 1·05	Similar type; bull with tail erect; above, water-fowl l.; beneath, river-fish l.: same border.	K ATA И A IOИ Nike, advancing l., wearing long chiton with diploïs, and fillet as zone, holding out olive-wreath in r., and raising her dress with l.

No.	Wt.	Metal. Size.	Obverse.	Reverse.
4	263·6	Æ 1·	Similar type; bull, with tail lowered; on his back, Seilen, kneeling r. on l. knee and stretching forward his l. hand over bull's head; beneath, pistrix r.: border of dots.	KATA N AION Nike, advancing l., wearing long chiton with diploïs, and bearing fillet in her outstretched r. hand.
5	267·7	Æ 1·	Man-headed bull, kneeling r. on r. knee; in ex., ornament of volutes: border of dots.	KAT AN A ION Similar type; Nike holds fillet and olive-wreath; in field l., H: border of dots.
6	262·1	Æ 1·	Man-headed bull, standing r.; above, Nike, flying r., holding fillet over bull's head: border of dots.	K AT A N AI OΣ Similar type; same letter.

7	259·3	Æ 1·	Same. (Same die.)	KATANA Similar type; Nike holds spray instead of wreath; in front, Ж.
8	10·7	Æ ·45	Head of Seilen l., with pointed ear: border of dots.	KAT [A]NE Thunderbolt with curled wings: border of dots.
9	12·7	Æ ·45	Similar type r.: same border.	Similar.
10	10·9	Æ ·45	Similar.	Same inscr. Similar type: border of dots.
11	4·2	Æ ·4	Similar.	K Winged thunderbolt.

No.	Wt.	Metal. Size.	Obverse.	Reverse.
			Catana under the name Ætna, B.C. 476–461.	
12	10·	Æ ·4	Head of Seilen r.: border of dots.	AIT NAI Winged thunderbolt.

13	9·6	Æ ·4	Similar.	AI N⊥ Winged thunderbolt: plain border.
14	9·3	Æ ·4	Similar head, wearing ivy-wreath: same border.	ΛI TN Similar type.
15	7·2	Æ ·4	Similar head, wearing wreath of laurel or olive: same border.	ΛW TIΛ Similar type.
16	14·4	Æ ·45	Similar head l., without wreath: same border.	AI TN Similar type.
			Period of Transition.	
17	261·2	Æ 1·05	KATANAI O N Head of Apollo r., laur.; hair turned up behind.	Quadriga r., driven by male figure, wearing long chiton, holding goad in r., reins in both hands; horses walking: border of dots.

18	267·2	Æ 1·05	Similar.	Similar.

No.	Wt.	Metal. Size.	Obverse.	Reverse.
19	266·4	Æ 1·05	KATAИAI Similar type.	Similar.

20	263·5	Æ 1·05	KATAИAIOИ Similar type.	Similar.
21	262·2	Æ 1·2	KATANAIO Σ Similar type; hair rolled behind.	Similar quadriga r.; charioteer holds goad in r. and reins in l.; above, Nike flying r., crowning horses: same border.
22	270·2	Æ 1·	KATAИAIOИ Similar type.	Similar type; charioteer holds reins in both hands: same border.
23	266·	Æ 1·	Similar.	Same. (Same die.)
24	265·5	Æ 1·05	KATAИAIOИ Young male head (Apollo?) l., laur.; hair short and wavy; behind, laurel-leaf with berry.	Quadriga r., driven by male charioteer, wearing long chiton, holding goad in r. and reins in both hands; horses walking; above, Nike, flying r., crowning horses.

No.	Wt.	Metal. Size.	Obverse.	Reverse.
25	269·3	Æ 1·05	ΚΑΤΑΝΑΙΟΣ Same head r.; behind, poplar-leaf?	Similar quadriga r.; above, Nike, flying l., crowning charioteer: border of dots.

No.	Wt.	Metal. Size.	Obverse.	Reverse.
26	258·3	Æ 1·	ΚΑΤΑΝΑΙΟ Head of Apollo? r., laur.; hair straight behind, and short.	Similar.

Period of Finest Art.

No.	Wt.	Metal. Size.	Obverse.	Reverse.
27	262·5	Æ 1·	ΚΑΤΑΝΑΙΩΝ Young male head l., diademed: border of dots.	Quadriga l.; charioteer holds reins in both hands; horses in high action, and the rein of the farthest hanging loose; above, Nike, flying r., holding wreath and fillet, crowning charioteer; line of ex. triple; in ex., H: border of dots.

No.	Wt.	Metal. Size.	Obverse.	Reverse.
28	244·4	AR ·95	Similar.	Same. (Same die.)
29	263·7	AR ·95	ΩΝ Similar head, bare: same border.	Same. (Same die.)

30	263·6	AR 1·05	ΚΑΤΑΝ Α ΙΩΝ Head of Apollo r., laur.; hair short: border of dots.	ΚΑΤΑΝΑΙΩΝ (in ex.) Quadriga l., driven by male charioteer, holding reins in both hands; horses in high action; above, Nike, flying r., crowning charioteer; in ex., fish l.

31	259·6	AR 1·	Head of Apollo, three-quarter-face towards l., laur.; hair long; in field r., ΗΡΑΚΛΕΙΔΑΣ.	Same inscr. Similar type; Nike holds wreath and fillet.

No.	Wt.	Metal. Size.	Obverse.	Reverse.
32	266·5	AR 1·1	Similar: border of dots.	Same inscr. Quadriga l., driven by male charioteer, wearing long chiton, holding reins in both hands; horses cantering, and the reins of the farthest hanging loose; above, Nike, floating erect r., holding wreath and caduceus bound with fillet; in ex., fish l.: border of dots.

33	259·2	AR 1·1	Same. (Same die.)	Same inscr. Quadriga r., driven by male charioteer, holding goad in r. and reins in both hands; horses in high action, and the rein of the farthest hanging loose; above, Nike, flying l., holding open wreath with both hands; beyond the horses, fluted Ionic column (meta); in ex., cray-fish r.
34	261·8	AR 1·05	Head of Apollo, facing; on either side, strung bow and lyre; beneath neck, ΑΓΟΛΛΩΝ; in field l., ΧΟΙ[ΡΙΩΝ]: same border.	Same. (Same die.)

No.	Wt.	Metal. Size.	Obverse.	Reverse.
35	267·2	AR 1·	ATANAIΩN Head of Apollo l., laur; hair turned up behind; on either side, knotted fillet, with bell attached, and cray-fish upwards.	Quadriga l., driven by charioteer, wearing long chiton, holding reins in both hands, and striking horses with goad; horses in high action; on this side the chariot, meta; above, Nike, flying r., bearing wreath and tablet inscribed EYAIN; under horses' feet, pellet; line of ex. double; in ex., crab: border of dots.

No.	Wt.	Metal. Size.	Obverse.	Reverse.
36	57·7	AR ·7	Head of young river-god Amenanos, three-quarter-face towards r., with short horns and flowing hair; on either side of neck, river-fish, upwards.	TANAI (in ex.) Fast quadriga r., driven by charioteer, holding goad and reins; rein of farthest horse hangs loose; above, Nike, flying l., crowning charioteer: border of dots.
37	64·	AR ·7	AMENANOΣ Head of young river-god l., with short horn, diademed; around, two river-fishes and cray-fish; beneath neck, EYAI.	KATANAIΩ N (in ex.) Similar.

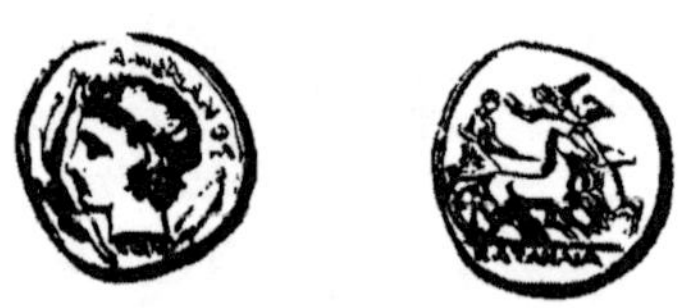

No.	Wt.	Metal. Size.	Obverse	Reverse.
38	63·1	AR ·7	ΑΜΕΝΑΝΟ Similar.	Same. (Same die.)
39	57·2	AR ·75	ΑΜΕΝΑΝΟΣ Similar head; around, three river-fishes; in field l., ΕΥΑΙ.	Same. (Same die.)
40	64·2	AR ·65	ΑΜΕΝΑ Similar head, both horns seen; in front, two river-fishes; behind, cray-fish.	Similar type and border.
41	64·	AR ·7	ΑΜΕΝΑΝ ΟΣ Similar head r., one horn seen; around, two fishes and cray-fish.	ΚΑ ΤΑ Ν ΑΙΟΝ Similar type and border.
			(Barbarous coin.)	
42	58·	AR ·65	ΑΜΕΝΑ Young head of river-god Amenanos, three-quarter-face towards l., hair diademed and wavy; on either side, cray-fish and fish; beneath neck, ΧΟΙ.	ΤΑ (in ex.) Fast quadriga r., driven by female charioteer, holding spear in r. and reins and shield in l.; above, Nike, flying l., crowning charioteer; in ex., mæander pattern; in field r., ΗΡΑΚΛΕΙΔΑ.
43	62·1	AR ·65	Head of Seilen, full-face, with pointed ears: border of dots.	ΚΛ ΤΛ ΝΑΙΩΝ Young male head l., diademed: border of dots.
			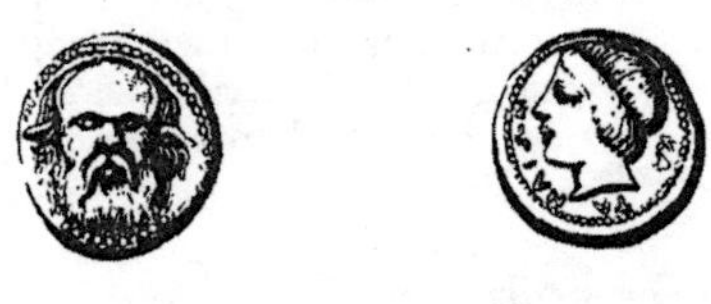	
44	28·7	AR ·5	Similar.	ΚΑΤΑΝΑΙΩ Ν Head of Apollo r., laur., hair rolled behind: plain border.
45	12·5	AR ·45	Head of Seilen r.: border of dots.	ΚΑΤΛΝ ΑΙΩΝ Thunderbolt with curled wings: border of dots.
46	13·4	AR ·45	Similar head l., crowned with ivy: same border.	Similar: no border.

No.	Wt.	Metal. Size.	Obverse.	Reverse.
47	12·1	AR ·45	Similar; behind head, Γ.	ΚΑΤΑ ΝΑΙΩΝ Similar.
48	2·3	AR ·25	Similar type: same border.	Κ Α Thunderbolt, not winged.
49	11·8	AR ·45	Head of nymph l., wearing sphendone: border of dots.	ΚΑΤΑΝΑΙΩΝ Bull butting r.; in ex., cray-fish r.
			COPPER.	
50		Æ ·75	ΑΤΑΝΑ Head of Persephone r., crowned with barley; behind, ivy-leaf: border of dots.	Thunderbolt with curled wings.
51		Æ ·55	ΑΜΕΝΑΝΟΣ Young head of river-god Amenanos l., with short horns; behind, ivy-leaf: plain border.	Κ Α Thunderbolt with spread wings.
52		Æ ·55	Similar.	Similar.
			Period of Decline; late.	
53		Æ ·65	ΚΑΤ Head of Pallas l., wearing crested Corinthian helmet, on which, griffin: border of dots.	Winged thunderbolt; in field, thyrsos: plain border.
54		Æ ·75	River-god reclining l.; in r., cornucopiæ, l. elbow resting on amphora; over l. shoulder, branch: border of dots.	ΚΑΤΑΝΑΙΩ[Ν] Helmets of the Dioskuri, surmounted by stars; beneath, lion's head r.; between, ΛΕ and Μ: plain border.
55		Æ ·75	Similar.	Similar.
56		Æ ·85	Similar.	ΚΑΤΑΝΑΙΩΝ Similar helmets; between them, ♀, above which, owl r.: border of dots.
57		Æ ·5	Head of Seilen r., crowned with ivy: border of dots.	ΚΑΤΑ ΝΑΙΩΝ Bunch of grapes: plain border.

No.	Wt.	Metal. Size.	Obverse.	Reverse.
58		Æ ·45	Similar.	Similar.
59		Æ ·55	Heads of Zeus Sarapis laur., and Isis, both r., wearing head-dresses of horns globe and plumes.	ΚΑΤΑ Ι Two ears of barley with leaves: plain border.
60		Æ ·5	Similar busts: border of dots.	ΚΑΤΑ ΝΑΙΩΝ Similar type: same border.
			With marks of value.	
			Litra.	
61	55·	Æ ·7	Head of Poseidon r., wearing tainia; over shoulder, trident.	ΚΑΤΑΝΑΙΩΝ Dolphin r.; above, ΧΙΙ: plain border.
			Dekonkion.	
62	69·	Æ ·8	Busts of Zeus Sarapis laur., and Isis, both r., wearing head-dresses as before, Isis with necklace; behind, ear of barley; in front, Χ: border of dots.	ΚΑ ΤΑ ΝΑΙΩΝ Apollo facing; he wears chlamys over l. shoulder, rests l. elbow on pillar, and holds laurel-branch and strung bow; at his feet, quiver and omphalos: plain border.
63	59·	Æ ·75	Similar.	Similar.
			Pentonkion.	
64	82·	Æ ·8	Head of Apollo r., laur.: border of dots.	ΚΑΤΑ ΝΑΙΩΝ Isis? wearing modius and long chiton, standing l., holding bird on r.; at her feet, dog; (Sothis?) in front, Π: plain border.
			Hexas.	
65	55·	Æ ·65	Similar type l.; behind, omphalos: same border.	Same inscr. Isis? r., wearing modius and long chiton, holding patera and bird; in field r., ΙΙ: plain border.

No.	Wt.	Metal. Size.	Obverse.	Reverse.
66	66·	Æ ·6	Similar type; behind, : same border.	Similar.
67	54·	Æ ·7	Similar.	Similar.
68	52·	Æ ·6	Similar type r.; behind, K.	ΚΑ ΤΑ ΝΑΙΩΝ Similar.
69	53·	Æ ·65	Similar type: border of dots.	ΚΑΤΑ ΝΑΙΩΝ Similar.
			Without marks of value.	
70		Æ ·8	ΛΑΣΙ Head of young Dionysos r., crowned with ivy; behind, 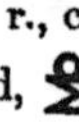.	ΚΑ ΤΑ ΝΑΙ Ω Ν The Catanæan brothers, wearing chlamydes, carrying their parents; one advancing l. with the father, who holds staff, the other r. with the mother.
71		Æ ·75	Similar.	ΚΑ Τ ΑΝΑΙΩΝ Similar.
72		Æ ·8	ΛΑΣΙΟ Similar.	Inscr. obscure. Similar type: plain border.
73		Æ ·85	Similar: border of dots.	ΚΛΤΑΝΑΙΩΝ Similar.
74		Æ ·7	One of the Catanæan brothers, advancing r., bearing draped male figure, with garments flying; between his legs, serpent.	ΚΑΤΑ ΝΑ ΙΩΝ One of the Catanæan brothers r., bearing draped female figure; between his legs, serpent.
75		Æ ·6	ΚΑΤΛ One of the Catanæan brothers l., bearing draped male figure seated r. on l. shoulder: plain border.	One of the Catanæan brothers r., bearing female figure; in field l., serpent: border of dots.
76		Æ ·5	No inscr. Similar type; father l., with staff: border of dots.	ΚΛΤΑ ΝΛΙΩΝ One of the Catanæan brothers l., bearing draped female figure, held r., in both arms.

No.	Wt.	Metal. Size.	Obverse.	Reverse.
77		Æ ·5	Similar.	Similar: plain border.
78		Æ ·45	Similar.	Similar.
79		Æ ·55	Similar.	Same inscr. Similar type; female figure l.: same border.
80		Æ ·9	KATANAI Ω N Head of young Dionysos r., crowned with ivy? hair in a bunch behind: border of dots.	Dionysos seated l., draped, holding bunch of grapes and thyrsos, in chariot, drawn by two panthers running r.; above, [monogram], [monogram], [monogram]: border of dots.
81		Æ ·85	Similar.	Similar.
82		Æ ·8	KATANAI ΩN Head of Hermes r., wearing winged petasos.	Nike, advancing l., holding wreath and palm; in field, [monogram], [monogram], [monogram]: border of dots.
83		Æ ·8	KATANAI Ω N Similar type.	Similar.
84		Æ ·85	KATANΛIΩN Bust of Hermes r., wearing winged petasos; over shoulder, caduceus: border of dots.	Similar.
85		Æ ·9	KATA NAIΩN Head of Zeus Ammon r., laur.: border of dots.	Æquitas l., holding scales and cornucopiæ; in field l., [monogram]? in field r., [monogram], [monogram]: border of dots.
86		Æ ·85	KATANAIΩN Similar type.	Similar; first mon. [monogram].

No.	Wt.	Metal. Size.	Obverse.	Reverse.
87		Æ 1·	Head of Zeus Sarapis r., laur., radiate, and surmounted by head-dress of globe horns and plumes.	ΚΑΤΑΝΑΙΩΝ Isis facing, veiled, and wearing head-dress of horns globe and plumes, and ears of barley; she holds in her r. a long sceptre, surmounted by animal's head? in field l., , , and traces of figure of Harpokrates; in field r., sistrum: border of dots.
88		Æ 1·05	Similar type.	Similar; visible in addition, in field l., , and small figure of Harpokrates l., with his r. hand on his lips, and in his l., cornucopiæ.
89		Æ 1·05	Similar.	Similar; no symbol in field r.
90		Æ 1·05	Similar.	Same inscr. Similar types; in field l., 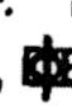 and sistrum; in field r., mon. : same border.
91		Æ ·95	Janiform head of Sarapis, surmounted by modius; in field l., 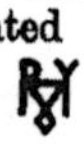 and ; in field r., : border of dots.	ΚΑΤΑ ΝΑΙ ΩΝ Persephone? l., holding in r. two ears of barley, in l., long torch: border of dots.
92		Æ ·95	Similar.	Similar.

No.	Wt.	Metal. Size.	Obverse.	Reverse.

CENTURIPA.

COPPER.

Period of Decline; early.

No.	Wt.	Metal. Size.	Obverse.	Reverse.
1		Æ 1·25	Head of Persephone l., wearing earring and wreath of corn; around, four dolphins: border of dots.	ΚΕΝΤΟΡΙΠΙΝΩΝ (in ex.) Leopard or lynx advancing l.: border of dots.

No.	Wt.	Metal. Size.	Obverse.	Reverse.
2		Æ 1·4	Similar.	Similar.

(The above two coins are restruck on coins of Syracuse. Obv. Head of Pallas. Rev. Star-fish between dolphins.)

Period of Decline; late.

With marks of value.

Dekonkion.

No.	Wt.	Metal. Size.	Obverse.	Reverse.
3	161·	Æ 1·05	Head of Zeus r., laur.; behind, eagle r.: border of dots.	ΚΕΝΤΟ ΡΙΠΙΝΩΝ Winged thunderbolt; beneath, Δ: plain border.
4	181·	Æ 1·05	Similar.	Similar.
5	158·	Æ 1·	Similar.	Similar.
6	160·	Æ 1·	Similar type, without eagle.	Similar.

No.	Wt.	Metal. Size.	Obverse.	Reverse.
			Hemilitron.	
7	150·	Æ ·95	Head of Apollo r., laur.: border of dots.	KENTO ΡΙΠΙΝΩΝ Lyre; (with four strings;) on either side, ●● ●● ●●: plain border.
8	116·	Æ ·9	Similar.	Similar.
			Trias.	
9	100·	Æ ·85	Bust of Artemis r., wearing stephane and earring; behind shoulder, top of bow and quiver: border of dots.	KENTO ΡΙΠΙΝΩΝ Tripod - lebes having neck and three handles; in field l., ●●●: plain border.
10	60·	Æ ·7	Similar.	Similar.
11	48·	Æ ·7	Similar.	Similar.
			Hexas.	
12	54·	Æ ·65	Bust of Persephone r., wearing necklace and earring, and wreath of barley; behind, stalk of barley: border of dots.	KENTO ΡΙΠΙΝΩΝ Plough r.; on the share, bird r.; behind, ●●: plain border.
13	45·	Æ ·65	Similar type and border.	Similar.
14	34·	Æ ·65	Similar.	Similar.
15	44·	Æ ·65	Similar type; behind, tripod: same border.	Similar.
16	35·	Æ ·7	Similar.	Similar.
			Uncertain denomination.	
17	33·	Æ ·5	Head of bearded Herakles r., laur.: border of dots.	KENTO ΡΙΠΙΝΩΝ Club l.; below, XI: plain border.
18	22·	Æ ·6	Similar.	Similar.

Without marks of value.

No.	Wt.	Metal. Size.	Obverse.	Reverse.
19		Æ ·5	Head of Apollo r., laur.: border of dots.	ΚΕΝ ΤΟ Laurel-bough: border of dots.
20		Æ ·5	Similar.	ΚΕ ΝΤΟ Similar type: same border.
21		Æ ·45	Similar?	Κ Ε Tree with two branches on each side: border of dots.

CEPHALOEDIUM.

COPPER.

Period of Decline; late.

No.	Wt.	Metal. Size.	Obverse.	Reverse.
1		Æ ·95	Head of bearded Herakles r., laur.: border of dots.	ΚΕ Φ Herakles facing, head l., holding in r., club, which rests on the ground, and in l., lion's skin: border of dots.
2		Æ ·85	Similar.	ΚΕ ΦΛ Similar.
3		Æ ·9	Similar.	ΚΕ ΦΑ Club downwards; behind which, lion's skin and bow-case, within which strung bow and three arrows: border of dots.
4		Æ ·8	Similar.	ΚΕΦ Α Club downwards; from the handle is suspended, on one side, lion's skin by the tail, on the other side, by the strap, case containing strung bow and three arrows: border of dots.

No	Wt.	Metal. Size.	Obverse.	Reverse.
5		Æ ·5	Bust of Hermes r., wearing winged petasos; over shoulder, caduceus: border of dots.	ΚΕ ΦΑ Winged caduceus: border of dots.

ENNA.

SILVER.

Period of Archaic Art.

No	Wt.	Metal. Size.	Obverse.	Reverse.
1	11·2	AR ·5	Quadriga r., driven by Demeter, holding torch and reins; horses walking: border of dots.	ΗΕΝ ΝΑΙ Ο Ν Female figure facing, head l., clad in long chiton, and with chlamys falling over both arms, sacrificing, with lighted torch in r., before altar.

COPPER.

Period of Decline; early.

No	Wt.	Metal. Size.	Obverse.	Reverse.
2		Æ 1·	ΔΑΜΑΤ Head of Demeter r., wearing earring necklace and wreath of barley.	ΕΝΝ Ox's head, with pendent fillets, towards r.; above, barleycorn.
3		Æ 1·	Traces of inscr. Similar type.	ΕΝΝΑ Ω Similar.
4		Æ ·6	Similar type.	ΕΝ between two barleycorns: all in olive-wreath.

No.	Wt.	Metal. Size.	Obverse.	Reverse.
			Period of Decline; late.	
5		Æ ·9	ENNA ΩN Female figure facing, head l., wearing long chiton and peplos; arms stretched out; in r. hand, a torch; l. holding end of peplos; on l. wrist what looks like a small figure in the same attitude as the larger one and holding torch: border of dots.	Bunch of grapes within wreath.
6		Æ ·9	ENNAI ΩN Young male figure facing, holding in r. spear; over l. arm, chlamys: border of dots.	Two winged serpents r., drawing plough; beneath, barley-corn: border of dots.
7		Æ ·85	Similar.	Similar.
8		Æ ·7	ENNA Bust of Hermes r., wearing winged petasos; over shoulder, caduceus.	Male figure standing r., his l. foot advanced, and grasping tree?
			(Much defaced.)	
			Colonial Coinage.	
9		Æ 1·2	L MVNA M·CESTIVS Head of Demeter l., wearing veil and stephane and bound with barley: border of dots.	MVN · HENNAE Hades in fast quadriga r.; his chlamys forming an arch over his head; in l., sceptre; his r. round the waist of Persephone, who throws herself backwards.
10		Æ 1·1	VNATIVS M·CESTIVS Similar type; in front of neck, torch.	Similar.
11		Æ ·85	MVN HENNA E Head of Artemis? r., wearing earring and necklace; hair in bunch behind: border of dots.	M: CESTIVS: L·MV NATIVS IIVIR Male figure l.; r. hand extended; chlamys over l. arm: border of dots.

ENTELLA.

SILVER.

Period of Archaic Art.

No.	Wt.	Metal. Size.	Obverse.	Reverse.
1	8·7	AR ·45	Female figure l., wearing long chiton with diploïs, and chlamys over both arms, sacrificing with patera at lighted altar.	ΛƎTᴎƎ Man-headed bull r.
2	12·8	AR ·55	Similar type: plain border.	EᴎTEΛ Similar type.

With marks of value.

Hemilitron.

No.	Wt.	Metal. Size.	Obverse.	Reverse.
3	4·7	AR ·35	Head of young Herakles l., wearing lion's skin.	ƐᴎT; around, ⁙⁙ (six pellets): border of dots.

CAMPANIANS AT ENTELLA.

COPPER.

Period of Decline; early.

No.	Wt.	Metal. Size.	Obverse.	Reverse.
4		Æ ·8	ENTEΛ Head of Persephone r., crowned with barley, wearing earring and necklace; hair falling behind and confined with a cord.	K AMΠ A NΩ N Pegasos flying l.; beneath, Corinthian helmet without crest r.

No.	Wt.	Metal. Size.	Obverse.	Reverse.
5		Æ ·85	ENTE Λ Λ Head of bearded warrior r., wearing close-fitting helmet with cheek-pieces and adorned with olive-wreath: border of dots.	K Pegasos flying r.; beneath, thunderbolt: border of dots.
6		Æ ·85	ΛΛ Ǝ Helmet r., with spike at the top and cheek-piece, bound with wreath.	Traces of inscr. Similar type; beneath, dolphin r.
7		Æ ·7	Traces of inscr. Similar type, without wreath.	Free horse r., prancing.

Period of Roman Dominion.

No.	Wt.	Metal. Size.	Obverse.	Reverse.
8		Æ ·75	ATPATINO Y Bust of Helios r., radiate and wearing chlamys.	ENTEΛ ΛIN ωN Concordia? l., holding patera and cornucopiae.

ERYX.

SILVER.

Period of Archaic Art.

No.	Wt.	Metal. Size.	Obverse.	Reverse.
1	62·	Ʀ ·65	IKVЯƎ NON Eagle, with wings closed, standing r. on meta: border of dots.	Crab; beneath, Ǝ.
2	9·1	Ʀ ·4	ERVKI ꟿOꟿ Eagle, with wings closed, standing l.: border of dots.	Crab.
3	9·4	Ʀ ·45	ERVK ꟿOꟿI Similar.	Similar.

Period of Transition.

No.	Wt.	Metal. Size.	Obverse.	Reverse.
4	10·5	AR ·45	Head of Aphrodite of Eryx, full-face; hair wavy, a formal curl hanging on each side: border of dots.	ΛO ΛI ꓘV ЯƎ Hound r., looking back, wearing collar.

No.	Wt.	Metal. Size.	Obverse.	Reverse.
5	12·8	AR ·45	Similar.	Similar.
6	13·1	AR ·45	ERYKA ꓭ I Ⲷ Female figure l., wearing long chiton with diploïs, sacrificing with patera at lighted altar.	Hound l.; above, wheel of four spokes: plain border.
7	12·4	AR ·45	Λ O Λ IꓘVЯƎ Similar; figure with both arms extended, and chlamys over r. shoulder.	Hound r., on the scent; above, branch of ivy with berries; in ex., volutes: border of dots.

No.	Wt.	Metal. Size.	Obverse.	Reverse.
8	10·4	AR ·5	Similar type; in field r., floral ornament.	Hound r.; above, honeysuckle ornament.
9	12·	AR ·5	Similar.	Similar type: border of dots.

Period of Finest Art.

No.	Wt.	Metal. Size.	Obverse.	Reverse.
10	14·3	AR ·5	Aphrodite, seated l., wearing long chiton; her l. hand resting on seat; on her r., dove r., with spread wings; behind, tree: border of dots.	EPV KIΛO Hound r.; above, archaic pattern, ✣.
11	12·4	AR ·5	Same. (Same die.)	Same. (Same die.)

No.	Wt.	Metal. Size.	Obverse.	Reverse.
12	7·1	AR ·45	Similar, but direction of type reversed; r. hand on chair, and dove on l. hand.	Similar type; above, archaic pattern, 卐.
13	10·7	AR ·5	ΕΡΥ ΚΙΝ Ο Ν Aphrodite, seated l., on throne, wearing long chiton, and chlamys over arms; in front, Eros, flying r., holding open wreath in both hands: border of dots.	Hound r.; above, star of eight rays, with as many dots between them; in front, floral ornament.
14	4·7	AR ·35	Head of Aphrodite r., wearing necklace and sphendone.	ΕΡΥ ΚΙΝ Ο Ν Hound r.

COPPER.

Period of Decline; early.

No.	Wt.	Metal. Size.	Obverse.	Reverse.
15		Æ 1·25	ΥΚΙΝΩΝ Head of Zeus Eleutherios r.: border of dots.	Aphrodite seated r.; her r. hand on seat, holding on l. dove, which stands l., with spread wings.

(Restruck on a coin of Syracuse. Obv. Head of Pallas. Rev. Starfish between dolphins.)

With marks of value.

Trias.

No.	Wt.	Metal. Size.	Obverse.	Reverse.
16	153·	Æ 1·05	ꓘVЯ Male head r., bearded.	Hound r.; around, ● ● ●

Hexas.

No.	Wt.	Metal. Size.	Obverse.	Reverse.
17	110·	Æ ·8	Similar type.	Similar type; above and below, ● ●

No.	Wt.	Metal. Size.	Obverse.	Reverse.
			Period of Decline; late.	
18		Æ ·85	Head of Aphrodite r., hair rolled and turned up behind: border of dots.	ЄΡΥΚΙ ΝΩΝ Herakles l., holding in r. club, which rests on the ground, and on l. arm lion's skin: border of dots.

GALARIA OR GALARINA.

SILVER.

Period of Archaic Art.

No.	Wt.	Metal. Size.	Obverse.	Reverse.
1	9·5	AR ·45	ꓤ ƎΤΟ Ƹ Zeus Soter, draped, seated l. on throne, on which l. hand rests; in outstretched r., sceptre resting on the ground, on the top of which is an eagle with closed wings l.: border of dots.	ϹΑ ΛΑ Young Dionysos towards l., wearing long chiton, with chlamys over l. shoulder; in r., kantharos; in l., bunch of grapes on long stalk: plain border.

No.	Wt.	Metal. Size.	Obverse.	Reverse.

GELA.

GOLD.

Period of Finest Art.

No.	Wt.	Metal. Size.	Obverse.	Reverse.
1	26·9	AV ·45	ΓΕΛΑΣ Fore-part of man-headed bull, swimming r.; above, barleycorn.	Horseman r., wearing Phrygian helmet, short tunic, and cothurni, holding reins and spear; horse walking.

No.	Wt.	Metal. Size.	Obverse.	Reverse.
2	17·7	AV ·45	ΣΩΣΙΠΟΛΙΣ Female head l. (Persephone?) wearing necklace and sphendone broad in front and behind: plain border.	ΓΕΛΑΣ Fore-part of man-headed bull, swimming l.: plain border.

SILVER.

Period of Archaic Art.

No.	Wt.	Metal. Size.	Obverse.	Reverse.
3	267·7	AR 1·05	ƧΑ Λ Ǝ) Fore-part of man-headed bull, swimming r.	Quadriga r., driven by charioteer wearing long chiton and holding goad and reins; horses walking; above, Nike r. crowning horses: border of dots.

No.	Wt.	Metal. Size.	Obverse.	Reverse.
4	268·7	Ʀ ·95	Similar.	Similar.
5	265·	Ʀ 1·	ϹΕΛΑΣ Similar type.	Similar.

6	265·1	Ʀ 1·05	Similar.	Same. (Same die.)
7		Ʀ ·9 plated	Similar?	Similar?
			(Fragment.)	
8	263·2	Ʀ 1·	ΕΛΑΣ Fore-part of man-headed bull, swimming r., l. foreleg bent.	Similar to no. 5.
9	267·5	Ʀ 1·	Ϲ Ε Λ ΑΣ Fore-part of man-headed bull, swimming r., r. foreleg bent.	Quadriga r., driven by bearded charioteer wearing long chiton, who holds goad in r. hand and reins in both, and looks back; horses galloping; above, Nike r. crowning them: border of dots.
10	262·9	Ʀ 1·	ϹΕΛΑ Similar type.	Quadriga r., driven by charioteer wearing long chiton, who holds goad in r. hand and reins in both; horses walking; beyond horses, Ionic column (meta).

No.	Wt.	Metal. Size.	Obverse.	Reverse.
11	264·1	AR 1·1	ϹΕΛΑΣ Similar type.	Similar type: border of dots.
12	264·3	AR 1·	Similar.	Similar.
13	253·7	AR 1·1	ϹΕΛΔΣ (*sic.*) Similar type.	Quadriga r., driven by charioteer, holding goad in r. hand and reins in both; horses trotting; above, Nike flying r., crowning horses: border of dots.
14	258·9	AR 1·05	ƧΑΛƎϽ Similar.	Quadriga r., driven by bearded charioteer wearing long chiton, who holds goad in r. hand and reins in both; horses walking; above, Nike flying r., crowning horses: border of dots.
15	259·1	AR 1·1	ϹΕΛΑΣ Similar type.	Quadriga r., driven by young male charioteer holding goad and reins; horses walking; beyond horses, Ionic column (meta): border of dots.
16	133·7	AR ·85	ƧΑΛƎϽ Fore-part of man-headed bull, swimming r.	Bearded horseman r., wearing only crested helmet; his r. holds aloft spear, his l. reins; horse prancing.

No.	Wt.	Metal. Size.	Obverse.	Reverse.
17	127·	AR ·8	ϹΕΛΑΣ Similar.	Similar.
18	133·4	AR ·85	ƧΑΛƎϽ Similar.	Similar type l.; horseman wears tall conical helmet.
19	134·1	AR ·8	ϹΕΛΑΣ Similar.	Similar type r.; horseman wears conical helmet with long neck-piece: border of dots.

No.	Wt.	Metal. Size.	Obverse.	Reverse.
20	134·	AR ·8	Similar.	Similar.
			(On neck of bull, deep incision.)	
21	135·9	AR ·75	Similar.	Similar.
22	128·7	AR ·8	ϹΕΛΑ≷ Similar.	Similar type.
23	127·4	AR ·85	ϹΕ ΛΑ≷ Similar.	Similar type: border of dots.
24	131·2	AR ·8	ϹΕ ΑΛ Similar.	Similar.
25	114·5	AR ·8 plated	Α Λ Ǝ Ͻ Similar.	Similar type.
26	127·2	AR ·85	ϹΕΛΑ≷ Similar.	Similar type: border of dots.
27	105·3	AR ·75	ΛΕVΑ≷ (*sic.*) Similar.	Similar.
28	12·2	AR ·5	Λ ƎϽ ƸΑ Fore-part of man-headed bull, swimming r.	Horse walking r., with bridle hanging down in the shape of a crescent; above, wreath: border of dots.
29	6·7	AR ·45	ϹΕΛΑ Similar.	Similar.
30	9·2	AR ·5	Similar.	Similar.
31	12·3	AR ·45	ϹΕ Λ Α Similar.	Similar.
32	8·	AR ·45	ϹΕΛΑ Similar.	Similar.
33	11·9	AR ·45	Similar type; beneath, barley-corn.	Similar.
34	7·5	AR ·35	ϹΕΛ Fore-part of man-headed bull, swimming r.	Wheel of four spokes.
35	11·3	AR ·35	ΕΛΑ Similar.	Similar.

No.	Wt.	Metal. Size.	Obverse.	Reverse.
			Period of Transition.	
36	264·8	Æ 1·1	ϹΕΛΑΣ Fore-part of man-headed bull, swimming r.: plain border.	Quadriga r., driven by male figure wearing long chiton, who holds goad in r. hand and reins in both; horses walking; above, Nike flying r., holding wreath and fillet; in ex., device consisting of honeysuckle between two volutes: border of dots.

No.	Wt.	Metal. Size.	Obverse.	Reverse.
37	269·6	Æ 1·1	<ΕΛΑΣ Similar.	Similar.
38	255·6	Æ 1·15	Similar.	Similar.
39	265·6	Æ 1·05	Inscr. obscure. Similar type.	Similar.
40	265·	Æ 1·05	ΛΑΣ Fore-part of man-headed bull, ear turned forward, swimming l.	Similar.
41	237·5	Æ 1·	ϹΕΛΑΣ Fore-part of man-headed bull, swimming r.; beneath, tunny-fish r. and spray of olive.	Similar quadriga r., driven by aged man wearing long chiton, who holds goad in r. hand and reins in both; above, Nike r., crowning horses with wreath, which she holds in both hands.
42	265·6	Æ 1·	Same. (Same die.)	Same. (Same die.)
43	260·	Æ 1·	ΕΛΑΣ Similar type; beneath, spray of olive.	Quadriga r., driven by aged man, who holds goad in r. hand and reins in both; horses walking; above, olive-wreath.

No.	Wt.	Metal. Size.	Obverse.	Reverse.
44	266·8	Æ 1·	ϹΕΛΑΣ Similar type; beneath, swan l.	Same. (Same die.)
45	266·5	Æ 1·	Similar type and symbol.	Quadriga l., driven by aged man, who holds goad in r. hand and reins in both; horses walking; above, olive-wreath.

No.	Wt.	Metal. Size.	Obverse.	Reverse.
46	260·4	Æ 1·1	ϹΕΛΑΣ Similar type; beneath, crane r.	Similar type r., and wreath.
47	262·7	Æ 1·	ƸΑΛƎ⅂ Fore-part of man-headed bull, swimming r.	Quadriga l., driven by bearded charioteer wearing long chiton, who holds goad in r. hand and reins in both; horses walking; above, Nike flying l., crowning horses: plain border.

No.	Wt.	Metal. Size.	Obverse.	Reverse.
48	268·3	Æ 1·05	ΓΕΛΑΣ Similar.	Same. (Same die.)
49	267·5	Æ 1·1	ΕΛΑΣ Fore-part of man-headed bull, swimming l.	Similar.

No.	Wt.	Metal. Size.	Obverse.	Reverse.
50	269·7	Æ 1·	Same die as no. 48.	Similar quadriga r., driven by bearded charioteer, who holds goad in r. hand and reins in both; above, Nike flying r., crowning horses; in ex., crane r.: plain border.
51	266·	Æ 1·	ΓΕΛΑΣ Similar type.	Same. (Same die.)
52	11·	Æ ·5	ΣΕΛΑΣ Fore-part of man-headed bull, swimming r.	Horseman l., bearded, helmeted, holding in r. reins, and in l. spear and round shield; horse prancing: plain border.
53	10·9	Æ ·55	Similar.	Similar.

Period of Finest Art.

No.	Wt.	Metal. Size.	Obverse.	Reverse.
54	264·6	Æ 1·05	Young head of river-god Gelas l., with short horn, diademed; around, three river-fishes.	ΓΕΛΩΙΟΝ (in ex.) Quadriga r., driven by Nike wearing charioteer's long chiton; horses trotting; above, olive-wreath: plain border.

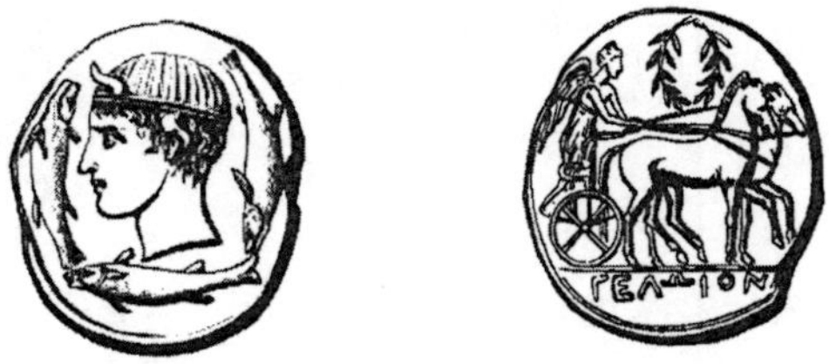

No.	Wt.	Metal. Size.	Obverse.	Reverse.
55	128·	Æ ·8	ΓΕΛΑ Similar head l.; in front, E ? all within wreath of olive.	Horseman, wearing helmet tunic and chlamys, galloping r., striking with spear at prostrate foot-soldier, who tries to shelter himself with his round shield.

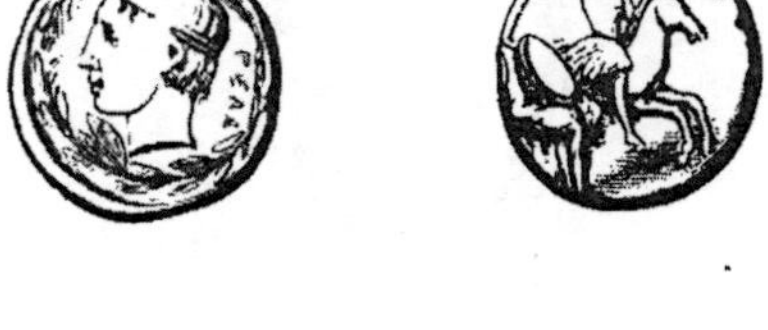

No.	Wt.	Metal. Size.	Obverse.	Reverse.
56	113·1	Æ ·8	Same. (Same die.)	Same. (Same die.)
57	258·7	Æ 1·05	ƸΑΛΛƎ⅂ Fore-part of man-headed bull, swimming r.; above, barleycorn; on edge, where bull's body is divided, ⅂Α ?	ΓΕ ΛΩ ΙΩ Fast quadriga r., driven by Nike holding goad and reins; above, eagle, flying r., holding serpent in its talons.

58	263·	Æ 1·	ƸΑΛΛƎ⅂ Similar.	ΕΛΩΙ ΩΝ Fast quadriga l., driven by Nike holding goad in l. hand and reins in both; above, eagle, flying towards r., with serpent in its talons; in ex., stalk of barley l.

59	266·	Æ 1·	Similar.	ΓΕΛΩΙΩΝ Fast quadriga l., driven by youth, wearing long chiton, who holds goad in r. hand and reins in both; above, eagle flying l.; in ex., stalk of barley l.: plain border.

No.	Wt.	Metal. Size.	Obverse.	Reverse.
60	7·8	AR ·35	Γ ΕΛΩΙΩΝ Bearded head of river-god Gelas l., crowned with barley; horn falling back from temple.	Head of young Herakles r., wearing lion's skin: behind, astragalos.
61	8·9	AR ·4	ΓΕΛΩΙΩΝ Similar.	Same.

Period of Decline; early.

No.	Wt.	Metal. Size.	Obverse.	Reverse.
62	16·2	AR ·5	ΓΕΛΑ Ϟ Bearded head of river-god Gelas r., with short horns falling back from forehead.	Free horse r., prancing.

COPPER.

Period of Finest Art.

With marks of value.

Trias.

No.	Wt.	Metal. Size.	Obverse.	Reverse.
63	56·	Æ ·65	Young head of river-god Gelas r., with short horns over forehead, hair erect; behind, barleycorn: border of dots.	ΓΕΛΑϞ Bull walking r., head lowered; in ex., ●●●: border of dots.
64	58·	Æ ·7	Similar.	Similar.
65	57·	Æ ·65	Similar.	Similar; above, barleycorn.
66	52·	Æ ·65	Similar.	Similar, the type l.
67	67·	Æ ·75	Similar.	Similar.
68	48·	Æ ·7	ΓΕΛΑ Similar head, and symbol: same border.	Bull walking r.; above, branch of olive r.; in ex., ●●●: border of dots.
69	55·	Æ ·65	Similar.	Similar.

No.	Wt.	Metal. Size.	Obverse.	Reverse.
70	·55	Æ ·7	ΓΕΛΑΣ Similar head: same border.	Similar.
71	·73	Æ ·75	ΓΕΛΑΣ Young head of river-god Gelas r., with short horns, wearing taenia: border of dots.	Bull walking l., head lowered; above, Π; in ex., ●●●: border of dots.
72	·65	Æ ·75	Similar.	Similar.
73	·57	Æ ·7	Similar type: same border.	ΓΕΛΑΣ Similar.

Uncia.

No.	Wt.	Metal. Size.	Obverse.	Reverse.
74	·75	Æ ·45	Young head of river-god Gelas r., short horns over forehead, hair erect; behind, barleycorn: border of dots.	ΓΕΛΑΣ Bull walking l., head lowered; above, barleycorn; in ex., ●: border of dots.

Without marks of value.

No.	Wt.	Metal. Size.	Obverse.	Reverse.
75		Æ ·85	Head of bearded Herakles r., wearing lion's skin; behind, astragalos?	ΓΕΛΩΙ ΩΝ Bearded head of river-god Gelas l., with short horns over forehead, and crowned with barley.
76		Æ ·45	Head of young Herakles r., wearing lion's skin.	ΓΕΛΩΙ Similar type; horn not visible.
77		Æ ·55	ΓΕΛΩΙ ΩΝ Head of Demeter or Persephone, three-quarter-face towards r., wearing wreath of barley, earring, and necklace.	Similar type: border of dots.

No.	Wt.	Metal. Size.	Obverse.	Reverse.
78		Æ ·55	Similar.	Similar.

No.	Wt.	Metal. Size.	Obverse.	Reverse.

Period of Decline ; early.

No.	Wt.	Metal. Size.	Obverse.	Reverse.
79		Æ 1·05	Youth r., wearing crested helmet, with feather at the side, and chlamys ; about to slay with sword a ram running r., which he seizes with l. hand : border of dots.	Free horse prancing r. ; above, star of eight rays.

No.	Wt.	Metal. Size.	Obverse.	Reverse.
80		Æ ·9	Similar.	Similar.

Period of Decline ; late.

No.	Wt.	Metal. Size.	Obverse.	Reverse.
81		Æ ·85	Young male head r., wearing tainia.	ΓΕΛ Youth r., wearing chlamys, about to slay with sword a ram running r., which he seizes with l. hand.
82		Æ ·85	Similar.	Similar type ; behind, Π.
83		Æ ·8	Young head of river-god Gelas r., crowned with reeds : border of dots. (On neck countermark : bucranium.)	ΛΩΙ ΩΝ Similar type, helmet seen ; behind, Η : plain border.
84		Æ ·75	Head of Persephone r., crowned with barley : border of dots.	ΓΕΛΩΙ ΩΝ Stalk of barley l.
85		Æ ·65	Bust of Persephone r., crowned with barley ; in field r., Α. (This letter perhaps remains from former striking.)	ΓΕΛΩΙ ΩΝ Similar type : plain border.

HIMERA.

SILVER.

Before B.C. 481.

No.	Wt.	Metal. Size.	Obverse.	Reverse.
1	89·5	Æ ·85	Cock advancing l.: border of dots.	Square device, consisting of four incuse triangles and four in relief, the whole arranged like the sails of a mill, and within incuse border of dots.

No.	Wt.	Metal. Size.	Obverse.	Reverse.
2	85·7	Æ ·85	Similar.	Similar.
3	85·8	Æ ·9	ΙИ M Similar.	Similar.
4	82·6	Æ ·8	HI M Similar type r.: same border.	Similar.
5	85·4	Æ ·8	Similar type: same border.	Similar.
6	88·4	Æ ·8	V⅃ Similar.	Similar.
7	89·3	Æ ·85	Similar type: border of dots.	Similar.
8	81·5	Æ ·85	Similar type l.: same border.	Similar.
9	12·2	Æ ·45	Similar. (Much injured.)	Similar.
10	12·	Æ ·45	Similar type r.: same border.	Similar.
11	13·6	Æ ·45	Hen l.	Similar.
12	13·6	Æ ·45	Similar type r.: plain border.	Similar.

No.	Wt.	Metal. Size.	Obverse.	Reverse.
13	2·9	Æ ·25	Cock advancing r.	Incuse square, divided into eight triangles by bars crossing.
14	79·1	Æ ·75	Cock advancing r.: border of dots.	Hen r., enclosed by linear square within incuse square.
15	89·9	Æ ·75	Cock l.: border of dots.	Similar.
16	86·5	Æ ·8	Similar.	Similar type, enclosed by border of incuse dots: all within incuse square.
17	87·5	Æ ·8	Similar.	Similar; type l.
18	87·	Æ ·75	Same type r.; above, [monogram]: same border.	Similar; type r.
19	89·	Æ ·8	Same type l.; above, ΓV: same border.	Similar; above hen, VΓ.
20	85·	Æ ·8	ƎMIH Similar type; above, ΓV V: border of dots.	Similar type: border not visible.
21	83·7	Æ ·75	HIMΕ Similar type: same border.	Hen l., in linear square within incuse square.
22	73·5	Æ ·75 plated	Similar type and same border.	Similar; type r.
23	87·5	Æ ·75	IATON Cock l.: border of dots.	Similar.

No.	Wt.	Metal. Size.	Obverse.	Reverse.
			Under Theron and Thrasydaeus, B.C. 481–467.	
24	132·6	AR ·8	HIMERA Cock l.	Crab.

No.	Wt.	Metal. Size.	Obverse.	Reverse.
25	132·	AR ·8	Similar.	Similar.
26	134·6	AR ·75	Similar.	Similar.
27	62·6	AR ·7	Cock l.: border of dots.	HIMER A Crab.
28	64·7	AR ·7	Similar.	HIME AЯ Similar.
29	64·8	AR ·7	Similar.	HIME R AION Astragalos.
			With marks of value.	
			Hexas.	
30	1·2	AR ·15	Astragalos.	●●.
			Period of Transition.	
31	263·2	AR 1·1	Nymph Himera, wearing sleeved chiton, and peplos of which ends fall over r. arm, facing, head l.; she holds in r. patera over altar with conical top, her l. hand extended open; to r., a Seilen r., bending backwards in trough, and receiving on his chest a jet of water from fountain in the shape of a lion's head.	Inscr. effaced. Quadriga l., driven by male figure wearing long chiton, who holds goad and reins; horses walking; above, Nike flying r., crowning charioteer: border of dots.

No.	Wt.	Metal. Size.	Obverse.	Reverse.
32	262·5	Æ 1·05	Similar type, the lion's head raised on steps; above l. arm of nymph, wheel of four spokes.	ΙΜΕΡΑΙΟΝ Similar type: same border.
33	265·3	Æ 1·1	Similar type, altar garlanded, the Seilen, facing, bends sideways to receive water on l. shoulder; above r. arm of nymph, barleycorn.	ΙΜΕΡΑΙΟΝ Similar type r., charioteer holds goad in r. hand and reins in both: border of dots.
34	265·1	Æ 1·1	Similar type, seilen towards r.; above l. arm of nymph, barleycorn; in ex., river-fish r.	Same. (Same die.)

35	128·4	Æ ·85	[Ι]ΑΤΟΝ (in ex.) Similar type, in place of seilen and fountain, erect caduceus bound with fillet; above r. arm of nymph, barleycorn.	ΙΜΕΡΑ Ι Ο Ν Naked youth, seated sideways on horse, galloping l., whose mane he grasps with r. hand, his l. hand, in which he holds whip, resting on horse's flank; in ex., crane flying l.: border of dots.

36	129·5	Æ ·9	Similar: ex. off coin.	Similar type: same border.

No.	Wt.	Metal. Size.	Obverse.	Reverse.
37	26·9	AR ·6	I O N Naked youth seated on he-goat, running r.; he holds in r. caduceus over shoulder, in l. buccinum which he blows: border of dots.	N Nike, wearing sleeved chiton, and peplos of which ends fall over r. arm, flying l., grasping in r. aplustre bound with long fillet, and holding up her dress with l.
38	30·9	AR ·6	ΛOI H Similar type l., buccinum in r., caduceus in l.: same border.	N I A K Similar.
39	32·3	AR ·6	Λ OIAΡƎ MI H Same. (Same die.)	Traces of legend. Similar.
40	31·2	AR ·6	Same. (Same die.)	Same. (Same die.)
41	12·5	AR ·45	Fore-part of monster l., having the horn of a goat, the head of a bearded man, the paw of a lion, with lion's head resting against shoulder, and a curled wing: border of dots.	H AIO N Naked youth seated on he-goat, running l.; he holds with l. hand horn of goat, his r. arm raised to strike him with whip.

No.	Wt.	Metal. Size.	Obverse.	Reverse.
42	11·9	AR ·45	Similar. (On body countermark: a vine-leaf.)	A I O N Similar type.
43	13·5	AR ·4	Similar type r., with pointed ear.	Similar type.
44	12·1	AR ·45	Similar.	Similar.
45	10·7	AR ·45	Bearded male head l., with pointed ear, wearing crested Athenian helmet: border of dots.	I ME A I O N Pair of greaves.

No.	Wt.	Metal. Size.	Obverse.	Reverse.
46	10·2	Æ ·4	Bearded head r., Kronos? border of dots.	ΒΙ ΜΕ Corinthian helmet without crest r.
47	8·3	Æ ·45	Similar head, wearing tainia: same border.	ΑЯ Ι Similar helmet, with volute on upper part.

Period of Finest Art

No.	Wt.	Metal. Size.	Obverse.	Reverse.
48	263·6	Æ ·95	Nymph facing, head l., wearing sleeved chiton and peplos the ends of which fall over r. arm; she holds in r hand patera over altar with square horns; behind her, a Seilen, facing, bending sideways to receive on his l. shoulder jet of water issuing from lion's-head fountain.	Quadriga r., driven by charioteer wearing long chiton, who holds reins in both hands horses in high action; above, Nike l., holding wreath and tablet; in ex., sea-horse l.

No.	Wt.	Metal. Size.	Obverse.	Reverse.
49	10·8	Æ ·45	ΙΜΕΡΑΙΩ Ν Head of young Herakles r., wearing lion's skin: border of dots.	Pallas facing, wearing chiton with diploïs, ægis, and three-crested helmet; she holds in raised r. spear by the middle, on l. arm, round shield: border of dots.

COPPER.

Period of Transition.

With marks of value.

Hemilitron.

No.	Wt.	Metal. Size.	Obverse.	Reverse.
50	102·	Æ ·8	Naked male figure, seated on he-goat running r.; he holds in r. buccinum aloft; in l. caduceus; beneath, grasshopper r.: plain border.	ΚΙΜ ΑΡ ∀ Nike, wearing chiton and peplos the ends of which fall over r. arm, advancing l.; she holds in r. aplustre, to the top of which is attached a wreath, to the bottom, a fillet; with l. she raises her dress; in field l., ⁝⁝: border of dots.

No.	Wt.	Metal. Size.	Obverse.	Reverse.
51	91·	Æ ·8	Similar; rider wears chlamys; beneath, Corinthian helmet r.: same border.	IMEPA Similar; no wreath.

Trias.

No.	Wt.	Metal. Size.	Obverse.	Reverse.
52	36·	Æ ·6	Similar type l.; beneath, ●●●.	Similar type; aplustre not seen.

Hexas.

No.	Wt.	Metal. Size.	Obverse.	Reverse.
53	35·	Æ ·55	Similar; beneath, grasshopper r.: border of dots.	ION Similar; aplustre seen; in field l., ●●.

Period of Finest Art.

Hemilitron.

No.	Wt.	Metal. Size.	Obverse.	Reverse.
54	60·	Æ ·65	IM E Head of nymph l., wearing sphendone, earring, and necklace; in front, ●●●●●●: plain border.	●●●●●● within laurel-wreath.
55	28·	Æ ·5	Head of nymph, three-quarter-face towards l., wearing ornamented ampyx and earring.	IME Cray-fish l.; above, ●●●●●●.

THERMAE HIMERAEAE.

SILVER.

Period of Finest Art.

No.	Wt.	Metal. Size.	Obverse.	Reverse.
1	129·3	AR ·9	ΘΕΡΜΙΤΑΝ Head of Hera r., wearing earring, necklace, and stephanos ornamented with fore-parts of griffins r.; behind, dolphin r., downwards: border of dots.	Young Herakles, naked, seated l., on rock covered with lion's skin, holding in r. club downwards, l. resting on rock; behind him, strung bow and quiver with strap: border of dots.

COPPER.

Period of Decline; early.

No.	Wt.	Metal. Size.	Obverse.	Reverse.
2		Æ ·6	Head of Hera r., wearing earring, necklace, and stephanos adorned with honeysuckle ornaments: plain border.	ΘΕΡΜΙΤΑΝ Head of young Herakles r., wearing lion's skin: plain border.
3		Æ ·55	Similar.	Similar.
4		Æ ·75	Female head r., wearing earring and necklace, hair bound with cord passing thrice round; behind, crescent, horns downwards: border of dots.	ΘΕΡΜΙΤΑΝ Head of young Herakles r., wearing lion's skin: border of dots.

No.	Wt.	Metal. Size.	Obverse.	Reverse.
			Period of Decline; late.	
5		Æ 1·1	Head of bearded Herakles r., wearing lion's skin; over shoulder, club: border of dots.	ΘΕΡΜΙΤΑΝ (in ex.) Three nymphs, facing, clad in chiton and peplos; the one on l. bears in r. bunch of grapes, the middle one is turreted and veiled; each holds in l. the end of her peplos: border of dots.
6		Æ ·85	Similar.	Similar.
7		Æ ·8	Similar.	ΘΕΡ ΜΙ ΤΑΝ Female figure l., veiled and turreted, wearing chiton and peplos; she holds patera and cornucopiæ: border of dots.
8		Æ ·5	Female head r., veiled: border of dots.	ΘΕΡΜ ΤΑΝ She-goat lying l.: border of dots.
9		Æ 1·	Female head r., veiled and turreted; behind, cornucopiæ: border of dots.	ΘΕΡΜΙΤΑΝ ΙΜΕΡΑΙΩΝ Draped figure of an old man, Stesichoros, r., leaning on long staff and reading book: border of dots.
10		Æ ·95	Similar.	Similar.

HYBLA MAGNA.

COPPER.

Period of Decline; late.

No.	Wt.	Metal. Size.	Obverse.	Reverse.
1		Æ ·75	Female bust r., veiled, wearing necklace and modius; behind, bee r.: border of dots.	ΥΒΛ ΑΣ ΜΕΓΑΛΑΣ Dionysiac female figure l., draped, holding amphora and thyrsos; at her feet, she-panther leaping up: plain border.

No.	Wt.	Metal. Size.	Obverse.	Reverse.
2		Æ ·9	Similar.	Similar.
3		Æ ·8	Similar.	Similar.

IAETIA.

COPPER.

Period of Decline; late.

No.	Wt.	Metal. Size.	Obverse.	Reverse.
1		Æ ·85	IAITI NΩ Head of bearded Herakles r., wearing lion's skin.	Triquetra of legs; at junction, winged Gorgon's head; between the legs, three ears of barley: border of dots.
2		Æ ·9	IAI TINΩN Similar type.	Similar.
3		Æ ·85	Bust of Artemis r.; behind shoulder, quiver: border of dots.	IAI TI NΩN Male figure l., wearing short chiton; he holds in r. patera, in l. long sceptre surmounted by Phrygian cap or helmet: border of dots.
4		Æ ·75	Head of young warrior r., wearing helmet surmounted by mural crown: border of dots.	IAITI NΩN Warrior l., wearing helmet surmounted by mural crown, and cuirass he holds spear and shield and wears sword slung round body: border of dots.
5		Æ ·8	Warrior l., wearing helmet surmounted by mural crown, and cuirass, holding spear and round shield: border of dots.	IAITI NΩN within laurel-wreath: border of dots.

LEONTINI.

SILVER.

Period of Archaic Art.

No.	Wt.	Metal. Size.	Obverse.	Reverse.
1	259·5	Æ 1·05	ИΟИΙΤИΟƎΛ Lion's head r., with open mouth; around, four barleycorns.	Quadriga r., driven by male charioteer wearing long chiton, holding goad in r. hand and reins in both; horses galloping; above, Nike flying r., crowning horses: border of dots.
2	263·7	Æ 1·	ΟИΙΤИΟƎΛ Similar.	Quadriga r., driven by bearded male charioteer, who holds reins in both hands; horses walking; above, Nike flying r., crowning horses: border of dots.
3	268·7	Æ 1·	ΛΕ Ο ΝΤ Ι ΝΟΝ Similar.	Similar; charioteer holds goad with reins.
4	261·	Æ 1·	No inscr. Similar type.	ΛΕΟΝΤΙΝΟΝ (in ex.) Similar.
5	267·8	Æ 1·	ΛΕΟΝΤΙΝΟΝ Similar type.	No inscr. Similar type: same border.
6	279·5	Æ 1·	ИΟИΙΤИΟƎΛ Similar.	Similar.
7	264·3	Æ 1·05	ΛΕΟ Ν ΤΙ Ν ΟΝ Similar; inscr. between lion's head and barleycorns.	Similar; charioteer holds goad in r. hand, reins in l.
8	261·	Æ 1·	Λ Ε ΟΝΤΙ ΝΟ Ν Similar.	Similar.

No.	Wt.	Metal. Size.	Obverse.	Reverse.
9	262·6	Æ 1·1	VO VIT VO ƎΛ Female head r., wearing necklace and earring; hair turned up behind, and bound with wreath; around, outside inscr., four barleycorns.	Similar type; in ex., lion running r.: border of dots.

10	260·	Æ 1·1	VEOИTI ИO И Head of Apollo r., laur.; hair cut short over forehead, in formal curls over temple, and plaited behind, with a long tress falling behind the ear; around, three laurel-leaves; beneath, lion running r.	Quadriga r., driven by young male charioteer, r. arm and shoulder bare; he holds branch in r. hand and reins in l.; above, Nike flying l., crowning him; in ex., lion running r.: border of dots.

11	270·	Æ 1·	Same. (Same die.)	Similar; charioteer fully draped.
12	128·	Æ ·8	ΛEOИTIИOИ Lion's head r., with open mouth; around, four barleycorns.	Naked horseman r., holding whip and reins; horse walking: border of dots.
13	129·7	Æ ·85	ΛE O И TI И O И Similar: plain border.	Similar; horse cantering.

No.	Wt.	Metal. Size.	Obverse.	Reverse.
14	125·	Ꞧ ·75	O ИIT И OƎ Λ Similar.	Similar.
15	133·	Ꞧ ·75	OИI ИOƎΛ Similar.	Similar.
16	66·3	Ꞧ ·6	ΛEONT I NO N Similar type: plain border.	Naked horseman r., holding reins in l. hand, r. resting on hip; horse trotting: border of dots.
17	64·3	Ꞧ ·55	Λ EONT I N ON Similar type.	Similar.
18	16·9	Ꞧ ·45	Lion's scalp facing: border of dots.	ΛE ON Barleycorn: plain border.
19	9·1	Ꞧ ·45	Similar.	ΛE ON Similar.
20	9·3	Ꞧ ·4	Similar.	Similar: border of dots.
21	9·8	Ꞧ ·4	Similar.	ƎΛ ON Similar type: plain border.
22	9·7	Ꞧ ·35	Lion's head r., mouth open: border of dots.	ИO ƎΛ Barleycorn: plain border.

With marks of value.

Hemilitron.

No.	Wt.	Metal. Size.	Obverse.	Reverse.
23	5·8	Ꞧ ·35	Lion's head r., mouth open: border of dots.	Λ E Barleycorn; on either side, ●●●●.

Pentonkion.

No.	Wt.	Metal. Size.	Obverse.	Reverse.
24	4·	Ꞧ ·25	Similar.	●●●●●
25	3·1	Ꞧ ·25	Similar.	Similar.

Hexas.

No.	Wt.	Metal. Size.	Obverse.	Reverse.
26	1·4	Ꞧ ·2	Similar.	I ●●

No.	Wt.	Metal. Size.	Obverse.	Reverse.
			Period of Transition.	
27	259·	Æ 1·05	Head of Apollo r., wearing laurel-wreath of two rows of leaves, hair cut short in front and tied in bunch behind with cord: border of dots.	ΛΕ Ο ΝΤΙ ΝΟ Ν Lion's head r., mouth open; around, four barley-corns; over type, ∴ (very small).
28	265·1	Æ 1·05	Similar type; hair turned up behind and bound with wreath: border of dots.	ΛΕ Ο ΝΤ ΙΝ ΟΝ Similar; pellets absent.

No.	Wt.	Metal. Size.	Obverse.	Reverse.
29	261·2	Æ 1·05	Similar type: (wreath with three rows of leaves:) same border.	ΛΕΟ ΝΤ Ι ΝΟ Ν Similar.
30	263·2	Æ 1·	Similar.	ΛΕ ΟΝ ΤΙ Ν Ο Ν Similar.
31	270·2	Æ 1·	Similar.	ΛΕΟ ΝΤ Ι Ν Ο Σ Similar.
32	270·3	Æ 1·1	Similar.	ΛΕΟ Ν ΤΙ ΝΟ Ν Similar.
33	268·4	Æ ·95	Similar.	ΛΕ Ο Ν Τ ΙΝΟ Ν Similar.
34	269·5	Æ 1·05	Head of Apollo r., wearing laurel-wreath, (with three rows of leaves,) hair rolled behind: border of dots.	ΛΕΟΝΤ ΙΝ Ο Similar.

No.	Wt	Metal. Size.	Obverse.	Reverse.
35	259·3	Æ 1·	Same. (Same die.)	ΛΕΟ ΤΙΝ ΟΝ Similar.
36	262·5	Æ 1·15	Similar type l.: same border.	Λ ΕΟΝ ΤΙΝΟ Ν Lion's head l., mouth open; around, four barleycorns.

No.	Wt	Metal. Size.	Obverse.	Reverse.
37	263·4	Æ 1·	Same. (Same die.)	ΛΕΟΝΤΙΝΟΝ (in one line.) Similar.
38	258·8	Æ 1·	Same. (Same die.)	ΛΕΟ ΤΙΝΟΝ Lion's head r., mouth open; around, four barleycorns.
39	263·	Æ 1·05	Similar.	ΛΕ ΟΝ ΤΙ ΝΟΝ Lion's head l., mouth open; three barleycorns, above, below, and in front; behind, laurel-leaf.
40	261·6	Æ 1·1	Similar.	ΛΕΟΝΤΙΝΟΝ Lion's head r., mouth open; around, three barleycorns; beneath, lyre on its side.
41	262·6	Æ 1·05	Similar type r. (wreath with two rows of leaves.)	ΛΕΟ ΝΤ ΙΝ ΟΝ Similar type; three barleycorns, above, in front, and beneath; behind, tripod-lebes.

No.	Wt.	Metal. Size.	Obverse	Reverse.
42	66·9	AR ·8	Head of Apollo r., wearing laurel-wreath, (with three rows of leaves,) hair turned up behind and bound with wreath : border of dots.	VE ON Lion's head l., mouth open ; above, in front, and beneath, a barley-corn : plain border.

No.	Wt.	Metal. Size.	Obverse	Reverse.
43	65·8	AR ·75	Same. (Same die.)	VEO N Same type r., with barleycorns.
44	61·	AR ·75	Head of Apollo l., wearing laurel-wreath, (with three rows of leaves,) hair turned up behind under wreath : border of dots.	VE ON Similar.
45	11·3	AR ·5	VEON Lion's head l., with open mouth : border of dots.	River-god naked l., holding in r. patera over altar, and in l., laurel-branch ; behind, barleycorn.
46	12·8	AR ·5	VEO N Similar type r. : same border.	Similar.
47	12·1	AR ·5	LEON Similar.	Similar ; on altar, ꓘ.
48	12·1	AR ·5	ΛE O N Similar.	Similar. (altar effaced.)
49	11·2	AR ·5	VEO N Similar.	Similar. (altar effaced.)
50	10·6	AR ·5	Head of Apollo r., laur., (wreath with two rows of leaves,) hair cut short in front, in formal locks over temple, and plaited behind, with long tress falling behind ear : border of dots.	V . E O N Barleycorn : plain border.
51	11·3	AR ·45	Similar.	Similar.

No.	Wt.	Metal. Size.	Obverse.	Reverse.
52	12·3	Æ ·55	Head of Apollo r., diademed, hair falling in tresses over temple, and rolled behind: border of dots.	Similar.

Period of Finest Art.

No.	Wt.	Metal. Size.	Obverse.	Reverse.
53	260·8	Æ 1·1	Head of Apollo r., laur.: border of dots.	VEONTINON Lion's head r., with open mouth; around, four barleycorns; in field l., tripod-lebes.
54	268·5	Æ 1·05	Head of Apollo r., laur.; hair short.	ΛΕΟΝΤΙΝΟ Ν Similar type; around, four barleycorns.
55	205·8	Æ 1· plated	Similar type: border of dots.	ΛΕΟΝ Τ ΙΝ Ο · Ν Similar type; above, in front, and behind, a barleycorn; beneath, river-fish r.

COPPER.

Period of Finest Art.

With marks of value.

Trias.

No.	Wt.	Metal. Size.	Obverse.	Reverse.
56	28·	Æ ·55	ΛΕΟΝ Head of Apollo r., laur., with short hair; behind, laurel-leaf with berry: plain border.	Tripod-lebes with three handles; between the legs, lyre and plectrum? on either side, barleycorn; in ex., ●●●.
57	23·	Æ ·55	Similar.	Similar.
58	21·	Æ ·6	ΛΕΟΝ Similar type l.; in front, same symbol: same border.	Similar.

No.	Wt.	Metal. Size.	Obverse.	Reverse.
			Period of Decline; late.	
59		Æ ·85	Bust of Apollo r., laur.; behind shoulder, top of quiver.	ΛΕΟΝΤΙΝ Ω Ν Demeter l., holding in r. two ears of corn, and in l. long torch; at her feet, plough l.: border of dots.
60		Æ ·85	Similar type: border of dots.	Similar.
61		Æ ·85	Head of river-god? bound with reeds; behind, crab.	ΛΕ ΟΝ ΤΙΝΩΝ Demeter or Isis? facing, wearing modius and veil; holds in r., two poppy-heads, in l. long torch.
62		Æ ·85	Bust of Demeter or Persephone, facing, wearing wreath of corn, shoulders draped; on l., plough r.: border of dots.	Λ ΕΟΝ Naked figure of river-god, seated r. on rock, holding cornucopiæ and branch; in field l., crab: border of dots.
63		Æ ·85	Similar.	Similar.
64		Æ ·9	Similar.	ИΩИI ΛΕΟΝΤ Similar type.
65		Æ ·8	Similar.	Similar: border of dots.
66		Æ ·6	Head of Demeter l., wearing corn-wreath and veil; behind, plough: border of dots.	ΛΕΟΝ ΤΙΝΩΝ Sheaf of barley: plain border.
67		Æ ·65	Similar; above symbol, ΛΕ.	ΛΕΟΝ ΤΙΝΩΝ Similar type.
68		Æ ·65	Jugate heads of Apollo and Artemis r., the former laur., the latter wearing stephane; behind, plough r.: border of dots.	ΛΕΟΝ ΤΙ ΝΩΝ Two ears of barley tied together: plain border.
69		Æ ·65	Similar.	Same inscr.; similar type.

No.	Wt.	Metal. Size.	Obverse.	Reverse.
70		Æ ·65	Female Dionysiac head r., bound with ivy: border of dots.	ΛΕΟΝ ΤΙΝΩΝ Warrior, facing, leaning with r. on spear, and holding in l. cornucopiæ? shield slung round neck.
71		Æ ·6	Similar.	Similar.
72		Æ ·55	Head of Apollo l., laur.; behind, plough: border of dots.	ΛΕΟΝ ΤΙΝΩΝ Lion walking l.: plain border.
73		Æ ·55	Similar.	ΛΕ ΟΝ ΤΙ ΝΩ Lion l.: plain border.
74		Æ ·55	Similar.	[monogram] Fore-part of running lion l.: plain border.
75		Æ ·55	Head of Apollo r., laur.; behind, plough.	ΛΕΟΝΤ ΙΝΩΝ Sacrificial galerus; border of dots.
76		Æ ·45	Similar type l.; behind, plough: border of dots.	Two fishes l.; beneath, [monogram]: plain border.
77		Æ ·5	Similar.	ΛΕΟΝ ΤΙΝΩΝ Similar type: same border.

Coin of Syracuse counterstruck by Leontini.

No.	Wt.	Metal. Size.	Obverse.	Reverse.
78		Æ ·8	Head of Pallas l., wearing Corinthian helmet without crest; on helmet, countermark:—ΛΕΟΝ Head of Apollo l., laur.	Sea-horse l. with curled wing: plain border.

No.	Wt.	Metal. Size.	Obverse.	Reverse.
			LILYBAEUM.	
			COPPER.	
			Period of Decline; late.	
1		Æ ·55	Head of Apollo r., laur., with long hair: border of dots.	ΛΥΒΑΙ ΙΤΑΝ Tripod-lebes with three handles: border of dots.
2		Æ ·9	Head of Apollo r., laur., with long hair; over shoulder, bow and quiver: border of dots.	ΛΙΛΥΒΑΙ ΙΤΑΝ Lyre: (with three strings:) border of dots.
3		Æ ·9	Similar.	Similar.
4		Æ 1·25	ΛΙΛΥ ΒΑΙ [ΙΤΑΙϹ] Female head r., wearing mural crown and veil, within a triangular enclosure: border of dots.	ΑΤΡΑΤΙΝΟ ΠΥΘΙΩΝ Serpent coiled around tripod: border of dots.
5		Æ 1·1	Similar.	Similar.
6		Æ 1·2	Similar.	Similar.
			Imperial.	
			AUGUSTUS.	
7		Æ ·65	AVGV within laurel-wreath: border of dots.	LILY BIT Lyre.
8		Æ ·7	Similar.	Similar.

LONGON.

SILVER.

Period of Transition.

No.	Wt.	Metal. Size.	Obverse.	Reverse.
1	11·3	Æ ·45	ИOIAИAΓΓoΛ Head of young Herakles r., in lion's skin: border of dots.	Young head l. of river-god Amenanos, with short horn above forehead.

MEGARA.

COPPER.

Period of Decline; late.

Trias.

No.	Wt.	Metal. Size.	Obverse.	Reverse.
1		Æ ·65	Bust of Pallas r., wearing necklace and crested Corinthian helmet: border of dots.	ΜΕ Bee; beneath, ●●●; in field l., uncertain letter: the whole within a wreath.

MENAENUM.

COPPER.

Period of Decline; late.

With marks of value.

No.	Wt.	Metal. Size.	Obverse.	Reverse.
			Tetras.	
1	61·	Æ ·65	Bust of Demeter r., wearing veil and corn-wreath: border of dots.	MENA INΩN Two torches crossed; below, ●●●●: plain border.
			Trias.	
2	42·	Æ ·65	Head of bearded Herakles r.: border of dots.	MENA INΩN Club r.; in field r., ●●●: plain border.
3	34·	Æ ·6	Similar.	Similar.
			Hexas.	
4	32·	Æ ·6	Bust of Hermes r., wearing petasos with wings at apex, and chlamys: border of dots.	MENAI NΩN Caduceus l.; in field r., ●●: plain border.

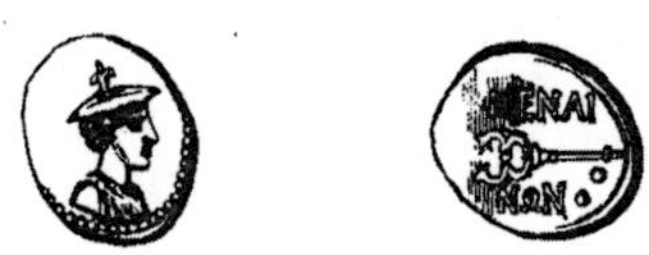

No.	Wt.	Metal. Size.	Obverse.	Reverse.
			Tetras.	
5	60·	Æ ·7	Bust of Demeter r., wearing necklace, wreath of corn, and veil: border of dots.	MENA INΩN Two torches crossed; beneath, IIII: plain border.
6	48·	Æ ·65	Similar.	MENA INΩN Similar.

No.	Wt.	Metal. Size.	Obverse.	Reverse.
			Without marks of value?	
7	58·	Æ ·65	Bust of Demeter r., wearing necklace, wreath of corn, and veil.	MENA INΩN Two torches crossed; beneath, Δ: plain border.
8	70·	Æ ·75	Bust of Zeus-Sarapis r., with laurel-wreath and Egyptian ornament; behind, E: border of dots.	MENA INΩN Fast biga r., driven by Nike, who holds whip and reins: plain border.
9	71	Æ ·75	Similar; no letter.	Similar; beneath horses, Π.
10	66·	Æ ·7	Bust of Apollo r., laur., with long hair; behind, Π: border of dots.	MENA INΩN Lyre (with four strings): plain border.
11	50·	Æ ·65	Similar.	MENA IN ΩN Asklepios, facing, holding in r. patera, and in l. rod, up which serpent twines.
12	66·	Æ ·7	Similar.	Similar: plain border.

MESSANA.

SILVER.

Under the name Zankle, before B.C. cir. 490.

No.	Wt.	Metal. Size.	Obverse.	Reverse.
1	84·9	Æ ·85	DANK Sickle - shaped object, on which are four equidistant projections, and within it a dolphin l. (harbour of Zankle): border of dots.	Incuse square of peculiar pattern, containing scallop.
2	63·1	Æ ·8	DANKL Similar type.	Similar.
3	75·1	Æ ·8	DANK Similar type, but without projections, and the tail of the dolphin outside sickle: border of dots.	Similar.
4	85·6	Æ ·9	DANKLE Similar type: border of dots between lines.	Similar.

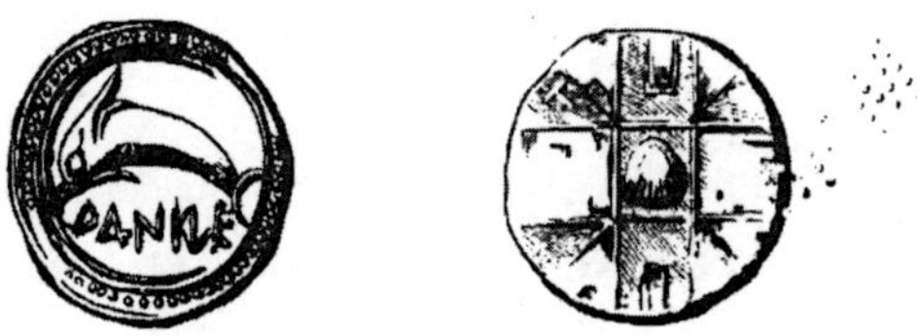

No.	Wt.	Metal. Size.	Obverse.	Reverse.
5	82·6	Æ ·95	Similar.	Similar.
6	85·	Æ ·9	Similar.	Similar.
7	11·3	Æ ·45	DANK Similar type: same border.	Similar.
8	1·7	Æ ·3	DAN Similar type: same border.	Similar.

No.	Wt.	Metal. Size.	Obverse.	Reverse.
			Period of Archaic Art. Time of Anaxilas, after B.C. cir. 490. With inscription ΜΕΣΣΕΝΙΟΝ.	
9	14·	Æ ·4	Lion's scalp: border of dots.	MEϟ: border of dots.

10	267·1	Æ ·95	Similar type: same border.	ΜΕ ϟϟΕ Ν ΙΟΝ Calf's head l.: border of dots.

11	269·7	Æ 1·	ΜΕϟϟΕ Ν ΙΟΝ Hare running r: border of dots.	Biga of mules (apene) r., driven by bearded male charioteer, who holds reins in both hands and goad, and sits drawn together on seat rising from the axle; mules walking; in ex., olive-leaf r.: border of dots.
12	259·9	Æ 1·05	ΜΕϟϟΕ ΝΙΟΝ Similar.	Similar.
13	244·	Æ 1·05 plated	Similar.	Similar.
14	266·2	Æ 1·05	ΜΕϟϟΕ Ν ΙΟ Ν Similar.	Similar.
15	265·3	Æ 1·1	ИOI И ƎϟϟƎM Similar type l.: same border.	Similar type l. and symbol l.: same border.
16	264·9	Æ 1·15	ΜΕϟϟΕ Ν ΙΟΝ Similar type r.; above, A: border of dots.	Similar type r.; above, Nike flying r., crowning mules; in ex., olive-leaf l.: border of dots.

No.	Wt.	Metal. Size.	Obverse.	Reverse.
			With inscription ΜΕΣΣΑΝΙΟΝ.	
17	236·	Æ 1· plated	MESSA N IO N Hare running r.: border of dots.	Biga of mules r., driven by male charioteer, seated as before, holding reins in both hands and goad; mules walking; above, Nike flying r., crowning mules; in ex., olive-leaf r.: border of dots.
18	264·5	Æ 1·1	ИOIИA MESS Similar type; beneath, spray of olive r.: same border.	Similar type; no goad; in ex., olive-leaf r., with fruit: border of dots.
19	269·5	Æ 1·	MESSAN I O N Similar type; beneath, B: same border.	Similar.
20	56·4	Æ ·7	MESSA N IO N Similar type; above, ꓭ: all within olive-wreath r.	Similar type and symbol: same border.
21	64·	Æ ·7	ИOIИ AƧƧƎM Similar type; within olive-wreath.	Similar.
22	13·7	Æ ·4	Hare running r.: border of dots.	ƧƎM: border of dots.
23	10·4	Æ ·5	Similar.	ƧƎM: same border.
24	11·9	Æ ·45	Similar.	ƧƎM within olive-wreath, inverted.
			Period of Transition. After B.C. cir. 476.	
25	258·7	Æ 1·05	MESSA N ION Hare running r.; beneath, spray of olive r.: border of dots.	Biga of mules r., driven by seated male charioteer, who holds reins in both hands; mules walking; above, Nike r., crowning mules; in ex., olive-leaf r.: border of dots.
26	267·3	Æ 1·	Similar; no symbol.	Similar.

No.	Wt.	Metal. Size.	Obverse.	Reverse.
27	256·8	Æ 1·1	WOIWA MEΣΣ Similar type; beneath, spray of olive r. with fruit: border of dots.	Similar.
28	263·7	Æ 1·05	MEΣΣANION Hare running r.: border of dots.	Similar type; Nike crowning charioteer; same symbol and border.
29	264·3	Æ 1·05	Similar.	Similar type; charioteer holds goad with reins; in ex., olive-leaf r. with fruit: border of dots.
30	262·3	Æ 1·15	Similar; above, bucranium.	Similar; mules standing.
31	61·3	Æ ·75	WOIW MEΣΣA Hare running r.: the whole within olive-wreath r.	Biga of mules r., driven by seated male charioteer, who holds reins in both hands; mules walking; above, Nike r., crowning mules; in ex., olive-leaf r. with fruit: border of dots.
32	62·6	Æ ·75	WO IW MEΣΣA Similar.	Similar.
33	9·1	Æ ·35	Dolphin r.; within olive-wreath r.	MEΣ Hare running r.: border of dots.

34	10·1	Æ ·35	Hare running r.: border of dots.	MEΣ plain border.
35	263·3	Æ 1·1	MEΣ Σ AN IO N Hare running r.; beneath, dolphin r.: border of dots.	Biga of mules r., driven by draped female charioteer (Messana) who stands erect in chariot, with chlamys flying, and holds reins in both hands and goad; mules walking; above, Nike r., crowning them; in ex., fish r.: border of dots.

No.	Wt.	Metal. Size.	Obverse.	Reverse.
36	266·9	Æ 1·	ΜΕΣΣΑΝΙΟΝ Similar.	Similar type; charioteer without chlamys and goad; in ex., two dolphins meeting: same border.
37	263·7	Æ 1·	ΜΕΣ ΣΑ Ν ΙΟ Ν Similar.	Similar type; Nike stepping on reins; in ex., leaf of olive with fruit r.: border of dots.

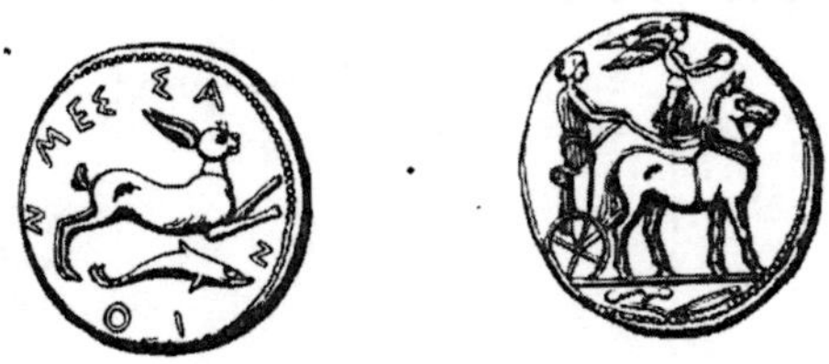

No.	Wt.	Metal. Size.	Obverse.	Reverse.
38	265·	Æ 1·05	ΜΕΣ Σ Α Ν ΙΟ Ν Similar.	ΜΕΣΣ ΑΝΑ Similar type; charioteer holding goad with reins, Nike wanting: same border.
39	262·7	Æ 1·05	Similar.	ΜΕΣΣΑ ΝΑ Similar type; in ex., two dolphins meeting: same border.
40	265·8	Æ 1·05	ΜΕΣΣΑΝΙ ΟΝ Similar.	ΑΝΑΣ ΣΕΜ Similar type; charioteer with chlamys; same symbols and border.
41	267·5	Æ 1·	Ν ΟΙ ΝΑΣΣ Ε Μ Hare running r.; beneath, dolphin l.: border of dots.	Same. (Same die.)
42	261·7	Æ 1·1	ΜΕΣΣΑ Ν ΙΟ Ν Hare running l.; beneath, ear of barley with leaves l.: border of dots.	ΜΕΣΣΑΝΑ (nearly obliterated). Similar type l.; same symbols and border.
43	264·7	Æ 1·	ΜΕΣ Σ ΑΝ ΙΟ Ν Similar type r.; beneath, fly r.: border of dots.	ΜΕΣΣΑΝ Α Similar.

No.	Wt.	Metal. Size.	Obverse.	Reverse.
44	255·3	AR ·95	ΜΕϟ ϟ Α ΝΙ Ο Ν Similar.	Traces of inscr. Similar type r.; in ex., olive-leaf r. with fruit: border of dots.
45	267·5	AR 1·05	ИO IИA ϟ ϟƎM Similar type r.; beneath, locust r., feeding on bunch of grapes with leaf: border of dots.	ΜΕϟϟΑ Similar type l.; in x., two dolphins meeting: border of dots.
46	266·3	AR 1·	ΜΕϟϟΑΝΙΟΝ (in ex.) Hare running l.; beneath, ear of barley l., with leaves; above, eagle flying l.	No inscr. Similar.
47	261·3	AR 1·	Same. (Same die.)	Similar type r.; in ex., olive-leaf with fruit r.: border of dots.

Period of Finest Art.

No.	Wt.	Metal. Size.	Obverse.	Reverse.
48	266·2	AR 1·05	ΜΕϟ ϟ Α ΝΙ Ο Ν Hare running r.; beneath, dolphin r.: border of dots.	Biga of mules l., driven by draped female figure (Messana), who stands and holds reins in both hands; mules walking; above, Nike r., crowning charioteer; in ex., two dolphins meeting: border of dots.
49	264·7	AR 1·	ИOI ИA ϟ ϟƎM Similar type l.; beneath, head of Pan? l., diademed with short horns: border of dots.	Same. (Same die.)
50	267·7	AR 1·	ΜΕϟϟΑΝ Ι ΟΝ Similar type r.; beneath, head of Pan r. and syrinx: border of dots.	Similar.
51	261·9	AR 1·05	ΜΕϟϟ ΑΝ ΙΟΝ Similar type; beneath, head of Pan r.: same border.	Similar; charioteer holds reins with goad.
52	262·1	AR ·95	ΜΕϟϟΑΝΙΟΝ Similar type; beneath, sea-horse l.: same border.	Similar.

No.	Wt.	Metal. Size.	Obverse.	Reverse.
53	265·5	Æ 1·15	Same. (Same die.)	Biga of mules l., driven by standing female figure, who holds reins in r. and goad in l.; mules trotting; around the neck of the nearer one, fillet; above, Nike, flying r., crowning charioteer: border of dots.
54	266·7	Æ ·9	ΜΕΣΣΑΝΙΟΝ (on band). Similar type; beyond, three ears of barley on one stalk: border of dots.	Same. (Same die.)
			With inscription ΜΕΣΣΑΝΙΩΝ.	
55	260·8	Æ 1·1	ΜΕΣΣΑΝΙΩΝ Hare running r.; beneath, dolphin r. above waves: border of dots.	Biga of mules l., driven by female charioteer, wearing long chiton with chlamys, who stands and holds reins in both hands with goad; mules walking; above, Nike r., crowning charioteer; in ex., two dolphins meeting: border of dots.
			(The rev. of this coin is from an older die than that of the obv.)	
56	265·2	Æ 1·05	ΜΕΣΣΑΝΙΩ Ν Hare running l.; beneath, eagle l., standing on rock, devouring serpent: border of dots.	Biga of mules l., driven by female charioteer, who holds goad and reins; mules walking; above, Nike r., holding wreath and caduceus; in ex., long fish l.; on line of ex., name of artist [ΚΙΜΩΝ ?]: border of dots

No.	Wt.	Metal. Size.	Obverse.	Reverse.
57	254·8	AR 1·05	ΜΕΣΣΑΝΙΩΝ Similar.	Same. (Same die.)
58	57·7	AR ·7	Head of Pelorias l., wearing necklace, earring, and wreath of corn; beneath, dolphin l.; in front, ΠΕΛΩΡΙΑΣ; behind, Α: border of dots.	Pheraimon, naked, advancing r., helmeted and holding spear and round shield; around, ΦΕ ΡΑ Ι ΜΩΝ: border of dots.
59	58·7	AR ·7	Similar; no letter behind.	Similar type; around, ΦΕΡΑΙΜ ΩΝ; in field r., I: same border.

No.	Wt.	Metal. Size.	Obverse.	Reverse.
60	12·3	AR ·5	Hare running r.; beneath, ivy-leaf l.: border of dots.	ΜΕΣ within olive-wreath r.
61	9·8	AR ·5	Similar type; beneath, spray of olive l.; above, Σ: border of dots.	Similar.
62	12·2	AR ·5	Similar type; beneath, olive-leaf l. with fruit: same border.	Similar.
63	11·4	AR ·55	Similar; beneath, scallop.	Similar.
64	11·4	AR ·5	Similar; beneath, Α.	Similar.
			Hemilitron?	
65	4·2	AR ·35	Hare running r.; beneath, Η: border of dots.	ΜΕ within olive-wreath r.
			COPPER.	
66		Æ 1·	ΜΕΣΣΑΝΑ Female head l., wearing necklace and earring; hair confined by crossing fillets; behind, uncertain symbol: (sickle enclosing scallop?) border of dots.	Biga of mules r., driven by draped female figure, who holds palm and reins; mules standing: plain border.
67		Æ 1·	ΜΕΣΣΑΝΙΟΝ Similar type: same border.	Similar type; in ex., Δ: same border.

No.	Wt.	Metal. Size.	Obverse.	Reverse.
68		Æ ·75	ΜΕΣΣΑΝΙΩΝ Hare running l.; in ex., locust l.: border of dots.	Cuttle-fish.
69		Æ ·8	Similar; locust r.	Similar.
70		Æ ·7	Head of Pelorias r., wearing sphendone and earring; in front, ΠΕΛΩΡΙΑΣ; on either side of neck, dolphin downwards: border of dots.	ΙΩ Ν Trident; in field r., hare downwards and scallop: plain border.
71		Æ ·7	Similar type l.; behind, dolphin l.: border of dots.	ΜΕΣΣ ΑΝ ΙΩ Ν Trident; between the prongs, Α Ρ; in field l., scallop; in field r., hare downwards: plain border.
72		Æ ·6	Similar type r.; in front, ΕΛΩΡ : border of dots.	ΜΕ ΑΝΙΩΝ Trident; on either side, scallop; in field r., hare downwards: plain border.

Period of Decline; early.

No.	Wt.	Metal. Size.	Obverse.	Reverse.
73		Æ 1·	Head of Poseidon l., laur.; in front, [ΠΟΣ]ΕΙΔΑΝ : border of dots.	ΜΕΣ ΣΑ ΝΙ ΩΝ Ornamented trident between two dolphins downwards; between the prongs, two smaller dolphins downwards: border of dots.
74		Æ ·95	Similar; behind, dolphin downwards.	Similar.
75		Æ 1·05	Similar type; around, ΠΟΣΕΙ ΔΑΝ : same border.	Μ [Ε] Σ ΣΑ Ν Similar; between prongs, honeysuckle ornaments in place of dolphins.
76		Æ 1·	Similar.	Μ Ε ΣΣ ΑΝ ΙΩ Ν Similar.
77		Æ 1·	Similar.	Similar.

No.	Wt.	Metal. Size.	Obverse.	Reverse.
78		Æ ·8	ΜΕϟϟΑΝΙΩΝ Head of young Herakles l., wearing lion's skin: border of dots.	Lion advancing r.; above, club r.; in ex., Δ: plain border.
79		Æ ·8	Similar.	Similar; in ex., pine-torch.
80		Æ ·85	Similar.	Similar.
81		Æ ·95	Head of Pelorias l., wearing wreath of corn, earring, and necklace; behind, ΠΕΛΩΡΙΑΣ; in front, two dolphins meeting: border of dots.	ΜΕΣΣΑΝΙΩΝ Warrior advancing l., wearing crested helmet, holding in r., spear, and on l. arm, round shield and chlamys: border of dots.
82		Æ 1·	Similar.	Similar: plain border.
83		Æ ·9	Similar.	ΜΕϟϟΑΝΙ ΩΝ Similar type: border of dots.
84		Æ ·85	Similar (legend off field).	ΜΕΣΣΑΝΙΩΝ (in ex.) Fast biga of horses r., driven by female figure, who holds goad in r. aloft, in l. reins: plain border.

MAMERTINI.

Occupied Messana B.C. 282.

COPPER.

No.	Wt.	Metal. Size.	Obverse.	Reverse.
1		Æ ·75	Head of Adranus l., bearded, wearing crested Corinthian helmet: border of dots.	ΜΑΜΕΡΤΙΝ (in ex.) Hound r.
2		Æ ·8	ΑΔΡΑΝΟΥ Similar.	Similar: plain border.
3		Æ 1·05	Head of Ares r., laur.; hair short; in front, ΑΡΕΟΣ; behind, Macedonian helmet: border of dots.	ΜΑΜΕΡ ΤΙΝΩΝ Eagle, with open wings, standing on thunderbolt l.: plain border.

No.	Wt.	Metal. Size.	Obverse.	Reverse.
4		Æ 1·1	Similar.	Similar; in field l., Φ.
5		Æ 1·1	Similar; behind head, arrow upwards.	Similar, without Φ.
6		Æ 1·1	Similar; behind head, axe-head.	Similar.
7		Æ 1·15	Similar; behind head, spear-head upwards.	Similar.
8		Æ 1·1	Similar; behind head, spear-head downwards.	ΜΑΜΕΡ ΤΙΝΩΝ Similar type.
9		Æ 1·15	Similar; no symbol.	Similar.
10		Æ 1·05	Similar; behind head, bucranium.	ΜΑΜΕΡΤΙΝΩ Ν Similar type; in field l., star of eight rays: border of dots.

No.	Wt.	Metal. Size.	Obverse.	Reverse.
11		Æ 1·1	Similar.	ΜΑΜΕΡΤΙΝΩΝ Similar type; in field l., Σ: same border.
12		Æ ·9	Similar head; behind, spear-head downwards: same legend and border.	ΜΑΜΕ Ρ Τ ΙΝΩΝ Similar type: plain border.
13		Æ ·85	Head of young Herakles l., wearing lion's skin; behind, bow.	ΜΑΜΕΡ ΤΙΝΩΝ Eagle, with spread wings, standing l. on thunderbolt.
14		Æ ·8	Head of young Zeus l., laur.; hair long; in front, ΔΙΟΣ: border of dots.	ΤΙΝΩΝ Similar type.
15		Æ ·75	Similar.	Similar; in field l., Я.
16		Æ ·75	Similar head; in front, ΔΙΟΣ ΜΕΣ	Similar; no mon.
17		Æ 1·1	Head of Ares r., laur.; hair short; in front, ΑΡΕ Ο Σ; behind, Macedonian helmet: border of dots.	ΜΑΜΕΡ ΤΙ ΝΩΝ Bull butting l.: plain border.
18		Æ 1·05	Similar.	Similar.
19		Æ ·85	Similar type and legend: same border.	ΜΑΜΕΡΤΙΝ ΩΝ Similar type: border of dots.
20		Æ ·75	Similar type l.; in front, legend; behind, helmet? same border.	ΜΑΜΕΡ ΤΙΝΩΝ Similar type: same border.
21		Æ ·65	Similar type r.; in front, ΑΡΕΟΣ; behind, bucranium: border of dots.	ΜΑΜΕΡΤΙ ΝΩΝ Similar type; above, club r.: border of dots.
22		Æ ·85	Head of Apollo r., laur., with long hair; behind, strung bow.	ΜΑΜΕΡΤΙΝΩΝ Naked warrior advancing r., striking with spear and holding round shield; on either side, Ξ and Ƭ.
23		Æ ·85	Similar.	Similar; without Ξ.

No.	Wt.	Metal. Size.	Obverse.	Reverse.
			With marks of value.	
			Hexas.	
24	117·	Æ ·9	Head of Ares r., laur.; hair short; in front, ΑΡΕΟΣ; behind, ⁚ : border of dots.	ΜΑΜΕΡΤΙΝΩΝ Pallas, in attitude of defence, r., with spear and shield which rests on the ground: border of dots.
			Pentonkion.	
25	156·	Æ 1·1	Head of Zeus r., laur.: border of dots.	ΜΑΜΕ ΡΤΙΝΩΝ Warrior, wearing crested helmet; he charges r., thrusting with spear and holding round shield; in field r., Π: border of dots.
26	177·	Æ 1·05	Similar.	ΜΑΜΕΡΤΙΝΩΝ Similar.
27	179·	Æ 1·05	Similar; behind head, club downwards.	Similar.
28	158·	Æ 1·	Similar; behind head, spear-head upwards.	Similar.
29	187·	Æ 1·1	Similar; behind head, thunderbolt.	Similar; on either side of type, Τ and Π.
30	167·	Æ 1·05	Similar; behind head, pentagram.	Same inscr. Warrior r., armed with helmet and sword, thrusting r. with spear in raised r. hand, and holding round shield; in field r., Π: border of dots.
31	51·	Æ ·8	Head of Zeus r., laur.: border of dots.	ΜΑΜΕΡΤΙΝΩΝ Warrior r., armed with crested helmet and sword, thrusting r. with spear in raised r. hand, and holding round shield; in front, Π: plain border.

No.	Wt.	Metal. Size.	Obverse.	Reverse.
32	165·	Æ 1·05	Head of Ares l., laur.; hair short: border of dots.	ΜΑΜΕΡΤΙΝΩΝ Horseman standing l., wearing chlamys over l. shoulder; holds with r. hand head of horse walking l.; in l., spear; in field l., Π: border of dots.
33	142·	Æ 1·05	Similar; behind head, Phrygian helmet r., terminating in griffin's head.	Similar; Γ.
34	181·	Æ 1·05	Similar; behind head, parazonium.	ΜΑ ΜΕΡΤΙΝΩΝ Similar.
35	191·	Æ 1·	Similar; behind head, altar?	Similar.
36	167·	Æ 1·	Head of Apollo l., laur.; hair long; behind, lyre.	ΜΑΜΕΡΤΙΝΩΝ Warrior, facing, wearing chlamys over l. shoulder; holds in r. parazonium, in l., spear, against which leans round shield; in field r., Π: border of dots.
37	168·	Æ 1·05	Similar type r.; behind, lyre: border of dots.	Similar; warrior turned l.
38	161·	Æ 1·05	Similar.	ΜΑΜΑΕΡΤΙΝΩΝ (*sic*) Similar.
39	228·	Æ 1·05	Similar.	ΜΑΜΕΡΤΙΝΩΝ Warrior seated l. on rocks, over which is spread chlamys; holds in r. spear, l. arm, which rests on round shield, supports head; in field l., Π: border of dots.
40	180·	Æ 1·05	Similar.	Similar.

Hemilitron.

No.	Wt.	Metal. Size.	Obverse.	Reverse.
41	204·	Æ 1·05	Head of Apollo r., laur.; hair long; behind, lyre, above which, ⁞⁞ (six pellets): border of dots.	ΜΑΜΕΡΤΙ ΝΩΝ Nike, clad in chiton with diploïs, l., holding wreath and palm: border of dots.

No.	Wt.	Metal. Size.	Obverse.	Reverse.
42	152·	Æ ·95	Similar type: same border.	Similar; in field r., ●●● ●●●
43	135·	Æ ·9	Similar; behind head, lyre.	Similar.
			Trias.	
44	108·	Æ ·9	Head of Apollo r., laur.; hair long; behind, lyre: border of dots.	Traces of inscr. Nike l., holding wreath and palm; in field l., III: border of dots.
45	111·	Æ ·85	Similar; behind head, tripod.	Similar.
			Uncia?	
46	45·	Æ ·6	Head of young Herakles r., wearing lion's skin; in front, ●? border of dots.	ΜΑΜΕΡΤΙΝΩΝ Nike l., holding wreath and palm.
			Without marks of value.	
47		Æ ·75	Head of Zeus r., laur.; behind, ΔΙΟΣ, over which, Ͳ: border of dots.	ΤΙΝΩΝ Hermes l., wearing chlamys over l. shoulder; holds patera and winged caduceus; at his feet ram l., looking up.

No.	Wt.	Metal. Size.	Obverse.	Reverse.
48		Æ ·8	Similar.	Similar.
49		Æ ·55	Female head r., wearing earring; hair in bunch behind; behind, cock r.: border of dots.	ΜΑΜΕ Warrior l., naked, holding spear in r., and in l. parazonium, which rests on the ground; in field l., trophy: border of dots.
50		Æ ·5	Head of Apollo l., laur.: border of dots.	ΜΑΜΕ Omphalos: border of dots.
51		Æ ·45	Head of Artemis r., wearing earring, necklace, and stephane; over shoulder, bow and quiver: border of dots.	ΜΑΜΕΡΤΙΝΩΝ Similar type; beneath, Λ? in field r., uncertain mon.

No.	Wt.	Metal. Size.	Obverse.	Reverse.

MORGANTIA.

SILVER.

Period of Archaic Art.

No.	Wt.	Metal. Size.	Obverse.	Reverse.
1	11·	AR ·45	Aged male head r., bearded and bound with tainia: border of dots.	ΑVΙΤΥΛ ΑϽЯΟΜ Ear of barley.

Period of Finest Art.

No.	Wt.	Metal. Size.	Obverse.	Reverse.
2	10·	AR ·45	ΜΟΡΓΑΝΤΙΝΩΝ Head of Artemis r.; hair rolled; over shoulder, quiver: border of dots.	Horseman l., wearing chlamys, thrusting with spear; horse prancing: border of dots.
3	10·5	AR ·45	Same. (Same die.)	Same. (Same die.)
4	12·5	AR ·45	ΜΟΡΓΑΝ Ν Head of Pallas, three-quarter-face towards r., wearing three-crested helmet; hair flowing: border of dots.	Μ ●ΡΓ Α Nike, wearing peplos, reclining l. on rocks? holds in r. wreath, l. rests on rock: plain border.

No.	Wt.	Metal. Size.	Obverse.	Reverse.
5	14·5	AR ·5	Traces of inscr. Similar.	Μ ΟΡΓΑΝΤ Ι Similar.
6	16·6	AR ·5	Similar type; ægis tied round throat: same border.	Traces of inscr. Similar type; beneath, grain of barley: same border.

COPPER.

Period of Decline; early.

No.	Wt.	Metal. Size.	Obverse.	Reverse.
7		Æ 1·05	ΜΟΡΓΑΝΤΙΝΩΝ Head of Pallas r., wearing highly ornamented three-crested Athenian helmet, on the side of which, serpent; behind, owl r.: border of dots.	Lion r., tearing stag's head; between his legs, serpent; above, Γ: border of dots.

No.	Wt.	Metal. Size.	Obverse.	Reverse.
8		Æ 1·	Same. (Same die.)	Same. (Same die.)
9		Æ 1·	Similar.	Similar type; no serpent; in ex., ꟼB: same border.
10		Æ ·75	Female head r., Sikelia? bound with myrtle-wreath.	. . . . . NTIN N Eagle, with spread wings, standing l. on serpent: border of dots.
11		Æ ·8	Similar.	ИΩИ ITИ ꟼOM Similar type: same border.
12		Æ ·6	Head of Apollo? r., laur.; in front, ΑΛΚ Ο Ƹ: border of dots.	Μ ΟΡΓΑΝ ΤΙΝΩΝ Tripod-lebes with neck and three handles: border of dots.
13		Æ ·65	Similar; behind, ꟼ.	Same. (Same die.)

MOTYA.

SILVER.

No.	Wt.	Metal. Size.	Obverse.	Reverse.
1	8·3	AR ·5	Eagle, with closed wings, standing l. on Ionic capital; holds in beak serpent; above, ivy-leaf: border of dots.	VOIAV TOM Dolphin l. and scallop.

No.	Wt.	Metal. Size.	Obverse.	Reverse.
2	132·2	AR ·9	Head of nymph r.; hair confined by fillet passing four times round; around, four dolphins r.	IOИ Naked male figure, seated sideways on horse galloping l.; in ex., tunny l.
3	127·5	AR ·9	MOTVAIOИ Head of nymph r.; hair tied at the back with a fillet; behind, cray-fish.	Hound standing r.; beneath, plant: border of dots.

No.	Wt.	Metal. Size.	Obverse.	Reverse.
4	134·5	AR ·85	Similar; hair rolled.	Same. (Same die.)

(See Siculo-Punic Class.)

MYTISTRATUS.

COPPER.

Period of Decline; early.

With marks of value.

Hemilitron.

No.	Wt.	Metal. Size.	Obverse.	Reverse.
1	427·	Æ 1·15	Head of Hephaistos r., bearded, wearing pilos.	ΥΜ in the midst of ●●●●●● : all within olive-wreath.
2	448·	Æ 1·15	Similar.	Similar? (defaced.)

(The above coins restruck on coins of Syracuse. Obv. Head of Pallas. Rev. Star-fish between dolphins.)

Uncia.

No.	Wt.	Metal. Size.	Obverse.	Reverse.
3	103·	Æ ·8	Similar type.	Υ Μ In centre, ● around which three fishes, with heads close to mark of value and tails at circumference: border of dots.

No.	Wt.	Metal. Size.	Obverse.	Reverse.

NACONA.

COPPER.

Period of Finest Art.

Trias.

No.	Wt.	Metal. Size.	Obverse.	Reverse.
1	65·	Æ ·65	NAKON Head of nymph r., wearing necklace and ear-ring; hair confined by fillet passing four times round.	Seilen, seated sideways on ass walking l.; holds in r. wine-cup, in l. thyrsos; in field, ●●●: border of dots.

NAXUS.

SILVER.

Period of Archaic Art.

No.	Wt.	Metal. Size.	Obverse.	Reverse.
1	83·5	Æ ·75	Head of Dionysos l., with pointed beard and long hair, and wearing wreath of ivy: border of dots.	ИOI NAX Bunch of grapes hanging from stalk between two leaves; to r. of stalk, A: the whole in incuse square.
2	84·9	Æ ·8	Similar type: border of dots on band.	NAXIOИ Similar type.
3	87·2	Æ ·85	Similar.	Similar: plain border.

No.	Wt.	Metal. Size.	Obverse.	Reverse.
4	11·2	Æ ·45	Similar.	ИOIX AИ Bunch of grapes: border of dots on band.
5	10·5	Æ ·45	Similar.	ИOI XAИ Similar.
6	11·5	Æ ·45	Similar: border of dots within plain border.	NAX IOИ Similar.

Period of Transition.

No.	Wt.	Metal. Size.	Obverse.	Reverse.
7	269·2	Æ 1·1	Head of Dionysos r., bearded; hair long and tied in a bunch behind, and bound with a wreath of ivy: border of dots.	N AXI OИ Bearded Seilen, naked, with pointed ears and long tail, seated on the ground, facing, head turned to l., towards wine-cup in his r. hand; supports himself with l. hand.
8	266·3	Æ 1·15	Same. (Same die.)	Same. (Same die.)
9	63·2	Æ ·7	Similar head; hair short: same border.	N A XI OИ Similar type towards l.: border of dots.

No.	Wt.	Metal. Size.	Obverse.	Reverse.
10	61·8	AR ·65	Similar.	ΝΑ ΧΙΟΝ Similar type; l. hand on knee.
11	63·5	AR ·75	Similar.	ΧΑΝ ΟΙ Similar type; l. hand on the ground: border of dots.
12	11·7	AR ·45	Similar head: border of dots.	ΝΑΧ ΙΟΝ Bunch of grapes.
13	11·	AR ·4	Similar.	ΙΧ ΑΝ Bunch of grapes on stalk: all within ivy-wreath.
14	10·7	AR ·5	Similar.	ΝΑΧ Bunch of grapes on stalk with leaves and tendrils.
15	11·1	AR ·5	Similar.	ΝΑ ΧΙ Bunch of grapes with two leaves connected with ivy-wreath.
16	10·9	AR ·5	Similar.	ΝΑΧ Bunch of grapes on branch with leaves.
17	10·	AR ·45	ΝΑΧΙ Similar.	Similar type: plain border.

Period of Finest Art.

No.	Wt.	Metal. Size.	Obverse.	Reverse.
18	264·7	AR 1·	Head of Dionysos r., bearded, bound with broad band adorned with ivy-wreath: border of dots.	ΝΑΞΙΟΝ Bearded Seilen, naked, with pointed ear and long tail, seated on the ground, facing; head turned to l., towards wine-cup in his r. hand; in l. hand, thyrsos; to l., vine growing with leaves and fruit.

No.	Wt.	Metal. Size.	Obverse.	Reverse.
19	267·7	Æ 1·1	Same. (Same die.)	Same inscr. Similar type: plain border.
20	130·4	Æ ·8	ΝΑΞΙΩΝ Head of Apollo l., laur.; hair turned up behind; behind, laurel-leaf with berry: border of dots.	Similar type; to r., term.

21	93·6	Æ ·75 plated.	Similar.	Similar.
22	124·3	Æ ·8	Same inscr. Similar type and symbol, direction reversed.	Seilen, facing, seated on r. heel; holding in r. wine-cup, and in l. thyrsos; to l., term; to r., vine: plain border.
23	31·7	Æ ·6	Young head of river-god Assinos l., with short horn, crowned with vine-leaves; in front, ΑΣΣΙΝΟ Σ: border of dots.	ΝΑΞΙ ΩΝ Seilen, facing, seated on l. heel, head turned to l., towards wine-cup in r. hand; in l. hand, pipes.
24	31·4	Æ ·55	Similar.	Similar.
25	10·4	Æ ·5	ΝΑΞΙ Head of bearded Dionysos r., crowned with ivy: border of dots.	Bunch of grapes on stalk with leaves and tendrils.
26	10·1	Æ ·45	ΝΑΞΙΩΝ (*sic.*) Young head of river-god Assinos l., crowned with vine-leaves: border of dots.	Similar type.

No.	Wt.	Metal. Size.	Obverse.	Reverse.
			PANORMUS. SILVER. *Period of Transition.*	
1	265·1	Æ 1·	И ΜЯ ΟИΑΠ Head of Apollo r., laur.; hair rolled.	Quadriga r., driven by charioteer clad in long chiton, holding goad in r. hand and reins in both; horses walking; above, Nike, flying r., crowning horses.

2	131·1	Æ ·9	ИΟΚ ΙΤΙΜꟼΟ И Π Head of nymph r., wearing earring, necklace, and sphendone ornamented in front; behind, 卐.	Hound r. looking back; above, murex: plain border.

3	128·4	Æ ·9	Head of nymph r.; hair tied at the back; behind, crayfish upwards.	Π ΑΝΟ Ρ ΜΟΣ Hound r: border of dots.
4	129·7	Æ ·85	Head of nymph r., wearing earring, necklace, and diadem; hair rolled.	Same. (Same die.)
5	13·3	Æ ·45	ΟꟼΜΟ ΑΠ Young male head r., (river-god?) wearing tainia; hair short: border of dots.	Fore-part of man-headed bull swimming r.; beneath, muscle.

No.	Wt.	Metal. Size.	Obverse.	Reverse.
			Before B.C. 254.	
			GOLD.	
6	8·3	AV ·3	Head of Pallas r., wearing crested Corinthian helmet: border of dots.	[monogram] Owl r.
7	5·4	AV ·25	Head of Apollo r., laur.: border of dots.	[monogram] Lyre (with three strings) bound with fillet: plain border.
			Period of Decline; late.	
			COPPER.	
8		Æ 1·05	ΠΑΝΟΡ N Bust of Pallas r., wearing crested Corinthian helmet: border of dots	Head of Persephone r., crowned with barley; in front, ear of barley? behind, poppy-head: border of dots.
9		Æ 1·15	ΠΑΝΟΡ ΜΙΤΑΝ Similar.	Similar type l.: same border.
10		Æ 1·	Similar type: same border.	ΠΑΝΟΡ ΜΙ ΤΑΝ Concordia? standing l., holding patera and cornucopiæ: border of dots.
11		Æ ·95	Π ΑΝΟ ΡΜΙΤΑΝ Similar.	Triquetra of legs; at the junction, winged head of Gorgon; between the legs, ears of barley: border of dots.
12		Æ ·85	ΠΑΝ ΜΙΤΑΝ Similar.	Similar.
13		Æ ·95	Head of Zeus l., laur.: border of dots.	ΠΑΝΟΡ ΜΙΤΑΝ Eagle with spread wings, standing l. on thunderbolt, looking back: border of dots.
14		Æ ·95	Similar.	Similar.
15		Æ ·85	Ram standing r.; between his legs, head of Janus: border of dots.	ΠΑΝΟΡΜΙΤΑΝ Eagle with spread wings, facing, standing on thunderbolt, head turned to l.: border of dots.

No.	Wt.	Metal. Size.	Obverse.	Reverse.
16		Æ ·8	Similar.	ΠΑΝΟΡ ΜΙΤΑΝ Similar.
17		Æ ·7	ΠΑΝ Ο ΡΜΙΤΑΝ Female head r., wearing stephane: border of dots.	Square altar with horns: border of dots.
18		Æ ·7	ΑΝΟ ΡΜΙΤΑΝ Similar.	Similar.
19		Æ ·7	ΠΑΝΟΡ ΜΙΤΑΝ Hermes seated l. on rock, holding caduceus: border of dots.	Circular altar, flaming, within laurel-wreath.
20		Æ ·65	Head of Persephone l., crowned with barley: border of dots.	ΡΜΙ ΤΑΝ Poppy-head between two stalks of barley: border of dots.
21		Æ ·7	Heads of the Dioskuri r., wearing laureate pilei: border of dots.	ΠΑΝΟΡ ΜΙΤΑΝ within laurel-wreath: border of dots.
22		Æ ·7	Ram standing r.: border of dots.	ΠΑΝ ΟΡΜΙ within laurel-wreath: border of dots.
23		Æ ·5	Head of Demeter l., veiled; behind, two ears of corn: border of dots.	[monogram] Prow r., adorned with wing.
24		Æ ·5	Similar.	Similar.
25		Æ ·45	Head of Aphrodite r., wearing stephane: border of dots.	[monogram] Dove r.: border of dots.
26		Æ ·6	Head of Zeus r., laur.: border of dots.	ΠΑ ΝΟΡ ΜΙΤΑΝ Military figure l., wearing helmet and cuirass, and holding patera and spear; shield rests against spear: border of dots.
27		Æ ·65	Similar.	Similar.
28		Æ ·65	Similar type l.: same border.	ΠΑ ΝΟΡ ΜΙΤΑΝ Similar.

No.	Wt.	Metal. Size.	Obverse.	Reverse.
			Bearing inscription PORTVS ?	
			With marks of value.	
			As.	
29	136·	Æ ·9	Head of Janus, laur.; above, I: border of dots.	PR within laurel-wreath: border of dots.
30	127·	Æ ·9	Similar.	Similar.
			Semis.	
31	47·	Æ ·7	Head of Zeus l., laur.	Similar.
			Doubtful denomination.	
32	44·	Æ ·65	Head of Demeter l., wearing veil and wreath of corn: border of dots.	Similar.
			With names of Roman magistrates.	
33		Æ ·85	Head of Zeus l., laur.: border of dots.	PR Military figure l., wearing helmet and cuirass, and holding patera and spear; shield rests against spear; in field r., [monogram]: border of dots.
34		Æ ·75	Similar.	Similar; figure wears sword; in field l., L·ME
35		Æ ·9	Similar type r.; behind, cornucopiæ: border of dots.	Similar; in field l., Q. FAB
36		Æ ·85	Similar.	Similar.
37		Æ ·85	Similar type l.: same border.	Similar; in field l., CATO
38		Æ ·8	Head of Zeus r., laur.; behind, sceptre.	ΠΑΝΟΡ ΜΙΤΑΝ Tetrastyle temple; beneath, C·D·
39		Æ ·8	Similar.	Similar.
40		Æ ·8	Similar.	Similar.
41		Æ ·45	Rudder and anchor: border of dots.	PR; beneath, L·GN: border of dots.

No.	Wt.	Metal. Size.	Obverse.	Reverse.
			Imperial.	
			AUGUSTUS.	
42		Æ ·9	ΠΑΝΟΡ ΜΙΤΑΝ Head of Augustus r., bare: border of dots.	Triquetra of legs; at the junction, winged Gorgon's head; between the legs, ears of barley: border of dots.
			AUGUSTUS AND LIVIA.	
43		Æ ·8	PANORMIT Head of Augustus r., bare.	GVS Head of Livia l., veiled, wearing earring and wreath of barley: border of dots.
44		Æ ·8	PANOR NORV Similar.	AVGVS Similar type r.: same border.
			AFTER DEATH OF AUGUSTUS.	
45		Æ ·95	PANHoRMI TANoRVM Head of Augustus l., radiate; in front, thunderbolt.	CN·DO·ROC .AETOR. IIVIR. Capricorn r.; beneath, triquetra of legs, at the junction of which, winged Gorgon's head, and between them, ears of barley.
46		Æ ·9	Similar.	CNDOMPROC AETO IIVIR Similar types.
47		Æ ·7	PANOR MITAN Livia as Demeter, veiled, seated r. on throne, holding patera and ears of corn.	CN·D LA Ram standing l.

COLONIA PANORMUS.

With marks of value.

Semis.

No.	Wt.	Metal. Size.	Obverse.	Reverse.
48	152·	Æ ·95	Head of Zeus l., laur.; behind, S: border of dots.	C· N Military figure l., wearing helmet, cuirass, sword, and chlamys; holds patera and spear; against spear rests round shield: border of dots.
49	69·	Æ ·9	Similar.	C· N Similar.
50	107·	Æ ·9	Similar.	C· N Similar.

With marks of value, and names of Roman magistrates, probably struck at Panormus.

MAN. ACILIUS, QUAESTOR.

As.

No.	Wt.	Metal. Size.	Obverse.	Reverse.
1	59·	Æ ·8	Head of Janus laur.; above, I: border of dots.	M / ACILI / Q within laurel-wreath: border of dots.

Semis.

No.	Wt.	Metal. Size.	Obverse.	Reverse.
2	97·	Æ ·85	Head of Zeus r., laur.: border of dots.	M.ACILI Eagle with wings spread, facing, on thunderbolt, head r.: border of dots.

AXIUS NASO.

As.

No.	Wt.	Metal. Size.	Obverse.	Reverse.
3	65·	Æ ·85	Head of Janus laur.; above, I: border of dots.	IASO (*sic*) within laurel-wreath: border of dots.

Semis.

No.	Wt.	Metal. Size.	Obverse.	Reverse.
4	38·	Æ ·65	Head of Zeus l., laur.	NA / SO within laurel-wreath: of dots.

No.	Wt.	Metal. Size.	Obverse.	Reverse.
			Q. BAEBIUS.	
			As.	
5	128·	Æ ·9	Head of Janus laur.; above, I: border of dots.	Q·B within laurel-wreath: border of dots.
			Quadrans.	
6	29·	Æ ·55	Head of young Herakles l., wearing lion's skin: border of dots.	Q·B Club: border of dots.
			FURIUS CRASSIPES.	
			As.	
7	121·	Æ ·8	Head of Janus laur.; above, I: border of dots.	CRAS SIPES within laurel-wreath: border of dots.
			Quadrans.	
8	19·	Æ ·45	Head of young Herakles r., wearing lion's skin: border of dots.	CRA SIP Club: border of dots.
			OPPIUS.	
			As.	
9	66·	Æ ·7	O P Head of Janus laur.; above, I: all within laurel-wreath.	Head of Zeus r., laur.: border of dots.
10	94·	Æ ·8	Similar.	Similar.
			P. TERENTIUS.	
			As.	
11	109·	Æ ·85	Head of Janus laur.; above, I: border of dots.	P·E Wolf r., suckling Twins and looking back: border of dots.
			Semis.	
12	72·	Æ ·75	Head of Zeus l., laur.: border of dots.	Similar.

No.	Wt.	Metal. Size.	Obverse.	Reverse.
			Without marks of value.	
			L. SEIUS, PROCONSUL.	
13		Æ ·7	SEPT·EIBA·D·IIVIR Triquetra of legs; at the junction, Gorgon's head.	L·SEIO PROCOS· D D
			Uncertain magistrates.	
			With marks of value.	
			As.	
14	106·	Æ ·85	Head of Janus laur.; above, I: border of dots.	AR within laurel-wreath: border of dots.
15	107·	Æ ·9	Similar.	Dove r. on bar, within laurel-wreath: border of dots.
16	122·	Æ ·9	Similar.	Laurel-wreath: border of dots.
17	79·	Æ ·85	Similar.	TRI Warrior, facing, wearing cuirass; holds in r. sceptre surmounted by bird; in l., large oval shield: border of dots.
18	102·	Æ ·9	Similar.	Spear-head r. and jaw-bone of boar: border of dots.
19	157·	Æ 1·	Similar.	Wing: border of dots.
			Semis.	
20	103·	Æ ·9	Head of Zeus l., laur.: border of dots.	Similar.
			Uncia.	
21	25·	Æ ·55	Head of young Her[illegible] wearing lion's [illegible] of [illegible]	Club upwards; in field l., Ẋ; in field r., bird r.: border of [illegible]s.

No.	Wt.	Metal. Size.	Obverse.	Reverse.
			Without marks of value.	
22		Æ 7	Square altar, with horns: border of dots.	D D Round edifice, surmounted by a line of battlements, and rising out of a basin, the sides of which are supported by pillars.
23		Æ ·7	Similar.	Similar: border of dots.

PAROPUS.

COPPER.

Period of Decline; late.

No.	Wt.	Metal. Size.	Obverse.	Reverse.
1		Æ ·8	Head of Apollo l., laur.: border of dots.	ΠΑΡΩΠΙΝΩΝ Hunter l., wearing short chiton and buskins, holding in r. patera? in l. long spear; beyond, hound running l.; in field l., wing: border of dots.

PETRA.

COPPER.

Period of Decline; late.

No.	Wt.	Metal. Size.	Obverse.	Reverse.
1		Æ ·75	Head of bearded Herakles r., wearing lion's skin: border of dots.	ΠΕΤΡΕΙ ΝΩΝ Female figure l., clad in long chiton with diploïs; r. raised, l. elbow resting on column: border of dots.

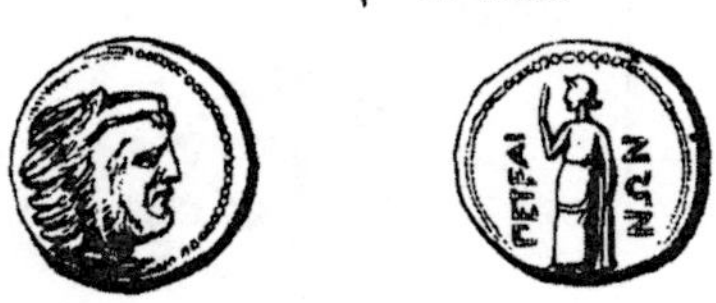

No.	Wt.	Metal. Size.	Obverse.	Reverse.
2		Æ ·75	Similar.	Similar.

No.	Wt.	Metal. Size.	Obverse.	Reverse.

PIACUS.

COPPER.

Period of Finest Art.

Hemilitron.

No.	Wt.	Metal. Size.	Obverse.	Reverse.
1	70·	Æ ·7	ΠΙΑΚΙΝ Head of young river-god l., with horns and pointed ear; wears wreath of olive; marks of value ●●●●●● between letters of inscription: plain border.	Dog r., seizing fawn by the throat; in front, leaf.

SEGESTA.

SILVER.

Period of Archaic Art.

No.	Wt.	Metal. Size.	Obverse.	Reverse.
1	124·7	AR ·85	Ʃ ΙΙΣΑΤ ƎƎ⅃ΑƎ Head of nymph Segesta r., wearing necklace; hair turned up behind under broad diadem, over which ends fall: border of dots.	Hound r., his nose to the ground: border of dots.
2	131·2	AR ·85	ƩΑΓΕƩ ⊥ΑΙΣΙ Β Similar type: plain border.	Similar.
3	132·4	AR ·8	Similar type.	Ʃ ΙΣ ΑΤƎƎ Similar.
4	125·3	AR ·85	Similar.	Ʃ ƎƎ⅃ƎƎ Similar.
5	125·1	AR ·85	ΙΜƎƩΙΙΣΑΤƎƎϽƎƎ Similar type.	Hound r., wearing collar, his nose to the ground: border of dots.

No.	Wt.	Metal. Size.	Obverse.	Reverse.
6	128·6	Æ ·85	ΕΓΕΣ ΣΙ ΙΑΤ Ε ΜΙ Similar type; diadem of beads.	Similar; hound without collar.
7	136·8	Æ ·9	ΣΙΙΑΤΣΕϽΕΣ Head of Segesta l., wearing earring and necklace; hair turned up behind under diadem of beads, over which ends fall.	Hound l.; above, murex: border of dots.
8	134·5	Æ ·85	Same. (Same die.)	Hound l., wearing collar; above, barleycorn: border of dots.
9	127·3	Æ ·95	Same. (Same die.)	Hound l., looking back; above, murex: border of dots.
10	127·5	Æ ·9	ΣΙΙΑΤΣΕΤΕΣ Similar head r.; diadem broad: plain border.	Hound r., wearing collar; above, barleycorn.
11	12·	Æ ·45	ΣΕϹΕΣΤΑΙΙ Β Head of Segesta r.; hair turned up behind under diadem of beads.	Hound running r.: border of dots.
12	9·5	Æ ·45	Similar type; diadem broad: border of dots.	Hound l., wearing collar; above, wheel of eight spokes.
13	10·7	Æ ·5	Similar.	ΑΤ Σ ΕϽΕΣ Hound r.; above, scallop.
14	14·8	Æ ·45	ΒΙΙΑΤΣΕΤΕΣ Head of Aphrodite Erycina? facing: border of dots.	Hound l.; above, wheel of seven spokes.

Period of Transition.

No.	Wt.	Metal. Size.	Obverse.	Reverse.
15	129·4	Æ ·9	Σ Ι Ι Α Τ Σ Α Σ Head of Segesta r.; hair turned up behind under broad diadem, over which ends fall: within inscr., plain border.	Hound r., wearing collar: border of dots.
16	133·	Æ ·9	Inscr. obscure. Similar.	Similar type l.: same border.

No.	Wt.	Metal. Size.	Obverse.	Reverse.
17	99·2	Æ ·7	ƎƎΓƎ ƧTAIIB Head of Segesta r.; hair confined by diadem, and rolled behind.	Hound l.
			(This coin has been clipped in ancient times.)	
18	128·8	Æ ·95	ƎIIATƧƎƆ Head of Segesta r., wearing earring, necklace, and sphendone: plain border.	Similar type: border of dots.
19	130·2	Æ ·9	Similar type.	Hound l., wearing collar, his nose to the ground: border of dots.
20	127·5	Æ ·95	Similar type: plain border.	Hound l., wearing collar: border of dots.
21	128·8	Æ ·9	Head of Segesta l.; hair turned up behind under diadem.	Similar.
22	121·2	Æ ·8	ΣΕCΕΣΤΑ ΙΙ Β Head of Segesta r., wearing necklace; hair rolled.	Hound l., wearing collar, his nose to the ground.
23	130·2	Æ ·9	ΣΕCΕΣ I Head of Segesta r., wearing earring and necklace; hair turned up behind under broad diadem.	Similar type r.
			(The above two coins are of somewhat barbarous work.)	
24	133·5	Æ ·85	Head of Segesta r., wearing earring, necklace, and diadem of beads.	Hound l., wearing collar.
25	131·5	Æ ·9	ΣΑΓΕ ΙΒ over which is struck ƆƎƧ Head of Segesta r.; hair waved and turned up behind under broad diadem.	Hound r., his nose to the ground; above, young male head r., diademed, hair long: border of dots.
26	124·3	Æ ·9	ΣΑΓΕΣ Β Same. (Same die.)	Hound advancing r., his r. fore-foot forward, his head near the ground; above, similar symbol: border of dots.

No.	Wt.	Metal. Size.	Obverse.	Reverse.
27	116·	Æ ·8	Traces of inscr. Same. (Same die.)	Similar type l.; above, female head l.
28	130·1	Æ ·9	ⵉΕΓΕⵉΤΑΙΙ Β Head of Segesta r., diademed; hair rolled.	Similar type r.; above, female head r., hair turned up behind under broad diadem: border of dots.
29	128·8	Æ ·85	ΒΙ ΤⵉΕ>Εⵉ Similar type.	Hound r., on the scent; above, same symbol: same border.

Period of Finest Art.

No.	Wt.	Metal. Size.	Obverse.	Reverse.
30	257·1	Æ 1·1	Head of Segesta r., wearing sphendone ornamented with stars.	ΕΓΕⵉ ΩΝ Youthful hunter r., standing with l. foot upon a rock; r. hand resting on hip; l. elbow on knee; he wears pilos suspended behind neck, a strap round shoulder, cothurni, and over l. arm chlamys; carries in l. hand two javelins; at his feet, two hounds r.: border of dots.
31	266·7	Æ 1·1	Same. (Same die.)	Same, but, visible in front, term l. (Same die.)
32	260·	Æ 1·2	ⵉΕLΕⵉΤΑΙΙΑ Head of Segesta r., wearing earring, necklace, and sphendone ornamented with stars behind; beneath, stalk of barley l.	ΤΑΙΩΝ Same. (Same die.)

No.	Wt.	Metal. Size.	Obverse.	Reverse.
33	264·4	Æ 1·05	Similar type to that on reverse of preceding coins.	ΣΕΓΕ ΣΤΑΙΙΑ (in ex.) Quadriga r., driven by female figure, who holds three stalks of barley in r. hand and reins in both hands; horses in high action; above, Nike l., crowning charioteer; in ex., grasshopper r.
34	256·5	Æ 1·05	Similar, but one hound only.	Same. (Same die.)

35	124·4	Æ ·95	Head of Segesta r., hair confined by fillet passing four times round; above and below, branches of ivy, meeting in front.	ΕΓΕΣΤ ΑΙ ΩΝ Hound r.; in front, murex.

36	118·8	Æ ·8	Head of Segesta r., wearing earring, necklace, and sphendone ornamented behind with stars; around, three barleycorns.	Hound advancing r., his nose near the ground; beyond, three ears of barley growing from one root.
37	127·8	Æ 1·05	ΣΕΓΕ Σ ΤΑΙΩΝ Head of Segesta r., hair bound with fillet passing thrice round.	ΣΕΓΕΣΤΑΙΙΒ (in ex.) Similar type: plain border.
38	130·8	Æ ·9	Head of Segesta r., wearing sphendone ornamented with stars.	ΒΙΙΑΤΣΞΓΞΣ (on band in ex.) Similar type.

(Obv. same die as no. 36.)

No.	Wt.	Metal. Size.	Obverse.	Reverse.
39	130·5	Æ 1·	ΕΓΕΣΤΑΙ ΟΝ Head of Segesta r.; hair rolled behind over narrow diadem.	ΕΓΕΣΤΑΙ (in ex.) Similar: plain border.

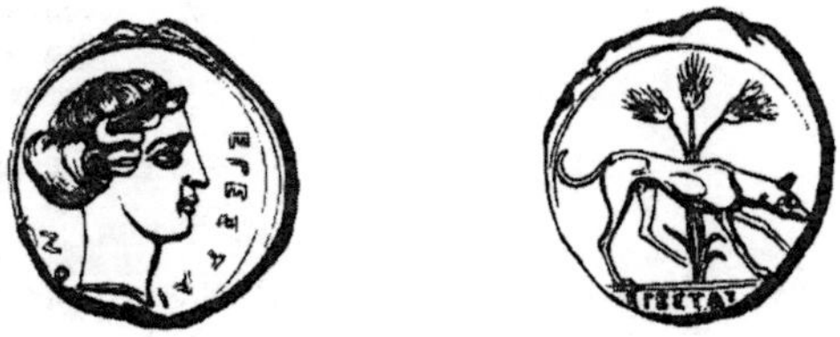

No.	Wt.	Metal. Size.	Obverse.	Reverse.
40	125·5	Æ ·9	Similar type.	Hound r.
41	131·5	Æ ·95	ΕΓΕΣΤΑΙΟΝ Similar type; behind, ivy-leaf.	Hound r., standing on stag's head, and seizing it by the nose; above, head r.: border of dots.
42	28·3	Æ ·5	Rude female head r.: border of dots.	ΕΡΕΣ Hound l., crouching; in front, Ρ.
			(Barbarous imitation.)	
43	11·5	Æ ·45	Head of Segesta, three-quarter face towards l.; hair turned up behind over diadem; on either side, branch of olive, tied by cord above: border of dots.	ΝΟ Ι ΑΤ Σ ΕΓΕ Hound l.; above, Gorgon-head surrounded by snakes; in front, murex.
44	12·	Æ ·45	Similar.	Similar.
45	6·1	Æ ·45	ΝΟ ΙΑΤ Head of Segesta r.: border of dots.	Hound l.; in front, plant or flower rising from ground.
46	5·2	Æ ·35	Young head r., wearing broad diadem; hair long.	Hound r., his nose to the ground; above, ivy-leaf: border of dots.

Hemilitron.

No.	Wt.	Metal. Size.	Obverse.	Reverse.
47	4·5	Æ ·35	Fore-part of crouching hound r.: border of dots.	Σ Ε Γ Ε around large Η.

No.	Wt.	Metal. Size.	Obverse.	Reverse.
				Hexas.
48	2·1	AR ·25	Head of hound r.: border of dots.	ΕΓΕ ΣΤΑ ●●
				COPPER.
				With marks of value.
				Tetras.
49	132·	Æ ·8	Head of Segesta r.; hair tied at the back by fillet with falling ends; behind, ivy-leaf: border of dots.	Hound r.; in front, plant; above and below, ○○ ○○
50	97·	Æ ·8	Head of Segesta r.; hair turned up behind under broad diadem.	Hound r.; in front, plant; around, ⊙ ⊙ ⊙ ⊙ (Marks of value added subsequently by punching.)
				Hexas.
51	86·	Æ ·85	Same. (Same die.)	Same; above and below, ● ● (Same die ?)
52	60·	Æ ·65	Similar type.	Similar type; above and below, ○ ○
53	81·	Æ ·7	Head of Segesta r., wearing sphendone.	Traces of inscr. Hound advancing l.; above and below, ● ●; in ex., weasel r.
54	95·	Æ ·65	Similar: border of dots.	ΕΓ ΕΣΤΑΙ Same. (Same die.)
55	113·	Æ ·65	Same. (Same die.)	ΕΣΤ Similar type r.; same marks of value; in ex., weasel l.
56	43·	Æ ·65	Head of Segesta r., wearing sphendone: border of dots.	Hound r., looking back; above and below, ● ●: border of dots.
57		Æ ·65	Traces of ƎAΣƎH Similar.	Similar type.

No.	Wt.	Metal. Size.	Obverse.	Reverse.
			Without marks of value.	
58		Æ ·4	Head of Segesta r.; hair wavy: border of dots.	Hound r., looking back.
			Period of Decline; late.	
59		Æ ·8	Bust of Segesta r., veiled and turreted.	ΓΕΣ ΤΑΙΩΝ Aeneas, holding in r. sword, and on his l. shoulder Anchises, both r.: border of dots.
60		Æ ·9	Similar.	ΣΕΓΕΣ ΤΑΙΩΝ Similar.
61		Æ ·85	Similar type; behind, countermark, sheep? r.: border of dots.	ΣΤ ΑΙΩΝ Similar; Aeneas facing; behind, eagle r., wings open: border of dots.
62		Æ ·85	Similar type: same border.	ΣΕΓΕΣΤΑΙΩ Military figure, facing, holding spear and sword; in field r., ⊙ and biga r.: border of dots.
63		Æ ·75	Similar type: same border.	ΙΩΝ Military figure l., spear over l. shoulder, holding by the bridle horse l.: border of dots.
64		Æ ·7	ΕΓΕΣ ΤΑΙΩΝ Bust of Segesta r., turreted: border of dots.	Similar type; in field l., murex: border of dots.
			Imperial Coinage.	
			AUGUSTUS.	
65		Æ ·95	ΕΓΕΣ ΤΑΙΩΝ Head of Augustus r., bare: border of dots.	Aeneas advancing, holding in r. Palladion, and with l. arm Anchises, both l.; above his head, crescent; behind him, eagle l., wings open: border of dots.
66		Æ ·95	Same. (Same die.)	Same. (Same die.)

SELINUS.

SILVER.

Period of Archaic Art.

No.	Wt	Metal. Size.	Obverse.	Reverse.
1	128·	AR ·95	Selinon-leaf.	Incuse square of twelve divisions, the alternate ones deeper.
2	111·2	AR 1· plated	Similar.	Similar.
			(This coin has been punched in ancient times.)	
3	131·3	AR ·85	Similar.	Incuse square of eight triangular divisions.
4	126·4	AR ·9	Similar.	Similar, but alternate divisions deeper.
5	133·4	AR ·95	Similar.	Incuse square of eight divisions, alternate ones deeper.

No.	Wt	Metal. Size.	Obverse.	Reverse.
6	130·	AR ·9	Similar.	Incuse square of ten divisions, six deeper.
7	134·5	AR ·8	Similar.	Incuse square of twelve divisions, the alternate ones deeper.
8	131·7	AR ·85	Similar.	Similar square of sixteen divisions.
9	127·3	AR ·9	Similar.	Incuse square of eight divisions, separated by double radiating lines.

No.	Wt.	Metal. Size.	Obverse.	Reverse.
			With marks of value.	
			Didrachm.	
10	134·	Æ ·9	Selinon-leaf; on either side of stalk, ● ●	Incuse square of twelve divisions, the alternate ones deeper.
11	136·3	Æ ·9	Similar.	Incuse square of ten divisions.
			Without marks of value.	
12	125·1	Æ ·8	Selinon-leaf.	Selinon-leaf in linear square within incuse.
13	131·8	Æ ·7	Similar.	Selinon-leaf in incuse square. (Traces of letters in corners.)
14	123·	Æ ·85	Similar.	ϟ Ǝ Λ I Similar.
15	121·2	Æ ·85	Similar.	Ƹ E I Λ Similar.
16	9·8	Æ ·45	Selinon-leaf.	Selinon-leaf in linear square within incuse square placed as lozenge.
			(Pierced with two holes.)	
17	5·8	Æ ·45	Similar.	Selinon-leaf: border of dots.
18	7·1	Æ ·45	Similar.	Similar type: linear circle within border of dots.
19	9·	Æ ·4	Similar.	Similar type: border of dots.
20	10·	Æ ·45	Similar.	Similar.
21	7·	Æ ·4	Similar.	Rose-like flower.
22	5·	Æ ·4	Similar.	Similar.
			Period of Transition.	
23	265·4	Æ 1·3	ƸEΛ OƸ River-god Selinos, naked, l., sacrificing with patera at an altar; holds in l. laurel-branch; on this side of altar, cock l.; in field r., bull standing l. on pedestal, above which, selinon-leaf.	ΛOI OΛΙΛƎ Ƹ Quadriga l., driven by Artemis, who holds reins in both hands; on her r. stands Apollo, his chlamys over shoulder, discharging an arrow; horses walking: border of dots.

No.	Wt.	Metal. Size.	Obverse.	Reverse.
24	269·	Æ 1·15	Σ ΕΛΙ ΜΟ Σ Similar; river-god horned and diademed, altar wreathed.	ΙΤΜ ΟΜΙΛƎΣ Similar.
25	266·8	Æ 1·1	Σ ΕΛ Ι ΝΟ Σ Similar.	Same. (Same die.)
26	268·8	Æ 1·1	Σ ΕΛΙΝ ΟΣ Similar.	Same. (Same die.)
27	262·1	Æ 1·1	ΣΕΛΙΝ ΟΣ Similar; river-god not horned.	ΣΕΛ ΙΝ ΟΝΤ ΝΟΙ Similar.
28	256·8	Æ 1·1	Σ ΕΛ Ι Ν Ο Σ Similar.	Same. (Same die.)
29	258·	Æ 1·1	ΟΝΤΙ Ο River-god l., wearing himation round body and over l. shoulder, sacrificing with patera at altar; he holds in raised l. hand laurel-branch; on this side of altar, cock l.; in field r., man-headed bull, standing l. on pedestal; above bull, selinon-leaf.	Similar; Apollo without chlamys.

No.	Wt.	Metal. Size.	Obverse.	Reverse.
30	268·8	Æ 1·05	ΣΕΛΙ ΝΟΝΤΙ ΟΝ River-god l., naked, sacrificing with patera at flaming altar; holds in l. laurel-branch; on this side of altar, cock advancing l.; in field r., bull l., his head lowered, standing on pedestal; above bull, selinon-leaf.	Quadriga r., the front ornamented with crane, driven by Artemis, who holds reins in both hands; on her r. stands Apollo, his chlamys over shoulder, discharging an arrow; horses walking: border of dots.
31	264·1	Æ 1·05	ΣΕΛ ΙΝΟΝΤ Ι ΟΝ Similar.	Similar type; Artemis holds goad with reins; in ex., barleycorn: border of dots.

No.	Wt.	Metal. Size.	Obverse.	Reverse.
32	259·1	Æ 1·1	ΣΕΛ ΙΝΟΝΤΙ ΟΝ Similar.	Similar type; front of chariot plain; same symbol: plain border.
33	261·6	Æ 1·15	ΣΕΛΙ ΝΟΝΤΙ ΟΝ Similar; bull, man-headed.	Similar type; no goad; above horses, olive-wreath; beneath their feet, bivalve shell; in ex., barleycorn.
34	131·3	Æ ·95	Σ Ε Λ Ι ΝΟ Ι ΤΟΝ (*sic*) Herakles, naked, r., seizing by the horn bull galloping r., which he presses with his l. knee, raising his club to strike: border of dots.	ΗΥΨ ΑΣ River-god Hypsas, towards l., naked, with short horn, sacrificing with patera at altar, round which bearded snake twines; he holds in l. laurel-branch; in field r., crane running r., over which, selinon-leaf.

No.	Wt.	Metal. Size.	Obverse.	Reverse.
35	124·7	Æ ·95	Similar.	ΗΥ ΨΑΣ Similar; altar wreathed.
36	134·1	Æ ·9	Similar. (Same die as last but one.)	Η Υ Ψ ΑΣ Similar.
37	128·4	Æ ·9	Ε Λ Ι Ν ΟΝΤ ΙΟΣ Similar.	ΗVΨ ΑΣ Similar.

With name of Eurymedon.

No.	Wt.	Metal. Size.	Obverse.	Reverse.
38	61·5	Æ ·75	ΟΔƎΜVϘVƎ Female head l., hair turned up behind under broad diadem; behind, crane r.: border of dots.	Ƨ Ο Ν Ι Λ Ǝ Ƨ Young head of river-god Selinos l., with long horn and pointed ear; behind, selinon-leaf.

No.	Wt.	Metal. Size.	Obverse.	Reverse.
39	10·8	AR ·45	Female figure, draped, seated l. on rock, on which l. hand rests, r. hand on the neck of a bearded snake, which advances towards her; above, selinon-leaf: border of dots.	ΣΕΛΙΝΟΕΣ Man-headed bull r.; in ex., long fish r.: plain border.
40	10·7	AR ·5	Similar; but female figure raises veil with l.	Similar.
41	10·3	AR ·45	Similar type; but female figure places l. hand on her breast: same border.	ΣΕΛ ΙΝΟ Σ Similar type; above, selinon-leaf.
42	11·2	AR ·4	Similar.	ΙΟΝ Similar type and symbol.
43	11·	AR ·5	Similar.	ΣΕΛΙΝ Similar type, and similar symbol inverted.

Period of Finest Art.

No.	Wt.	Metal. Size.	Obverse.	Reverse.
44	264·	AR 1·1	ΣΕΛΙΝΟΝΤ ΙΟΝ River-god l., naked, sacrificing with patera at flaming altar; holds in l. laurel-branch; on this side of altar, cock l.; in field r., bull l., his head lowered, standing on pedestal bound with wreath; above bull, selinon-leaf; in ex., fish l.	ΣΕΛΙΝΟΝΤΙΟΝ (in ex.) Quadriga r., driven by Nike, who holds reins in l. and raises r.; horses in high action; above, olive-wreath; in ex., ear of barley r.: border of dots.

No.	Wt.	Metal. Size.	Obverse.	Reverse.
45	264·6	AR 1·15	Same. (Same die.)	die.)

No.	Wt.	Metal. Size.	Obverse.	Reverse.
46	125·8	Ʀ ·85	Herakles r., naked, seizing by the horn bull, struggling r., which he presses with l. knee, raising his club to strike: border of dots.	ΣΕΛΙΝΟΝΤΙΟΝ River-god l., naked, sacrificing with patera at round-topped altar, around which snake twines; he holds in l. long branch of laurel; in field r., crane r., above which, selinon-leaf: border of dots.
47	29·	Ʀ ·6	Head of bearded Herakles r., wearing lion's skin.	ΝΟΝΤΙΟΝ (in ex.) Quadriga l., driven by male charioteer, who holds reins with goad; horses in high action; above, selinon-leaf.
48	26·1	Ʀ ·65	Head of young Herakles, three-quarter face towards l.: border of dots.	ΣΕΛΙΝΟΝΤΙΟΝ (in ex.) Similar type and symbol.
49	30·	Ʀ ·65	Same. (Same die.)	Same. (Same die.)

COPPER.

Trias.

No.	Wt.	Metal. Size.	Obverse.	Reverse.
50	138·	Æ ·75	Head of young river-god l., horned.	Selinon-leaf; around, ● ● ●

SOLUS.

COPPER.

Period of Decline; late.

No.	Wt.	Metal. Size.	Obverse.	Reverse.
1		Æ ·7	Head of young Herakles r., wearing lion's skin.	Sea-horse, with curled wing, r.; behind, scallop: border of dots.

No.	Wt.	Metal. Size.	Obverse.	Reverse.
2		Æ ·85	ϹΟΛΟ N Bust of Poseidon l., laur.? over shoulder, trident: border of dots.	Head of Pallas? r., wearing crested helmet: border of dots.
3		Æ ·9	Similar.	Similar.
4		Æ ·9	Head of Pallas? r., wearing crested Corinthian helmet: border of dots.	ϹΟΛΟΝ ΤΙΝѠΝ within laurel-wreath: border of dots.
5		Æ ·7	Head of Poseidon r., laur.; over shoulder, trident: border of dots.	ИΩИΙ Τ ИΟΛΟϽ Naked warrior, advancing l., helmeted, holding spear and shield: border of dots.

No.	Wt.	Metal. Size.	Obverse.	Reverse.
6		Æ ·9	Similar.	ϹΟΛΟΝ ΤΙΝ ѠΝ Similar type r.: same border.
7		Æ ·7	Naked warrior, advancing r., holding spear and shield: border of dots.	ϹΟΛΟΝ ΤΙΝѠΝ within laurel-wreath.

See Siculo-Punic Class.

STIELA.

SILVER.

Period of Finest Art.

No.	Wt.	Metal. Size.	Obverse.	Reverse.
1	62·5	AR ·65	Young male head l., laur., with slight whisker; in front, branch of plant: (selinon?) border of dots.	ΣΤΙΑ Fore-part of man-headed bull, advancing l. (River Alabon.)
2	31·5	AR ·55	Similar.	Similar. (Ι obliterated.)

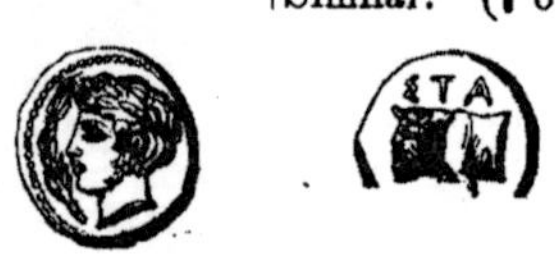

SYRACUSE.

Period of Archaic Art.

Oligarchy of the Geomori, before B.C. 485.

SILVER.

With Ϙ in inscription.

No.	Wt.	Metal. Size.	Obverse.	Reverse.
1	267·4	Æ 1·	ΣVRA Quadriga r., driven by male charioteer, holding reins in both hands; horses advancing slowly: border of dots.	Granulated incuse square, divided into quarters; in the centre, an incuse circle, containing a female head l.; hair indicated by dotted lines, and falling formally over the neck.
2	265·3	Æ 1·	ΣVRAϘO ΣION Similar.	Similar.

No.	Wt.	Metal. Size.	Obverse.	Reverse.
3	130·8	Æ ·75	ΣVRA Naked horseman r., leading a second horse; horses walking in step: border of dots.	Similar.

[Head. Coinage of Syracuse, Pl. I. 2.]

No.	Wt.	Metal. Size.	Obverse.	Reverse.
			Rule of Gelon? B.C. 485–478.	
4	263·6	AR 1·05	ΣV RAϘ OΣI ON Linear circle, within which female head r.; hair indicated by dotted lines, and falling formally over neck; she wears diadem and necklace; around, four dolphins r.	Quadriga r., driven by male charioteer, holding reins in both hands, goad in l.; above, Nike r., wings spread, alighting upon the yoke, holding wreath in r. and placing her l. upon the forelock of the third horse; horses walking: border of dots.

No.	Wt.	Metal. Size.	Obverse.	Reverse.
5	130·3	AR ·8	Similar.	Naked horseman r., leading a second horse: horses walking in step: border of dots.
6	128·6	AR ·8	ΣVRAϘOΣION Female head r., wearing earring and necklace; hair indicated by lines, falling in formal tress, and bound with diadem of oval beads: around, three dolphins r.	Same. (Same die.)
7	262·7	AR 1·05	ΣVR AϘ OΣI ON Female head r., wearing necklace; hair enclosed in net and bound with narrow diadem; around, four dolphins r.	ΣVRA (in ex.) Quadriga l., driven by male charioteer, holding reins in both hands, goad in r.: above, Nike, flying r., crowning him; horses walking: border of dots.
8	261·4	AR 1·15	ΝΟΙΣΟϘΑЯVΣ Sim[illegible]	[illegible]

No.	Wt.	Metal. Size.	Obverse.	Reverse.
9	266·7	Ʀ 1·05	ΣVRA ϘO ΣI OΝ : Female head r., wearing necklace; hair indicated by dots, the ends turned up behind, bound with narrow diadem; around, four dolphins r.	Quadriga r., driven by male charioteer, holding reins in both hands, goad in l.; horses walking; above, Nike, with spread wings, flying r. and crowning horses: border of dots.
			With K in inscription.	
10	265·1	Ʀ 1·	ΣVR AK OΣI OΝ Female head l., wearing necklace; the hair, indicated by dots and bound with narrow diadem, falls in a long tress tied near the end; around, four dolphins l.	Quadriga r., driven by bearded male charioteer, holding reins in both hands, goad in r.; horses walking; above, Nike, with spread wings, flying r. and crowning horses: border of dots.
11	264·	Ʀ 1·	Same. (Same die.)	Similar; Nike wears peplos, and her wings are thrown back.
12	267·6	Ʀ 1·	ΣVRAK OΣI OΝ Female head r., wearing necklace and diadem of beads; hair indicated by dots, turned up behind and tied, the ends falling over the cord; around, four dolphins r. [Head. Pl. I. 4.]	Same as no. 10. (Same die.)
13	267·7	Ʀ ·95	ΣVRA K OΣIO Ν Same type, but the ends of the hair passing under diadem, and not tied with cord; around, four dolphins r.	Similar type and same border.
14	269·	Ʀ ·95	ΣVRAKO ΣIO Ν Similar.	Similar.
15	258·7	Ʀ 1·05	ΣVR A K OΣ I O Ν Similar.	Similar.
16	260·9	Ʀ ·95	ΣVRAKO ΣI OΝ Similar; no necklace.	Similar.

No.	Wt.	Metal. Size.	Obverse.	Reverse.
17	263·7	AR ·95	ΣVR AKO ΣI OM Female head r., wearing necklace; hair bound with two diadems, a plain one, above which is a beaded one, the hair indicated by dots in front, and by lines at the back, the ends turned up behind and falling over the diadems; around, four dolphins r.	Similar.
18	265·7	AR 1·05	ΣVRA K OΣ I O N Similar head r., with single diadem of beads; hair indicated by dots; around, four dolphins r.	Similar.
19	268·2	AR ·95	ΣVRA K O ΣIO N Similar.	Similar.
20	134·	AR ·9	ΣVRA KOΣ ION Female head r., wearing necklace and diadem of beads; hair, indicated by dots, turned up behind under diadem, over which the ends fall; around, three dolphins r.	Horseman r., naked, bearded leading a second horse horses walking in step: border of dots.
				[Head. Pl. I. 5.]
21	65·3	AR ·65	ΣVRAKOΣION Similar head; no dolphins.	Naked horseman r.; horse walking: border of dots.
22	263·5	AR 1·	ΣVRAKO ΣION Female head r., wearing necklace and diadem of beads; hair turned up behind under diadem, over which the ends fall; around, four dolphins r.	Quadriga r., driven by male charioteer, holding goad in r. hand, reins in l.; horses walking; crowned by Nike with spread wings, flying r. border of dots.
23	263·4	AR 1·	Σ V RA KOΣ I OM Similar.	Similar.
24	266·6	AR ·95	ΣVRAKOΣIO N Similar.	Similar.

No.	Wt.	Metal. Size.	Obverse.	Reverse.
25	266·	AR ·95	ΣVRAKOΣIO N Female head r., wearing necklace and diadem of beads; hair, indicated by dots in front and by lines behind, hanging down over neck; around, four dolphins r.	Quadriga r., driven by bearded male charioteer, holding goad in r. hand, reins in l.; horses walking, crowned by Nike, flying r.: border of dots.
26	267·1	AR ·95	ΣV RAK OΣI ON Similar.	Similar.
27	266·1	AR ·95	ΣVRAKO Σ IO N Similar.	Similar.
28	266·4	AR 1·	ΣVRAKOΣI O N Female head r., wearing necklace and diadem of beads; hair indicated by dots in front and by lines at the back, the ends turned up under and falling over diadem; around, four dolphins r.	Similar.
29	263·	AR 1·	ΣVRAKOΣION Similar.	Similar.
30	265·4	AR 1·	Σ VRAK O ΣI O N Similar.	Similar.
31	263·6	AR ·95	ΣAVRA KOΣ I ON Female head r., wearing plain necklace and diadem; the ends of the hair turned up under and falling over the diadem; around, four dolphins r.	Similar.
32	267·5	AR ·95	ΣVRAKOΣI O N Female head r., wearing necklace and diadem of beads; hair indicated by dots in front and by lines at the back, the ends turned up under and falling over diadem; around, four dolphins r.	Similar; line of ex. double: border not visible.

No.	Wt.	Metal. Size.	Obverse.	Reverse.
33	267·3	Æ ·95	Same inscr. Female head r., wearing necklace and broad diadem, above which, diadem of beads; hair indicated by dots in front and by lines at the back, the ends turned up under and falling over the broad diadem; around, four dolphins r.	Similar; line of ex. border of dots.
34	261·7	Æ ·95	ΣVRA KOΣIO N Female head r., wearing necklace and diadem of beads; hair indicated by lines; it is turned up behind under diadem, over which the ends fall; around, four dolphins r.	Similar.
35	264·9	Æ 1·	ΣVRAK OΣ IO N Similar head r.; hair slightly waved, and parted from the crown of the head to the ear; around, four dolphins r.	Similar.
36	270·	Æ 1·1	ΣVRAK OΣI ON Similar.	Similar type 1. Nil spread wings: bo dots.
37	266·2	Æ ·95	ΣVRAKOΣI ON Similar; hair not waved nor parted; dolphins larger.	Similar to no. 35.
38	263·6	Æ 1·	ΣVRAKO ΣIO N Similar.	Similar.
39	266·7	Æ ·9	ΣVRAKOΣION Similar.	Similar; line of ex. d
40	220·1	Æ ·95 plated.	ΣV RA ON M N (Inscr. blundered.) Similar.	Similar; line of ex. si

(This coin is an ancient forgery.)

No.	Wt.	Metal. Size.	Obverse	Reverse.
41	269·	Æ ·95	Ƹ VꞦA KOƸIO Ʌ Female head r., wearing necklace, earring, and diadem of large beads; hair projecting over forehead, and turned up behind under diadem, over which the ends fall; around, four dolphins r.	Similar.
42	268·9	Æ ·95	ƸVꞦ AKO ƸIO Ʌ Similar.	Similar. [Head. Pl. I. 6.]
43	263·1	Æ 1·	ƸVꞦVK OƸ I OɅ Similar.	Similar.
44	267·	Æ 1·	ƸVꞦA KOƸI OɅ Similar.	Similar.
45	269·	Æ ·95	ɅOIƐ OꓘA ᖉVƐ Similar.	Similar.
46	127·6	Æ ·85	ƸVR AKO ƸIOɅ Female head r., wearing necklace and diadem of beads; hair slightly waved, and parted from the crown of the head to the ear as on no. 35; around, three dolphins r.	Horseman r., naked, bearded, leading a second horse; horses walking in step: border of dots.
47	65·2	Æ ·65	ƸVᴙAKOƸ IO Ʌ Female head r., wearing necklace and plain diadem; hair projecting over forehead, and turned up behind under diadem, over which the ends fall.	Horseman r., naked, bearded: border of dots. [Head. Pl. I. 7.]
48	13·7	Æ ·5	Female head r., wearing earring, necklace, and diadem of beads; hair indicated by lines and projecting over forehead; it is turned up behind under diadem, over which the ends fall: border of dots.	ƸV R A Cuttle-fish.
			ƸVRA Similar.	No inscr. Similar.

No.	Wt.	Metal. Size.	Obverse.	Reverse.
50	12·6	Æ ·5	Similar.	Similar.
51	12·6	Æ ·45	Similar; necklace plain.	Similar.
52	11·5	Æ ·45	No inscr. Similar.	ΣV Ʀ A Similar.
53	10·1	Æ ·45	Σ V Ʀ A Similar.	No inscr. Similar.
			[Head. Pl. I. 8.]	
54	7·6	Æ ·4	No inscr. Similar.	A Ʀ VΣ Similar.
55	11·4	Æ ·35	Female head r., wearing necklace and diadem of beads; hair turned up behind under diadem, over which the ends fall: border of dots.	Wheel of four spokes.
56	10·5	Æ ·4	Similar.	Similar.
57	10·1	Æ ·35	Similar.	Similar.
58	9·8	Æ ·3	Similar.	Similar.
59	9·7	Æ ·35	Similar.	Similar.
60	7·2	Æ ·35	Similar; diadem plain?	Similar.
			(Barbarous.)	
61	6·8	Æ ·35	Similar to no. 59.	Similar.
			[Head Pl. I. 9.]	
62	10·2	Æ ·35	Female head r., wearing earring, necklace, and diadem of beads; hair turned up behind under diadem, over which the ends fall.	Σ V Ʀ A within wheel of four spokes.
			[Head. Pl. I	

No.	Wt.	Metal. Size.	Obverse.	Reverse.
			Demaretion-class. (Struck B.C. 480–479.)	
63	685·6	Æ 1·4	ΣV ϘA KOΣ ION outside linear circle, within which, female head, Nike? r., wearing olive-wreath, earring, and necklace with pendants; hair waved in front and turned up behind, leaving one loose lock, which falls behind the ear; the ends of the hair gathered up and tied with double cord; around the whole, four dolphins r.	Quadriga r., driven by male figure, holding goad in r. and reins in both hands; horses walking; above, Nike flying r., crowning them; in ex., lion running r.: border of dots.

No.	Wt.	Metal. Size.	Obverse.	Reverse.
64	268·2	Æ 1·	ΣV ϘAK OΣI ON Similar.	Similar. [Head. Pl. I. 11.]
65	258·2	Æ 1·05	Similar.	Similar.
66	9·7	Æ ·4	Similar head: border of dots.	Σ V R A within wheel of four spokes. [Head. Pl. I. 12.]

No.	Wt.	Metal. Size.	Obverse.	Reverse.
			Period of Transition. (Time of Hieron I., B.C. 478–467; Thrasybulos, B.C. 467–6, and Democracy, B.C. 466–412.) SILVER.	
67	254·8	AR 1·1	ΣV ΡA KOΣI OV Female head r., wearing ear-ring, necklace, and diadem of beads; hair waved in front and turned up behind under diadem, over which the ends fall; around, four dolphins r.	Quadriga r., driven by male charioteer, goad in r. hand, reins in both; horses walking, crowned by Nike, flying r.; in ex., pistrix r.: border of dots.
68	257·3	AR ·9	ΣVRAKOΣ IO N Similar.	Quadriga r., driven by male charioteer, holding reins with both hands; horses walking; above, Nike flying l., and crowning charioteer; in ex., pistrix r.: border of dots.
69	269·3	AR 1·	Similar.	Same. (Same die.)
70	266·5	AR ·95	Same. (Same die.)	Similar.
71	267·5	AR 1·1	ΣVΡ A KO ΣIOV Similar.	Quadriga r., driven by male charioteer, holding goad in r. hand and reins in both; horses walking, crowned by Nike, flying r.; in ex., pistrix r.: border of dots.

No.	Wt.	Metal. Size.	Obverse.	Reverse.
72	266·5	AR 1·05	ΣVRAKOΣI O N Female head r., wearing ear-ring, necklace, and diadem of beads; hair waved and turned up behind under diadem, over which the ends fall; around, four dolphins r.	Similar.

No.	Wt.	Metal. Size.	Obverse.	Reverse.
73	266·4	Æ 1·05	ΣVRAK OΣ I O N Similar.	Similar.
			[Head. Pl. II. 2.]	
74	265·2	Æ 1·05	ΣVRAKOΣIO Similar.	Similar.
75	132·5	Æ ·9	Σ VRAKOΣI O N Female head r., wearing necklace and diadem of beads; hair waved and tied behind with double cord, leaving short ends; three loose tresses hang over the cheek; around, four dolphins r.	Horseman r., naked, bearded, leading a second horse; horses walking in step; behind, Nike flying r., about to crown horseman; in ex., pistrix r.: border of dots.

No.	Wt.	Metal. Size.	Obverse.	Reverse.
76	67·1	Æ ·65	ΣVR[A]KOΣION Female head r., wearing necklace and diadem of beads; hair waved in front and turned up behind under diadem, over which the ends fall.	Horseman r., naked; horse walking: border of dots.
77	11·7	Æ ·45	ΣVRA Female head r., wearing diadem of beads, earring, and necklace; hair waved in front and turned up behind under diadem: border of dots.	Cuttle-fish.
			[Head. Pl. II. 4.]	
78	11·7	Æ ·45	ΣVRA Similar.	Similar.
			Tetras.	
79	4·1	Æ ·35	Similar type: same border.	Wheel of four spokes, within which, marks of value, ••••
			[Head. Pl. II. 5.]	

No.	Wt.	Metal. Size.	Obverse.	Reverse.
80	268·7	AR 1·	ΣVRAKOΣIO N Female head r., wearing earring and necklace; hair waved in front, and bound with cord once round the head and twice round the back hair; around, four dolphins r.	Quadriga r., driven by male figure, holding goad in r. hand, reins in both; horses walking; above, Nike flying l., about to crown charioteer; in ex., pistrix r.: border of dots.
			[Head. Pl. II. 6.]	
81	266·3	AR 1·05	ΣVRAKOΣI O N Female head r., wearing earring and necklace; hair waved in front, bound with cord, and in rolls behind; around, four dolphins r.	Similar; Nike flying r. and crowning horses: [pistrix not visible in ex.:] border of dots.
82	263·7	AR ·95	Similar.	Similar type; in ex., pistrix r.
83	268·7	AR 1·	Same inscr. and similar type; hair bound with string of beads; around, four dolphins r.	Similar: border of dots.
84	267·9	AR 1·05	ΣVRAKOΣ I ON Similar.	Similar.
			[Head. Pl. II. 7.]	
85	266·2	AR 1·	ΣVRAKOΣ IO N Female head r., wearing earring and necklace; hair waved in front, bound with cord, and in rolls behind; four loose tresses hang over the cheek; around, four dolphins r.	Similar.
86	266·3	AR ·95	Σ V P A K O Σ I O N Female head r., wearing earring, necklace, and cord, over which the hair is rolled five times, leaving four loose tresses, which hang over the cheek; around, four dolphins r.	Similar type and symbol.
87	264·	AR 1·25	ΣYPAKOΣION Similar.	Similar: Nike flying l., crowning charioteer.

No.	Wt.	Metal. Size.	Obverse.	Reverse.
88	267·5	AR ·95	ΣVPAKO ΣIOΝ Female head r., wearing earring, necklace with pendants, and diadem; hair caught up by diadem in front, and rolled behind; around, four dolphins r.	Similar type and symbol; Nike flying r., crowning horses.
89	268·6	AR 1·15	ΣVPAKOΣ I O Ν Similar.	Similar.
90	269·2	AR ·95	ΣY RAKOΣIO Ν Similar type, but broad necklace, upon which a string of beads; around, four dolphins r. [Head. Pl. II. 8.]	Similar.
91	263·	AR 1·05	ΣVRAKOΣIOΝ Female head r., wearing earring and necklace; hair waved, in a bunch behind, and bound with string of beads; around, four dolphins r.	Similar; charioteer holding reins only.
92	264·	AR 1·	Same. (Same die.)	Similar; charioteer holding goad in r. hand, reins in both.
93	267·2	AR 1·	Similar. [Head. Pl. II. 9.]	Similar; charioteer holding reins in both hands. (Same die as no. 91.)
94	267·5	AR 1·	ΣVRAKOΣI OΝ Female head r., wearing earring and necklace; hair waved, and bound with cord passing three times round the head and twice round back hair; around, four dolphins r. [Head. Pl. II. 10.]	Similar type and symbol; charioteer holding goad in r. hand, reins in both.
95	268·2	AR 1·05	Similar.	Similar: border of dots.

No.	Wt.	Metal. Size.	Obverse.	Reverse.
96	261·4	Æ 1·05	ΣY RAKOΣIOΝ Female head r., wearing earring and necklace; hair waved over the whole head, with a bunch behind, and bound with crossed diadem, the ends of which hang down behind the neck; around, four dolphins r.	Similar type and symbol l.: border of dots.
97	267·8	Æ 1·	ΣVRAKOΣI ON Female head r., wearing earring and necklace; hair waved in front and rolled behind, and bound with string of beads; around, four dolphins r.	Same type and symbol r.: border of dots.
98	266·9	Æ ·95	Same. (Same die.)	Similar; charioteer holding reins in both hands.
99	266·1	Æ 1·	Similar; hair bound with plain cord.	Similar; charioteer holding goad in r. hand, reins in both.
100	268·5	Æ ·95	ΣVPAKOΣI O N Female head r., wearing earring and broad necklace, upon which a string of beads; hair bound with plain broad diadem, wound twice round the head and fastened with a cord, the back hair turned up under diadem and protruding in bunch above; around, four dolphins r.	Similar type and symbol.

No.	Wt.	Metal. Size.	Obverse.	Reverse.
101	266·5	Æ ·95	ΣΥΡΑΚΟΣΙΟΝ Similar type; necklace narrow; around, four dolphins, meeting in pairs.	Similar type; on front of chariot, crane r.: plain border.
102	268·8	Æ 1·05	Similar.	Same. (Same die.)
103	269·4	Æ 1·05	ƧOK A ꟼVƧ Female head r., wearing earring and necklace; hair in korymbos; around, four dolphins r.	Quadriga l., driven by male figure, holding goad in r. hand and reins in both; horses prancing; above, Nike flying r. and crowning charioteer; in ex., pistrix l.: border of dots.

No.	Wt.	Metal. Size.	Obverse.	Reverse.
104	265·8	Æ 1·05	ΣVΡΑΚΟΣΙ Ο Ν Similar.	Same. (Same die.)
105	267·8	Æ 1·15	ΣΥΡΑΚΟΣΙΟΝ Similar. [Head. Pl. II. 12.]	Similar.
106	65·8	Æ ·65	Σ V Ρ Α Κ Ο Σ Ι Ο Ν Female head r., wearing earring and necklace; hair in korymbos. [Head. Pl. II. 13.]	Horseman l., wearing chlamys; horse prancing: border of dots.

No.	Wt.	Metal. Size.	Obverse.	Reverse.
107	262·8	Æ ·95	ΣΥ ΡΑΚΟΣ Ν Female head r., wearing earring and necklace; hair bound with sphendone, the long ends of which are wound three times round the head; around, four dolphins (three visible).	Quadriga r., driven by male figure, holding goad in r. hand, reins in both; horses walking; above, Nike flying l., about to crown charioteer.

No.	Wt.	Metal. Size.	Obverse.	Reverse.
108	264·7	Æ ·95	ΣΥΡ ΑΚ Ο ΣΙ ΟΝ Similar; a lion's head ornament attached to necklace; around, four dolphins r.	Same; upon the front of the chariot is seen A. (Same die.)
109	270·7	Æ ·95	ΣΥ Ρ Α ΚΟΣΙ Ο Similar.	Similar; no letter visible.
110	262·5	Æ 1·	[Σ]ΥΡΑΚΟΣΙΟΝ Similar; no lion's head on necklace.	Similar: border of dots.

No.	Wt.	Metal. Size.	Obverse.	Reverse.
111	266·5	Æ 1·05	Σ ΥΡΑ ΚΟΣΙΟΝ Female head r., wearing earring and necklace; hair waved over forehead, the rest enclosed in sakkos, bound with broad diadem, the ends of which hang down behind the neck; around, four dolphins.	Quadriga r., driven by aged male figure, bald and bearded, holding goad in r. hand, reins in both; horses walking; above, Nike flying r. and crowning them: border of dots.

No.	Wt.	Metal. Size.	Obverse.	Reverse.
112	265·5	Æ ·9	ΣΥΡΑΚΟΣΙΟΝ Female head r., wearing earring, necklace, and ampyx adorned with olive-wreath; the hair enclosed in sakkos, drawn together by a string at the crown of the head, and ornamented with a band of mæander and zig-zag patterns; around, four dolphins.	Same. (Same die.)

(Head. Pl. III. 8. Obv.)

No.	Wt.	Metal. Size.	Obverse.	Reverse.
113	269·6	Æ 1·15	Same inscr. Similar.	Similar type; charioteer, Nike, and horses all varied: same border.
114	261·4	Æ 1·1	ΣYRAKOΣIOΝ Similar.	Similar.
115	265·1	Æ 1·05	ΣVR AKO Similar; necklace with lion's head ornament attached to it.	Quadriga r., driven by male charioteer, holding reins with outstretched arms, goad in r. hand; horses walking: border of dots.
116	265·	Æ ·95	ΣYPAKOΣ IO Ν Similar; on neck below earring, A.	Similar type; Nike l. crowns charioteer: border of dots.
117	261·5	Æ 1·	ꓘAЯVƧ Similar; necklace without lion's head ornament; no letter on neck.	Similar type.
118	262·	Æ 1·	ΣYPAKOΣ Similar; the ends of two strings, with which the sakkos is tied, hang loose from the crown of the head.	Same. (Same die.)
119	265·5	Æ 1·	Traces of inscr. Female head r., wearing earring and necklace, and bound with cord wound four times round the hair; around, four dolphins.	Similar.
120	268·4	Æ ·95	ΣYPAKOΣIOΝ Similar.	Similar; Nike r. crowns horses: border of dots. (Chariot nearly off field.)
121	267·1	Æ 1·1	ΣYP A K O Σ Similar.	Same; on front of chariot, representation of crane r. (Same die.)

No.	Wt.	Metal. Size.	Obverse.	Reverse.
122	263·3	AR 1·05	ΣΥΡΑΚΟΣΙΟΝ Similar.	Similar.
123	262·2	AR 1·05	ΣΥΡΑΚ ΙΟ Similar.	Similar.
124	267·	AR 1·25	ΣΥΡΑΚΟΣΙ ΟΝ Female head r., wearing earring, necklace, and ampyx ornamented with mæander pattern; the back hair enclosed in a net attached to the ampyx by a buckle; around, four dolphins.	Quadriga r., driven by male charioteer, holding rein with outstretched arms goad in r. hand; horse walking; above, Nike, flying r., crowns them; in ex locust r.: border of dots.

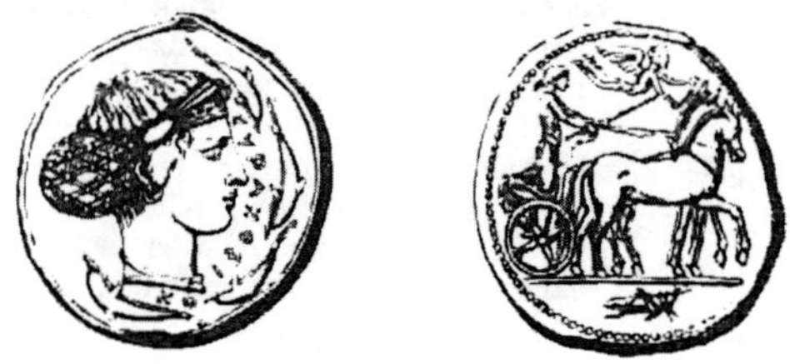

No.	Wt.	Metal. Size.	Obverse.	Reverse.
125	265·5	AR 1·15	ΣΥ ΡΑ ΚΟΣΙΛΛ (*sic*) Female head l., wearing earring and necklace, and bound with cord wound five times round the hair, leaving loose locks at the crown of the head; around, four dolphins.	Same. (Same die.)

COPPER.

Trias.

No.	Wt.	Metal. Size.	Obverse.	Reverse.
126	62·	Æ ·65	ΣΥΡΑ Female head r., wearing necklace; hair in korymbos; in front and behind, dolphin, downwards: plain border.	Cuttle-fish, the feelers of which are connected by a web; around, ● [●] ●

[Head. Pl. III. 7.]

No.	Wt.	Metal. Size.	Obverse.	Reverse.
127	50·	Æ ·65	Similar.	Similar [●] ● [●]
128	47·	Æ ·6	Similar.	Similar; around, ● ● ●
129	52·	Æ ·6	Similar.	Similar.
130	41·	Æ ·6	Similar.	Similar.
131	44·	Æ ·55	Traces of inscr. Same head l.	Similar. (Marks of value not visible.)

Uncia?

No.	Wt.	Metal. Size.	Obverse.	Reverse.
132	21·	Æ ·45	No inscr. Same head r.	Similar; no mark of value.

[Head. Pl. III. 8.]

Period of Finest Art.

Class I.—Transition from Ο to Ω, both in use.

Democracy after the Athenian Siege, B.C. 412–406.

GOLD.

No.	Wt.	Metal. Size.	Obverse.	Reverse.
133	18·1	AV ·4	ΣΥΡ Head of young Herakles l., wearing lion's skin: plain border.	Σ Υ / Ρ Α in the four quarters of an incuse square, in the centre of which is an incuse circle, containing a female head l., wearing sphendone, earring, and necklace.

[Head. Pl. III. 9.]

No.	Wt.	Metal. Size.	Obverse.	Reverse.
134	18·	AV ·4	ΣΥΡΑ Similar.	Similar.

No.	Wt.	Metal. Size.	Obverse.	Reverse.
135	17·9	AV ·4	ϟYP Similar (no border visible).	Similar.
136	17·9	AV ·4	[ϟ]YP A Similar.	Similar.
137	17·7	AV ·4	No inscr. Similar (no border visible).	No inscr. Similar.
138	10·4	AV ·4	ϟ Y P A Head of Pallas l., wearing crested Athenian helmet: plain border.	Eight-sided ægis, with border of serpents intertwined; upon it gorgon-head: plain border.
				[Head. Pl. III. 10.]
139	8·8	AV ·3	ϟYP Similar.	ϟ Y P A in the four quarters of an incuse square, in the centre of which an incuse circle, containing a wheel of four spokes.

SILVER.

Tetradrachms by Eumenos.

No.	Wt.	Metal. Size.	Obverse.	Reverse.
140	266·1	AR 1·15	ϟYPAKOϟIOꟽ Female head l., wearing earring and necklace; hair rolled; across front of head, ampyx, on which, EVMH ꟽOY; around, four dolphins.	Quadriga l., driven by charioteer, holding goad in r. hand, reins in both; horses galloping in step; above, Nike flying r., carrying an untied wreath, and about to crown the charioteer: border of dots.

No.	Wt.	Metal. Size.	Obverse.	Reverse.
141	262·1	Æ 1·05	ΣVPAKOΣIO Λ Similar head, without ampyx; beneath, EVΜHNOV; around, four dolphins.	Similar.
142	259·1	Æ 1·05	Same. (Same die.)	Similar type; beneath horses, a crane l.; in ex., a fish swimming l., followed by a dolphin.
143	267·	Æ 1·15	ΣYPAKOΣIOΝ Female head l., wearing earring and necklace; hair bound with a crossed cord, locks of hair flying loose over the head; beneath, traces of EYΜHNOV; around, four dolphins.	Similar type; no symbol; in ex., scallop: same border.
144	264·5	Æ 1·05	ΣYPAKOΣIOΝ Female head l., wearing earring and necklace; hair bound with a diadem crossed; behind, EVΜHN OV; around, four dolphins.	Quadriga l., driven by charioteer, holding goad and reins; horses galloping in step; above, Nike about to crown charioteer with untied wreath; in ex., EVΜHNOV: border of dots.
145	222·	Æ 1·05 plated.	Similar; behind head, EYΜHΛOV; around, four dolphins.	Similar type; ex. plain: border of dots.

(Ancient forgery.)

No.	Wt.	Metal. Size.	Obverse.	Reverse.
146	276·2	Æ ·9	[ΣY]PAKOΣIOΝ Female head l., wearing earring and necklace; hair rolled; behind neck, EY; around, four dolphins.	Quadriga l., driven by charioteer, holding reins in both hands, goad in r.; horses galloping in step; above, Nike flying r., about to crown charioteer; beneath horses, EY; in ex., a fish swimming r., followed by a dolphin: border of dots.
147	265·5	Æ 1·	Similar; beneath, EY.	Same. (Same die.)

No.	Wt.	Metal. Size.	Obverse.	Reverse.
			Tetradrachms by Eumenos and Euainetos.	
148	262·5	Æ 1·05	ΣΥΡΑ ΚΟΣΙΩΝ Female head l., wearing earring and necklace; hair rolled; beneath, ΕΥΜΕΝΟΥ; around, four dolphins.	Quadriga r., driven by bearded male figure, holding goad and reins; horses galloping; the rein of the farthest horse broken and trailing upon the ground; above, Nike flying l., carrying a wreath with which she is about to crown the charioteer, in one hand, and in the other, a label suspended by a cord, bearing the legend ΕΥΑΙΝ ΕΤΟ; in ex., two dolphins meeting: border of dots.
			[Head. Pl. III. 13.]	
149	267·6	Æ 1·05	Same. (Same die.)	Same. (Same die.)
150	265·7	Æ 1·05	ΣΥΡΑΚΟΣΙΩΝ Female head l., wearing earring and necklace hair bound with sphendone, tied above and ornamented with stars; in field below ΕΥΜΕ ΝΟΥ; around, four dolphins.	Same. (Same die.)
151	264·9	Æ 1·05	ΣΥΡΑ Female head l., wearing earring and necklace; hair rolled; beneath, ΕΥ; around, four dolphins.	Quadriga r., driven by female charioteer, holding goad and reins; horses galloping; the rein of the farthest horse broken and trailing upon the ground; above, Nike flying l., about to crown charioteer; in ex., a chariot-wheel lying on the ground, and [illegible] of ex., ΕΥΑ [illegible] minute [illegible] dots.

No.	Wt.	Metal. Size.	Obverse.	Reverse.
			Tetradrachms by Eumenos and Euth——.	
152	266·8	Æ 1·	Traces of inscr Similar type to no. 150; legend EVMENO V.	Quadriga r., driven by naked winged youth, looking upwards towards Nike, flying l., who crowns him; in ex., EYΘ, and Skylla swimming r., her r. arm extended towards a fish, which swims before her, her l. holding a trident over her shoulder; behind her, a dolphin r.: border of dots.
153	263·9	Æ ·95	ΣVPAKO Σ Head of Persephone l., wearing earring and necklace to which is attached a lion's head ornament; her hair is rolled and bound with ears of barley; beneath, EVM; around, four dolphins.	Same. (Same die.)
			Tetradrachms by Soson and Eumenos?	
154	266·8	Æ 1·15	ΣYPAKO ΣIO N Female head l., wearing earring and necklace to which is attached a ram's head ornament; across front of head, ampyx, on which, Σ[ΩΣ] ΩN; around, four dolphins.	Quadriga l., driven by charioteer, holding goad in r. hand, reins in both; horses galloping in step; above, Nike flying r., carrying an untied wreath, and about to crown charioteer; in ex., two dolphins meeting: border of dots.
155	266·5	Æ 1·2	ΣYPA KOΣIO N Similar; hair bound with broad diadem seen in front.	Same. (Same die.)

Tetradrachm by Phrygillos and Euth——.

No.	Wt.	Metal. Size.	Obverse.	Reverse.
156	255·9	AR 1·	ΣΥ ΡΑΚ ΟΣ Ι ΟΝ Head of Persephone l., wearing earring and necklace; hair bound with wreath of barley and poppy, the latter with one leaf and a poppy-head over forehead; beneath, [ΦΡ]ΥΓΙΛΛ; around, four dolphins.	Same. (Same die.)

No.	Wt.	Metal. Size.	Obverse.	Reverse.
157	263·9	AR ·95	Same.	Same.

(Same dies.)

Tetradrachms by Phrygillos.

No.	Wt.	Metal. Size.	Obverse.	Reverse.
158	263·5	AR 1·3	ΣΥΡΑ ΚΟΣΙ ΟΝ Female head l., wearing earring, necklace, and sphendone ornamented with stars of eight rays and having on the front part ΦΡΥ; around, four dolphins.	Quadriga l., driven by female figure, (Persephone?) carrying flaming torch and holding reins; above, Nike flying r., about to crown charioteer; in ex., ear of barley with three leaves l.: border of dots.

No.	Wt.	Metal. Size.	Obverse.	Reverse.
159	255·8	Æ 1·	Σ Υ Ρ Α ΚΩ ΣΙ ΟΝ Similar type and same engraver's name; around, four dolphins.	Similar; Nike carries wreath and palm.
160	264·4	Æ 1·	ΣΥΡΑΚΟΣΙΟΝ Similar.	Same. (Same die.)
161	261·	Æ 1·1	ΣΥ ΡΑΚ Female head l., wearing earring, necklace, and sphendone, tied above, ornamented behind with stars of eight rays, and having on the front part ΦΡΥ? around, four dolphins.	Similar; Nike carries wreath only.

Drachms by Eumenos.

No.	Wt.	Metal. Size.	Obverse.	Reverse.
162	65·4	Æ ·65	ΣΥ Ρ Α Κ ΟΣΙΟΝ Female head r., wearing earring and necklace; hair bound with diadem crossed; beneath, ΕVΜΕΝΟV; around, four dolphins r.	ΛΕV Κ Α Σ ΠΙΣ Leukaspis advancing r., in attitude of attack, wearing crested helmet with feather at the side, and carrying on l. arm oval shield, and in r. hand sword, the scabbard of which hangs behind him, suspended by a strap passing over r. shoulder: border of dots. [Head. Pl. III. 15.]
163	58·4	Æ ·7 plated.	Similar.	Similar.

Half-Drachms by Euainetos?

No.	Wt.	Metal. Size.	Obverse.	Reverse.
164	33·1	Æ ·65	ΣΥΡΑΚΟΣΙΟΝ Female head l., wearing earring, necklace, and sphendone, tied in front; on either side, a dolphin downwards.	Quadriga l., driven by charioteer holding reins in both hands, goad in r.; horses prancing; the rein of the farthest horse broken and trailing; above, Nike flying r., crowning charioteer; in ex., a chariot-wheel lying on the ground: border of dots. [Head. Pl. III. 16.]
	31·	Æ ·6	Similar.	Similar.

No.	Wt.	Metal. Size.	Obverse.	Reverse.
166	31·	AR ·6	ΣΥΡΑΚΟΣΙΟ Ν Similar.	Quadriga r., driven by charioteer holding reins in both hands, goad in r.; horses galloping; above, Nike flying l., crowning charioteer; in ex., two dolphins meeting.
167	29·4	AR ·65	ΣΙΟΝ Similar.	Similar: border of dots.

Period of Finest Art.

Class II.—Ω in general use.

Dionysios the Elder, B.C. 405–367; Dionysios II., B.C. 367–356; Dion, Kallippos, and Hipparinos, 356–350, and Interval, 350–345.

GOLD.

By Kimon?

No.	Wt.	Metal. Size.	Obverse.	Reverse.
168	88·9	AV ·55	ΣΥΡΑΚΟΣΙΟΝ Female head l., (Arethusa?) wearing earring, necklace, and sphendone, upon which are three stars; behind, a barley-corn and ΚΙ: border of dots.	ΣΥΡΑ Herakles kneeling on r. knee, and strangling lion with both arms; behind, club; above, ivy-leaf.

By Euainetos?

No.	Wt.	Metal. Size.	Obverse.	Reverse.
169	44·1	AV ·4	ΣΥΡΑΚΟ ΣΙΩΝ Young male head l.: border of dots.	ΣΥ ΡΑΚΟΣ ΙΩ[Ν] on a bar beneath an incuse square, within which a free horse prancing r.
170	44·5	AV ·4	Similar.	Similar.
171	44·7	AV ·45	Similar.	Similar.
172	44·4	AV ·4	ΣΥΡΑ Same type; behind, Ε: same border.	Similar; above, star of eight rays.

[Head. Pl. IV. 2.]

No.	Wt.	Metal. Size.	Obverse.	Reverse.
			SILVER.	
			Decadrachms by Euainetos (signed).	
173	660·9	AR 1·45	ΣY PA KOΣ IΩN Head of Persephone l., wearing earring and necklace; hair turned up behind, arranged in wavy curls, and bound with wreath of corn-leaves; around, four dolphins; in field, under chin, Δ; beneath the whole, traces of EY AINE: border of dots.	Quadriga l., driven by charioteer holding goad and reins; horses in high action; above, Nike flying r., about to crown the charioteer; in ex., a ledge or step, on and against which is placed a suit of defensive armour, consisting of helmet and shield, cuirass and greaves; beneath, AΘΛA: border of dots.
			[Head. Pl. IV. 3.]	
174	667·6	AR 1·35	KOΣIΩN Similar.	Similar.
175	665·	AR 1·45	ΣY PAK O ΣI ΩN Similar; no Δ; beneath, EY AINE: border of dots.	Similar.

176	659·4	AR 1·45	ΣY PA KO ΣIΩN Similar.	Similar.
177	650·5	AR 1 35	Similar.	Similar.
178	663·1	AR 1·4	Similar.	Same. (Same die.)
			Decadrachms by Euainetos, without signature.	
179	669·3	AR 1·35	Similar; beneath chin, a dot.	Similar.
180	669·5	AR 1·35	Similar.	Same. (Same die.)
181	659·9	AR 1·35	Similar.	Same. (Same die.)

No.	Wt.	Metal. Size.	Obverse.	Reverse.
182	661·3	AR 1·35	Similar; under chin, a dot; behind neck, a star of four rays.	Similar.
183	659·4	AR 1.4	Similar.	Similar.
184	666·6	AR 1·35	Similar; under chin, a dot; behind neck, a star of eight rays.	Similar.
185	669·4	AR 1·3	Similar; no dot; behind neck, a star of eight rays.	Same. (Same die.)
186	664·1	AR 1·45	Similar; behind neck, a scallop-shell.	Similar.
187	667·8	AR 1·4	Similar; beneath chin, griffin's head r.	Similar. (Same die as no. 183).

Tetradrachm by Euainetos.

No.	Wt.	Metal. Size.	Obverse.	Reverse.
188	266·9	AR 1·	ΣΥΡΑΚΟΣΙΩΝ Female head l., (Arethusa?) wearing earring and necklace; hair bound with sphendone, tied above, and ornamented in front, with a dolphin l. above waves, and behind, with three stars of eight rays; around, four dolphins; on the lower dolphin in front, ΕΥΑΙ.	Quadriga r., driven by bearded male figure holding goad and reins; horses galloping; the rein of the farthest horse broken and trailing upon the ground; above, Nike flying l., carrying a wreath, with which she is about to crown the charioteer in one hand, and in the other, a label suspended by a cord, bearing the legend ΕΥΑΙΝ ΕΤΟ; in ex., two dolphins meeting: border of dots. (Same die as no. 150.)

Tetradrachm by Euainetos and Eumenos?

No.	Wt.	Metal. Size.	Obverse.	Reverse.
189	266·	AR 1·	Same. (Same die.)	Quadriga l., driven by charioteer holding goad and reins; horses galloping in step; above, Nike flying r., about to crown the charioteer; in ex., two dolphins meeting: border of dots. (Style of Eumenos.)

Tetradrachm by Eukleides and Euainetos.

No.	Wt.	Metal. Size.	Obverse.	Reverse.
190	268·2	AR 1·	ΣΥΡΑΚΟΣΙΟΣ Female head l., wearing earring and necklace; hair bound with sphendone, tied above, and ornamented in front with a swan swimming l., and at the back with stars of eight rays, and with engraver's name EVKΛEI; around, four dolphins.	Quadriga r., driven by female figure holding goad and reins; horses galloping; the rein of the farthest horse broken and trailing upon the ground; above, Nike flying l., about to crown charioteer; in ex., a chariot-wheel lying on the ground; on exergual line, EYAINETO in minute characters: border of dots. (Same die as no. 151.)

Tetradrachms by Eukleides and Eumenos.

No.	Wt.	Metal. Size.	Obverse.	Reverse.
191	265·7	AR 1·05	Same. (Same die.)	Quadriga l., driven by charioteer holding goad and reins; horses galloping in step; above, Nike flying r., about to crown the charioteer; in ex., two dolphins meeting: border of dots. Style of Eumenos. (Same die as no. 189.)
192	263·6	AR ·95	ΣΥΡΑΚΟ Similar; ornaments on sphendone and engraver's name not visible.	Similar; beneath horses, EY.
193	265·3	AR 1·	ΣΥΡΑΚΟΣΙΟΣ Female head l., wearing earring and necklace; hair rolled; beneath chin, a diptych, on the tablets of which, EVKΛ/ΕΙΔΑ; around, four dolphins.	Quadriga l., driven by charioteer holding goad and reins; horses galloping in step; above, Nike flying r., about to crown charioteer; in ex., EYMHNOV: border of dots.

Tetradrachms by Eukleides and ——— ?

No.	Wt.	Metal. Size.	Obverse.	Reverse.
194	266·7	AR ·95	ΚΟ ΣΙΩ Ν Female head l., wearing earring and necklace; hair bound with sphendone, over which several tresses fly back; beneath head, on a scroll, slightly incuse, ΕVΚΛΕΙ; around, four dolphins: plain border.	Quadriga l., driven by male figure holding reins in both hands, goad in r.; horses prancing; above, Nike flying r., about to crown the charioteer; in ex., dolphin l.: border of dots.
195	265·9	AR 1·05	ΣΥΡ Α Κ ΟΣ Ι Ω Ν Similar; beneath head, traces of same engraver's name?	Similar.

No.	Wt.	Metal. Size.	Obverse.	Reverse.
196	267·	AR 1·05	Ν ΩΙ ΣΟΚ Similar; without engraver's name.	Same. (Same die.)
197	267·5	AR 1·05	Σ Υ ΣΙΩΝ Similar.	Similar.
198	265·6	AR 1·05	ΣΥΡ Α ΚΟΣΙΩΝ Head of Pallas, three-quarter-face l., wearing necklace of pendants with medallion in centre, and richly-ornamented Phrygian helmet having three crests, on the front of which, ΕV Κ ΛΕΙΔ Α; around, four dolphins: plain border. Head, [illegible]	Quadriga l., driven by female figure (Persephone?) holding flaming torch and reins; above, Nike flying r., about to crown her; the horses in high action in ex., ear of barley l.: border of dots.

No.	Wt.	Metal. Size.	Obverse.	Reverse.
199	264·5	AR 1·1	Same; medallion of necklace bears a gorgon-head. (Same die.)	Same. (Same die.)

Decadrachms by Kimon.

No.	Wt.	Metal. Size.	Obverse.	Reverse.
200	667·2	AR 1·35	ΣΥΡΑΚΟΣΙΩΝ Female head l., Arethusa? wearing earring, necklace, band tied above, and net; on front of band, ΚΙ/Μ; around, four dolphins.	Quadriga l., driven by charioteer holding goad and reins; horses in high action; above, Nike flying r., about to crown charioteer; in ex., a ledge or step, on and against which is placed a suit of defensive armour, consisting of helmet and shield, cuirass and greaves. [Beneath, ΑΘΛΑ; on the horizontal surface of the exergual line, ΚΙΜΩΝ: border of dots.] ΑΘΛΑ and ΚΙΜΩΝ are more or less legible on the other specimens of this reverse-die.

No.	Wt.	Metal. Size.	Obverse.	Reverse.
201	669·1	AR 1·4	Similar, but differing in style; band not tied above, and without legend; around, four dolphins; on that below the neck, ΚΙΜΩΝ : border of dots.	Same. (Same die.) ΑΘΛΑ.

No.	Wt.	Metal. Size.	Obverse.	Reverse.
202	661·	AR 1·45	[ΣΥΡΑΚ]ΟΣΙΩ Similar; inferior in style; Κ on band.	Same. (Same die.)
203	625·3	AR 1·4	ΣΥΡΑΚΟΣΙΩ Same. (Same die.)	Same. (Same die.)
204	661·8	AR 1·4	ΣΥΡΑΚΟΣΙΩΝ Similar, but superior in style; on band, ΚΙ/Μ ? (effaced;) dolphin uninscribed.	Similar.
205	664·6	AR 1·6	Similar; signature on band Κ ? (effaced.)	Similar.
206	667·5	AR 1·55	Same. (Same die.) Κ ? (effaced.)	Same. (Same die.)

Tetradrachms by Kimon.

No.	Wt.	Metal. Size.	Obverse.	Reverse.
207	268·0	AR 1·1	Similar; band tied above; no signature.	Quadriga l., driven by male charioteer holding goad and reins; horses prancing; above, Nike flying r., and crowning charioteer; in ex., dolphin l. : border of dots.

[Head. Pl. IV. 8.]

No.	Wt.	Metal. Size.	Obverse.	Reverse.
208	266·3	Æ 1·2	Head of Arethusa, three-quarter-face l., wearing earring and necklace; hair flowing in loose tresses; across her forehead, ampyx, on which, ΚΙΜΩΝ; around, four dolphins, two on either side, swimming among the locks of the hair: border of dots, lower half of which double-struck: above, outside border, ΑΡΕΘΟΣΑ.	ΣΥΡΑΚ ΟΣΙΩΝ Quadriga l., driven by male charioteer, holding goad in r. hand, reins in both, with head turned, looking behind him; horses galloping; beneath them, a prostrate column; (meta;) above, Nike r., stepping upon the heads of the two nearer horses, and carrying wreath with which she is about to crown the charioteer; in ex., ear of barley l.: plain border.

209	254·7	Æ 1·05	Same. (Same die.)	ΣΥΡΑΚΟΣΙΩΝ (in ex.) Quadriga l., driven by charioteer, holding goad in r. hand, reins in both, touching with goad the head of the third horse; horses prancing; above, Nike flying r., about to crown charioteer; on line of ex., ΚΙΜΩΝ: plain border.
			Tetradrachms by Parme——	
210	265·	Æ 1·	ΣΥΡΑΚΟΣΙ ΩΝ Female head l., wearing earring, necklace, and sphendone, tied above and ornamented at the back with stars of eight rays; around, four dolphins.	Quadriga l., driven by male charioteer, holding goad in r. hand, reins in both; above, Nike flying r., about to crown him; in ex., dolphin l.: border of dots.

No.	Wt.	Metal. Size.	Obverse.	Reverse.
211	266·7	AR ·95	Α ΟΣΙΩΝ Similar.	Similar type; beneath hind legs of horses, a broken chariot-wheel. (Ex. off coin.)
212	260·6	AR 1·05	ΣΥΡΑΚΟΣΙΩΝ Similar; beneath, ΠΑΡ[ΜΕ]: plain border.	Quadriga l., driven by charioteer, with r. raised, and holding goad and reins in l.; above, Nike flying r., crowning charioteer; horses prancing, the rein of the farthest broken and trailing; in ex., ear of barley l.
				[Head. Pl. V. 1.]
213	264·9	AR 1·	Same; signature ΠΑΡΜΕ. (Same die.)	Same. (Same die.)

Tetradrachms by various engravers.

No.	Wt.	Metal. Size.	Obverse.	Reverse.
214	264·6	AR 1·05	ИΩΙƧΟΚΑꟼΥƧ Female head l., wearing necklace and earring; hair bound with diadem, visible only above forehead; behind, ΙΜ; beneath, three dolphins: plain border.	Quadriga l., driven by charioteer, extending r. and holding reins in l.; horses prancing; the rein of the farthest horse hanging loose; above, Nike flying r., about to crown charioteer; in ex., lion devouring bull l.: border of dots.

No.	Wt.	Metal. Size.	Obverse.	Reverse.
215	268·6	AR 1·	No inscr. Female head r., wearing earring, necklace, and ampyx; hair rolled; around, four dolphins.	Quadriga l., driven by charioteer, holding goad and reins; horses prancing; above, Nike flying r., and crowning the charioteer: border of dots.

No.	Wt.	Metal. Size.	Obverse.	Reverse.
216	263·6	Æ 1·	Same. (Same die.)	Quadriga l., driven by charioteer, holding in r. goad, with which he touches the head of the farthest horse, and in l. reins; horses prancing; above, Nike flying r., and crowning charioteer; in ex., swan flying l.: border of dots.
217	265·3	Æ 1·	ΣΥΡΑΚΟΣΙ Ω Ν Female head l., wearing earring and necklace; hair bound with sphendone, broader than usual in front, and ornamented with stars behind; around, four dolphins.	Quadriga l., driven by bearded male charioteer, holding goad in r. hand, reins in both; horses prancing; above, Nike flying r., crowning charioteer; in ex., ear of barley l.
218	266·3	Æ ·95	Same. (Same die.)	Same. (Same die.)
219	264·7	Æ 1·	ΣΥΡΑΚΟΣΙ ΩΝ Female head l., wearing earring, necklace, and sphendone, tied above and ornamented behind with three stars of eight rays; beneath, head of bearded satyr r.; around, four dolphins: plain border.	Quadriga l., driven by charioteer, holding goad in r. hand, reins in both, the rein of the near horse attached to front of chariot; above, Nike flying r., about to crown charioteer; horses prancing, the rein of the farthest broken and trailing; beneath their hind legs, a broken chariot-wheel; in ex., ear of barley: border of dots.
				[Head. Pl. V. 2.]
220	267·	Æ 1·1	ΣΥΡΑΚΟΣΙΩ Ν Female head l., wearing earring, necklace, and sphendone, tied above; around, four dolphins: plain border.	Same. (Same die.)
221	260·5	Æ 1·1	ΣΥΡ Α ΚΟΣ ΙΩ Female head r., wearing earring, necklace, and sphendone, tied above and ornamented behind with stars: plain border.	Similar; no broken rein or wheel under horses.
222	254·7	Æ 1·05	ΣΥΡΑΚΟΣΙ Similar; behind neck, ꓘ.	Same. (Same die.)

No.	Wt.	Metal. Size.	Obverse.	Reverse.
223	262·3	AR 1·1	ΣΥΡΑ Κ ΟΣ ΙΩΝ Head of Persephone r., wearing earring and necklace; hair falling over neck, and bound with wreath of barley; around, four dolphins: plain border.	Similar; rein of farthest horse broken and trailing.

No.	Wt.	Metal. Size.	Obverse.	Reverse.
224	267·	AR 1·	ΚΟΣΙΩΝ Female head r., wearing earring and necklace; hair in korymbos; around, four dolphins: plain border.	Quadriga l., driven by female charioteer, holding lighted torch and reins; above, Nike flying r., about to crown her; horses prancing; in ex., ear of barley l.: border of dots. (Same die as no. 198.)
			[Head. Pl. V. 5.]	
225	259·3	AR ·95	Α ΚΟΣΙΩ Ν Similar.	Same. (Same die.)
			Drachms and smaller divisions.	
226	63·4	AR ·75	ΣΥ Ρ Α Κ ΟΣΙ Ω Ν Head of Pallas, three-quarter-face l., wearing necklace and Phrygian helmet with three crests, on the front of which honeysuckle ornament; around, four dolphins: plain border. (Work of Eukleides: cf. tetradrachm, no. 198.)	ΣΥΡΑΚΟΣΙ ΩΝ Leukaspis, naked, in attitude of attack, r., wearing crested Athenian helmet, carrying spear in r. and large oval shield on l. arm; at his l. side, a sword, the handle of which only is visible, suspended by strap passing over r. shoulder; behind him, a square altar, garlanded; in front, a sacrificial ram lying on its back l.; in ex., ΛΕVΚΑΣΠ[ΙΣ]: plain border.
			[Head. Pl. V. 6.]	
227	64·6	AR ·65	Same. (Same die.)	Same. (Same die.)

No.	Wt.	Metal. Size.	Obverse.	Reverse.
228	64·8	Æ ·65	Same. (Same die.)	Ι ΩΝ Similar type; fire upon altar; legend in ex. not visible: same border.
229	64·1	Æ ·75	Same. (Same die.)	ΣΥΡΑΚΟΣΙ ΩΝ Same. (Same die.)
230	64·8	Æ ·7	Same. (Same die.)	Same; in ex., [ΛΕV]ΚΑΣ ΠΙΣ. (Same die.)
231	30·	Æ ·55	[Σ] Υ Head of Pallas, three-quarter-face l., wearing necklace and Phrygian helmet with three crests; around, four dolphins: plain border.	Quadriga l., driven by charioteer, holding goad in r. hand, reins in both; horses prancing; above, Nike flying r., crowning charioteer; in ex., two dolphins meeting: plain border. [Head. Pl. V. 7.]
232	31·6	Æ ·55	Σ [Υ] Same. (Same die.)	Same. (Same die.)
233	29·8	Æ ·65	[ΣΥΡΑ]ΚΟΣΙΩΝ Female head r., wearing diadem, earring, and necklace; hair flowing; above, ΙΜ; in front, a dolphin l., upwards: plain border. (Cf. tetradrachm, no 214.)	Quadriga l., driven by charioteer, holding reins in both hands; horses prancing; above, Nike flying r., crowning charioteer; in ex., pilos and ΚΙ Μ: plain border. (By Kimon?) [Head. Pl. V. 8.]
234	12·4	Æ ·45	ΣΥΡΑΚ Female head r., wearing earring, necklace, and sphendone; behind, a dolphin l., downwards: plain border.	Cuttle-fish. [Head. Pl. V. 9.]
235	11·9	Æ ·5	ΣΥΡΑ Female head l., wearing earring, necklace, and sphendone tied above; behind, barleycorn: plain border.	Similar.
236	12·3	Æ ·45	ΣΥΡΑΚΟΣΙΩΝ Female head l., wearing necklace and sphendone; behind, dolphin r., downwards: border of dots.	Similar. [Head. Pl. V. 10.]

No.	Wt.	Metal. Size.	Obverse.	Reverse.
237	5·5	AR ·35	Female head l., wearing ear-ring and sphendone: border of dots.	ΣΥ ΡΑ in the upper quarters of a wheel of four spokes, in the lower quarters of which are two dolphins r. and l.
			[Head. Pl. V. 11.]	
238	4·	AR ·35	Similar.	Similar.
			(This coin is broken, and is consequently under weight.)	
239	4·7	AR ·35	Female head r., wearing ear-ring and necklace: border of dots.	Σ Υ / Ρ Α in the four quarters of a wheel.
			Trias or Quarter-Litra.	
240	2·8	AR ·3	ΣVΡΑ Female head r., wearing necklace and sphendone: border of dots.	Cuttle-fish; around which, ●●●
			[Head. Pl. V. 12.]	
			COPPER.	
			Struck between B.C. 412–345.	
241		Æ ·65	Female head l., wearing ear-ring and sphendone, ornamented behind with star of eight rays, and having in front ΦΡV indistinct: plain border. (By Phrygillos.)	Incuse square of four quarters in different planes, in the centre of which is an incuse circle containing a star of sixteen rays.
242		Æ ·7	ΣΥΡΑ Similar.	Same.
			[Head. Pl. V. 13.]	
243		Æ ·65	Female head l., wearing ear-ring, necklace, and sphendone; behind, dolphin: plain border.	ΣΥ ΡΑ in the upper quarters of a wheel of four spokes, in the lower quarters of which are two dolphins r. and l.
244		Æ ·65	Similar. (Dolphin off coin.)	Similar.
245		Æ ·6	Similar.	Similar.
246		Æ ·6	Similar.	Similar.
			[Head. Pl. V. 14.]	

No.	Wt.	Metal. Size.	Obverse.	Reverse.
247		Æ ·6	Similar type; behind, ear of barley: plain border.	Similar.
248		Æ ·6	Similar; no symbol.	Cuttle-fish: plain border.

[Head. Pl. V. 15.]

No.	Wt.	Metal. Size.	Obverse.	Reverse.
249		Æ ·5	Female head r., laur., wearing necklace.	Cuttle-fish.
250		Æ ·45	Similar.	Similar.
251		Æ ·45	ΣΥΡΑΚΟ ΣΙ Female head l., wearing earring, necklace, and sphendone: plain border.	Trident downwards, on either side of which, Μ Η: border of dots.

[Head. Pl. V. 16.]

Period of Decline; early.

Democracy restored by Timoleon, B.C. 345–317.

ELECTRUM.

No.	Wt.	Metal. Size.	Obverse.	Reverse.
252	106·4	El. ·7	ΣΥΡΑΚΟΣΙΩΝ Head of Apollo l., laur., hair hanging over neck; behind, strung bow: border of dots.	Head of Artemis r., wearing earring and necklace, hair turned up behind over diadem; behind neck, quiver, and in field l., strung bow; in front, ΣΩΤΕΙΡΑ: border of dots.

No.	Wt.	Metal. Size.	Obverse.	Reverse.
253	58·4	El. ·6	No inscr.; same type; behind, horse's head r.: border of dots.	ΣΥΡΑΚ ΟΣΙΩΝ Tripod-lebes with neck and three handles: plain border.

[Head. Pl. VI. 2.]

No.	Wt.	Metal. Size.	Obverse.	Reverse.
254	57·8	El. ·55	Similar; no symbol.	Similar.
255	57·1	El. ·6	Similar; behind, altar?	Similar.

No.	Wt.	Metal. Size.	Obverse.	Reverse.
256	56·4	El. ·55	Similar; behind, cornucopiæ.	Similar.
257	55·6	El. ·6	Similar; behind, lamp.	Similar.
258	55·3	El. ·55	Similar; behind, star of eight rays.	Similar.
259	55·2	El. ·55	Similar; behind, Corinthian helmet without crest l.	Similar.
260	55·1	El. ·55	Similar; behind, lyre.	Similar.
261	54·8	El. ·65	Similar; behind, pilos.	Similar.
262	54·3	El. ·6	Similar; behind, kantharos.	Similar.
263	53·	El. ·55	Similar; behind, amphora.	Similar. [Head. Pl. VI. 3.]
264	54·	El. ·55	Same type and border; behind, wreath.	Similar; between legs of tripod, Π. (Π mark of value = 5 Corinthian staters or 50 litræ Æ ?)
265	32·8	El. ·45	ΣΕΥΣ ΕΛΕΥ ΘΕΡΙΟΣ Head of Zeus Eleutherios l., laur.	ΣΥΡ Α Κ Pegasos flying l.; in front, Æ; beneath, ● ● ● (Mark of value = 3 Corinthian staters or 30 litræ Æ.) [Head. Pl. VI. 4.]
266	28·6	El. ·45	Head of Apollo l., laur.; hair falling over neck.	ΣΥΡΑΚ ΟΣΙΩΝ Lyre of five strings. [Head. Pl. VI. 5.]
267	28·	El. ·4	Similar.	Similar.
268	28·4	El. ·45	Similar.	ΣΥΡΑΚΟ ΣΙΩΝ Similar.
269	27·3	El. ·45	Similar.	ΣΥΡΑΚ ΟΣΙΩΝ Similar.
270	11·	El. ·35	Female head r., wearing ear-ring, necklace, and sphendone.	Cuttle-fish. [Head. Pl. VI. 6.]
271	10·8	El. ·35	Similar.	Similar.

No.	Wt.	Metal. Size.	Obverse.	Reverse.
			SILVER.	
			For the silver staters, 1st Syracusan issue, as described below, see Colonies of Corinth.	
	135 grains, full weight	Æ ·85	ΣΥΡΑΚΟΣΙΩΝ Head of Pallas l., wearing plain Corinthian helmet, with neck-piece and covering to protect the ear, but without crest.	Pegasos flying l.
			[Head. Pl. VI. 7.]	
272	36·3	Æ ·55	Female head l., laur., wearing earring and necklace; around, three dolphins: border of dots.	Pegasos flying l.
			[Head. Pl. VI. 8.]	
273	38·7	Æ ·6	Female head (Kyane ?) l., wearing earring and necklace; hair rolled, and with a bunch over the forehead; behind, a lion's head l.; beneath, ΕΥ.	ΣΥΡΑΚΟΣΙΩΝ Pegasos flying l.
			[Head. Pl. VI. 10.]	
274	19·6	Æ ·5	Similar.	ΣΥΡΑΚ[ΟΣΙ]ΩΝ Half-Pegasos, with curled wing, flying l.
275	19·5	Æ ·5	Similar.	Similar.
			[Head. Pl. VI. 11.]	
276	19·8	Æ ·5	ΣΥΡ ΑΚΟΣΙΩΝ Female head l., wearing earring and necklace; hair rolled; around, three dolphins: border of dots.	Half-Pegasos, with curled wing, flying l.; above, a star of eight rays.
			[Head. Pl. VI. 9.]	
277	17·4	Æ ·5	Σ[ΥΡΑΚΟ]ΣΙΩΝ Similar.	Similar; no symbol.
278	17·2	Æ ·45	ΚΟΣΙΩ Similar.	Similar.

No.	Wt.	Metal. Size.	Obverse.	Reverse.
279	11·4	AR ·45	Female head (Kyane ?) l., wearing earring and necklace hair rolled, and with a bunch over the forehead; behind, ΕΥ and lion's head l.	ΣΥ ΡΑ Κ[Ο]Σ ΙΩΝ Cuttle-fish.
			[Head. Pl. VI. 12.]	
280	31·3	AR ·6	ΣΥ ΡΑΚΟ Ν Head of Pallas, three-quarter-face l., wearing necklace and Phrygian helmet with three crests; around, three dolphins.	Naked horseman r., his hair in krobylos; horse walking; behind, a star of ten rays: plain border.
			[Head. Pl. VI. 14.]	
281	28·9	AR ·6	ΣΥΡΑΚ Ο ΣΙ Similar; in field l., two dolphins: plain border.	Similar; symbol, star of fourteen rays; beneath it, an ear of barley r., and beneath horse, Ν.
			[Head. Pl. VI. 13.]	
282	29·4	AR ·55	Traces of inscr. Similar to no. 280.	Similar; no symbols or letter.
283	23·4	AR ·5	ΣΥΡΑΚΟΣΙ ΩΝ Youthful janiform head, laur.; in field r., two dolphins: plain border.	Free horse prancing r.; above, ear of barley r.; beneath, Ν: plain border.
			[Head. Pl. VI. 15.]	
284	23·5	AR ·5	ΑΚΟΣ ΙΩΝ Similar.	Free horse prancing r.
285	23·5	AR ·55	ΣΥΡΑΚΟΣ ΙΩΝ Similar; in field r., dolphin r., downwards: border of dots.	Free horse prancing l.; above, star of fourteen rays: plain border.
286	16·1	AR ·45	Similar.	Horse prancing r., with loose rein; above, star of eight rays: plain border.
			[Head. Pl. VI. 16.]	

No.	Wt.	Metal. Size.	Obverse.	Reverse.
			COPPER.	
287		Æ 1·25	ΣΥΡΑ Head of Pallas l., wearing Corinthian helmet bound with wreath of olive: plain border.	Two dolphins, between which, star-fish or jelly-fish, with eight rays, the points of which are connected by a web: plain border.

No.	Wt.	Metal. Size.	Obverse.	Reverse.
288		Æ 1·15	Similar.	Similar.
289		Æ ·75	ΣΥΡΑ (inverted.) Similar; in front and behind, a dolphin, downwards: plain border.	Sea-horse l., with curled wing; rein hanging loose: plain border.

No.	Wt.	Metal. Size.	Obverse.	Reverse.
290		Æ ·8	Similar; no dolphins.	Similar.
291		Æ ·85	Similar.	Similar.
292		Æ ·7	Similar: no border visible.	Similar: (no loose rein:) plain border.
293		Æ ·75	Similar: with circular countermark, enclosing a female head l.	Similar.
294		Æ ·75	Similar: with two countermarks, one circular, enclosing female head l., the other square, enclosing lion's head l.	Similar.

No.	Wt.	Metal. Size.	Obverse.	Reverse.
295		Æ ·7	Similar: no countermark.	Similar; with circular countermark; within which, wheel.
296		Æ ·7	Similar; with circular countermark, enclosing head of young river-god l.	Similar.
297		Æ ·7	Similar; with circular countermark, containing fish within a border of dots.	Similar; no countermark.
298		Æ ·7	Similar; with circular countermark, containing star.	Similar.
299		Æ ·65	ΣΥΡΑΚΟΣΙΩΝ Head of Aphrodite? l., wearing earring and necklace; hair bound with crossed cord, and with a loose tress at the back of the head.	Half-Pegasos, with curled wing, flying l.: beneath, Σ.
				[Head. Pl. VII. 3.]
300		Æ ·65	Same.	Same.
301		Æ ·65	Female head l., wearing earring and necklace; hair in sphendone, ending in band, which passes round the top of the head and outside the sphendone; behind neck, a spray of laurel or olive.	ΣΥ ΡΑ. Dolphin r.; beneath which, scallop-shell; between them, ●: plain border.
302		Æ ·6	Similar: plain border.	Similar.
				[Head. Pl. VII. 7.]
303		Æ ·6	Head of youthful river-god (Anapos), three-quarter-face l.: border of dots.	ΣΥ ΡΑΚΟΣΙΩ Ν Half-Pegasos flying r; beneath, stalk of barley r.: plain border.
				[Head. Pl. VII. 6.]
304		Æ ·55	Similar.	ΣΥΡΑ Κ ΟΣ ΙΩΝ Half-Pegasos, with curled wing, flying l.: plain border.
305		Æ ·5	Female head (Kyane?), three-quarter-face l., wearing necklace: plain border.	Cuttle-fish.
306		Æ ·5	Similar.	Similar.

No.	Wt.	Metal. Size.	Obverse.	Reverse.
307		Æ ·25	Pegasos flying r.	Cuttle-fish.
			(It is not certain that this coin is of Syracuse.)	
308		Æ 1·05	ΣΥΡΑΚΟΣ ΙΩΝ Bearded head of hero (Archias?) l., wearing Corinthian helmet: border of dots.	Pegasos flying l.; beneath, dolphin l.; between them, Σ: border of dots.
			[Head. Pl. VII. 4.]	
309		Æ ·85	ΣΥΡΑΚΟ ΣΙΩΝ Head of Persephone l., wearing ear-ring and necklace; hair rolled, and bound with wreath of corn: border of dots.	Pegasos flying l.; beneath, Σ: border of dots.
			[Head. Pl. VII. 5.]	
310		Æ ·75	Similar.	Similar.
311		Æ 1·05	ΖΕΥΣ Ε Λ ΕΥΘΕΡΙΟΣ Head of Zeus Eleutherios l., laur.; hair falling over neck.	ΣΥΡΑ Κ ΟΣΙΩ Ν Free horse prancing l.: plain border.
			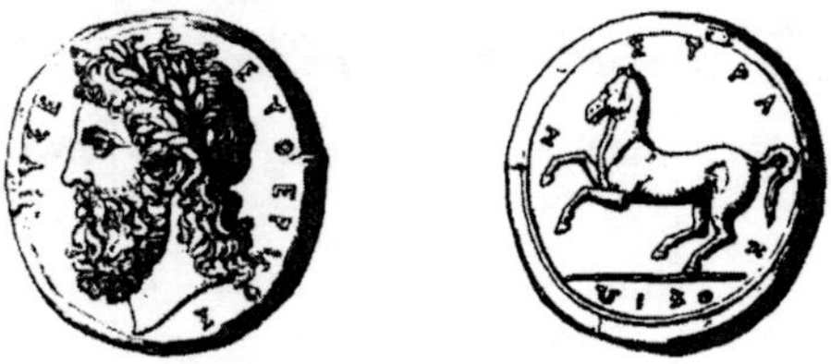	
312		Æ 1·	ΖΕΥΣ ΕΛ ΕΥΘΕΡΙΟΣ Similar.	Similar.
313		Æ ·95	ΖΕΥΣ ΕΛ ΕΥ ΘΕΡΙΟΣ Head of Zeus Eleutherios r., laur.; hair short: plain border.	ΣΥΡΑΚΟ ΣΙΩΝ Thunderbolt upright; in field r., eagle r.: plain border.
			[Head. Pl. VII. 10.]	
			(Cf. AR of Locri Brutt. Cat. Gr. C. Italy, p. 364, no. 1.)	(Cf. AR of Alexander of Epirus, struck in Italy B.C. 332–326.)

No.	Wt.	Metal. Size.	Obverse.	Reverse.
314		Æ ·95	Similar.	ΣΥ ΡΑ ΚΟΣΙΩΝ Similar.
315		Æ 1·	Similar.	ΣΥΡΑΚΟ ΣΙΩΝ Similar; in field r., barleycorn.
316		Æ 1·	ΖΕΥΣ ΕΛΕ ΥΘ ΕΡΙΟΣ Similar.	ΣΥΡΑΚ ΟΣΙΩΝ Similar.
317		Æ ·95	ΖΕΥΣ ΕΥ ΘΕΡΙΟΣ Similar.	ΣΥΡΑΚΟ ΣΙΩΝ Similar; in field l., barleycorn.
318		Æ 1·05	ΖΕΥΣ ΕΛ ΕΥ ΘΕΡΙΟΣ Similar.	Similar; no symbol.
319		Æ ·65	Ε ΛΕΥΘΕΡΙΟΣ Similar type l.: plain border.	ΣΥΡΑ Σ Similar.
			[Head. Pl. VII. 11.]	
320		Æ ·65	ΖΕΥΣ ΕΛ Similar.	ΣΙΩ Ν Cuttle-fish.
321		Æ ·7	ΣΥΡΑΚΟΣΙΩΝ Head of Apollo l., laur.; hair falling over neck; behind, pilos: border of dots.	Pegasos flying l.; beneath, Α: plain border.
			[Head. Pl. VII. 12.]	
322		Æ ·75	Similar; behind, pentagram.	Similar; beneath, ΑΓ.
323		Æ ·7	Similar; behind, club downwards.	Similar.
324		Æ ·7	Similar; behind, bunch of grapes.	Similar; beneath, ⊢Ρ.
325		Æ ·7	Similar; behind, strung bow in case.	Similar.
326		Æ ·75	Similar; behind, amphora.	Similar.
327		Æ ·8	Similar; behind, wreath.	Similar; beneath, monogram.
328		Æ ·7	Similar; behind, lion's head l.	Similar; above, monogram.
329		Æ ·7	Similar; behind, pine-torch flaming.	Same type; beneath, ΝΙ: plain border.

No.	Wt.	Metal. Size.	Obverse.	Reverse.
330		Æ ·75	Similar.	Similar.
331		Æ ·7	Similar; behind, cornucopiæ.	Similar.
332		Æ ·8	Similar; behind, club downwards.	Similar type; above, ΣΩ: plain border.
333		Æ ·7	Similar; no symbol.	Similar; beneath, Δ.
334		Æ ·7	Similar.	Pegasos flying r.; beneath, Δ: plain border.
335		Æ ·7	Similar type: border of dots.	ΣΥΡΑΚΟΣΙΩ Ν Pegasos flying l.; above, Ƒ? plain border.

Agathokles B.C. 317–289.

1st coinage, B.C. 317 to B.C. circ. 310.

(Without name or title.)

GOLD.

No.	Wt.	Metal. Size.	Obverse.	Reverse.
336	66·2	AV ·6	Young male head (Apollo?) l., laur.	ΣΥΡ Α ΚΟΣΙΩΝ Biga r., driven by charioteer, holding goad and reins; horses galloping; beneath, triquetra of legs.

No.	Wt.	Metal. Size.	Obverse.	Reverse.
337	66·2	AV ·65	Similar; beneath, Σ.	ΣΥΡ Α ΚΟ ΣΙΩΝ Similar.
338	66·4	AV ·65	Similar type; behind, ear of barley: border of dots.	Similar.
339	66·2	AV ·55	Similar type; behind, kantharos.	ΣΥΡ ΑΚ Ο ΣΙ Similar.
340	65·	AV ·65	Similar; no symbol.	ΣΥΡ Α ΝΩΙΣΟΚ Similar.

(Semi-barbarous.)

No.	Wt.	Metal. Size.	Obverse.	Reverse.
341	65·9	AV ·6	Similar.	ΣΥΡ Α Κ ΟΣΙΩ Ν Similar.
			(Semi-barbarous.)	
342	44·	AV ·5	Young male head (Apollo ?) l., laur. : plain border.	Biga r., driven by charioteer, holding goad and reins; horses galloping; beneath, triquetra of legs; in ex., —
			[Head. Pl. VIII. 2.]	
343	44·	AV ·5	Similar type.	Similar; in ex., Σ ?
344	21·2	AV ·4	Head of Persephone l., wearing wreath of barley, earring, and necklace.	ΣΥΡΑΚΟ ΣΙΩΝ Bull (Anapos ?) walking l., head lowered.
			[Head. Pl. VIII. 3.]	
345	21·8	AV ·4	Similar.	Similar.
			SILVER	
346	264·9	AR 1·	Head of Persephone l., wearing wreath of corn, earring, and necklace; around, three dolphins; beneath, NK : border of dots.	ΣΥΡΑΚΟΣΙΩΝ (in ex.) Quadriga l., driven by charioteer, holding goad and reins; horses in high action; above, triquetra of legs; beneath the inscr., in ex., ΑΙ : border of dots.

347	261·	AR 1·	Similar; beneath, NK.	Similar.
348	263·9	AR 1·05	Similar; beneath, NI.	Similar: plain border.
349	261·	AR 1·05	Similar; letters not visible.	Similar.
350	263·5	AR ·95	Similar; beneath, NI.	Similar: border of dots.
351	266·1	AR ·95	Similar. (Border not visible.)	Similar.
352	263·8	AR 1·	Similar type; around, three dolphins; beneath, ΦΙ : border of dots.	Similar.

No.	Wt.	Metal. Size.	Obverse.	Reverse.
			For the silver staters of the 2nd Syracusan issue as described below, see Colonies of Corinth.	
	135 full wt.	Ʀ ·85	Head of Pallas l., wearing Corinthian helmet, ornamented with griffin, and having neckpiece, covering to protect the ear, and crest; behind, sometimes, trophy.	ΣΥΡΑΚΟΣΙΩΝ Pegasos r. or l.; in field, triquetra, and sometimes also ear of barley.
			[Head. Pl. VIII. 5, 6.]	
353	59·4	Ʀ ·65	Σ[ΥΡ]ΑΚΟΣΙΩΝ Young male head (Apollo or Herakles?) l., laur.; behind, trophy? border of dots.	Triquetra of legs; in the centre, a circle, containing a gorgon-head; on the feet are winged talaria: plain border.
			[Head. Pl. VIII. 7.]	
			COPPER.	
354		Æ ·75	ΣΥΡΑΚΟΣΙΩΝ Young male head (Apollo or Herakles?) l., laur.; behind, trophy? beneath, ΑΙ? border of dots.	Similar.
			[Head. Pl. VIII. 8.]	
355		Æ ·75	Similar; behind, trophy.	Similar.
356		Æ ·85	ΣΥΡΑΚΟΣΙΩΝ Head of Persephone l., wearing wreath of barley and necklace; behind, star of eight rays: border of dots.	Bull butting l.; above, ΑΙ and dolphin l.; beneath, another dolphin l.: plain border.
			[Head. Pl. VIII. 9.]	
357		Æ ·9	Similar; behind, barleycorn.	Similar; but above bull, ΝΙ.

No.	Wt.	Metal. Size.	Obverse.	Reverse.
358		Æ ·85	Similar.	Similar; but NK.
359		Æ ·95	Similar; behind, scallop.	Similar.
360		Æ ·85	Traces of inscr. Similar head; behind, traces of symbol: border of dots.	Similar; above upper dolphin, ΑΓ.
361		Æ ·9	ϹΥΡΑΚΟϹΙΩΝ Similar head varied; behind, long flaming torch: border of dots.	Similar; ΑΙ: (ΑΙ or ΑΓ) plain border.
362		Æ ·9	Similar; behind, scallop.	Similar; beneath upper dolphin, ϡΝ.
363		Æ ·8	ΑΚΟϹΙΩΝ Head of Persephone l., wearing earring and necklace; hair bound with wreath of barley; behind, cornucopiæ: border of dots.	Bull butting l.; above, dolphin l., beneath which, Φ; in ex., another dolphin l.: plain border.
364		Æ ·75	Similar.	Similar; no letter.
365		Æ ·8	ΟϹΙΩΝ Similar, varied: border of dots.	Similar; ex. plain.
366		Æ ·65	ϹΥΡΑΚΟϹΙΩΝ Female head l., wearing earring and necklace; hair rolled; behind, cornucopiæ: border of dots.	Bull butting l.; above, ΝΙ: plain border.
367		Æ ·7	Similar.	Similar; above, dolphin, beneath which, Ο; in ex., ΝΙ.
			[Head. Pl. VIII. 11.]	
368		Æ ·6	Similar; behind, bucranium.	Bull butting l.: plain border.
369		Æ ·6	No inscr. Similar type; behind, scallop.	[Ϲ]ΥΡΑΚΟϹΙΩΝ (in ex.) Similar type; above, Ε: plain border.

No.	Wt.	Metal. Size.	Obverse.	Reverse.
370		Æ ·65	ΣΥΡΑΚΟΣ[Ι]ΩΝ Similar type; no symbol: border of dots.	Similar; above, dolphin l.; in ex., wreath?
371		Æ 6	No inscr. Similar type; behind, ear of barley?	Traces of inscr. Bull butting l.; above, trident r.; in ex., Π? plain border.
372		Æ ·7	Similar; in front, dolphin l., downwards; behind, ear of barley.	ΣΥΡΑΚΟΣ Ι ΝΩ Similar; above, Ѧ; in ex., Γ.
373		Æ ·6	Similar.	Similar. [Head. Pl. VIII. 12.]
374		Æ ·65	Similar.	Similar.
375		Æ ·65	Similar.	No inscr. Similar; above, dolphin l.; in ex., ΣΑ.
376		Æ ·65	Similar; behind neck, scallop?	Similar; above, axe; in ex., ΣΩ.
377		Æ ·5	ΣΥΡΑΚΟΣΙΩΝ Head of Apollo l., laur.: border of dots.	Dog lying l. and looking back; in field l., X: plain border.

2nd coinage B.C. circ. 310–306.

SILVER.

Tetradrachms with ΑΓΑΘΟΚΛΕΙΟΣ; and later ΑΓΑΘΟΚΛΕΟΣ.

(A) Fine work; struck at Syracuse.

No.	Wt.	Metal. Size.	Obverse.	Reverse.
378	260·1	AR ·9	ΣΥΡΑΚΟ Head of Persephone r., wearing earring and necklace (effaced); hair long and bound with wreath of barley; behind, ΚΟΡΑΣ (obscure): border of dots.	ΚΛΕΙΟΣ Nike, half-draped, standing r., holding in r. a hammer and in l. a nail, with which she is about to fix the helmet to a trophy; in field r., triquetra of legs: plain border.

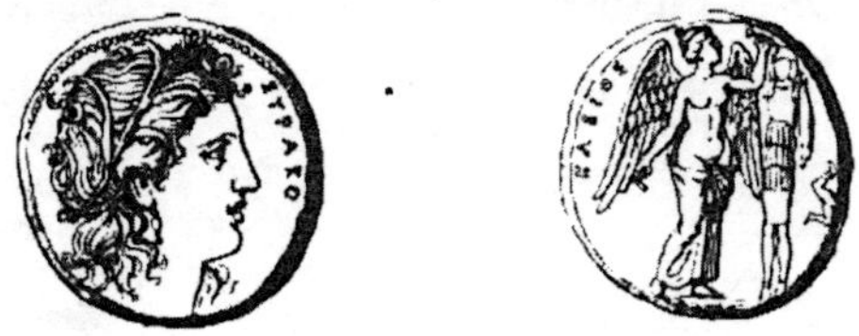

No.	Wt.	Metal. Size.	Obverse.	Reverse.
379	247·5	AR 1·1 plated.	No inscr. Similar; behind, ΚΟΡΑΣ upwards.	ΑΓΑΘΟΚΛΕΙΟΣ Similar.
			[Head. Pl. IX. 2.]	
380	259·6	AR 1·	Similar.	Inscr. off coin. Similar.
			(B) Barbarous work; struck in Africa?	
381	266·5	AR 1·	Similar; behind, ΚΟΡΑΣ downwards.	ΑΓΑΘΟΚΛΕΙΟΣ Similar; triquetra in field l.: border of dots.
382	265 2	AR 1·05	Similar.	Similar.
383	262·7	AR 1·	Similar.	Similar.
384	260 5	AR 1·1	Similar.	Similar.
385	228·8	AR 1·05	Similar.	Similar.
			(Probably plated.)	
386	257·4	AR 1·05	Similar type l.; behind, ΚΟΡΑΣ upwards.	Inscr. off coin. Similar.
387	259·2	AR 1·	Similar type r.; behind, ΚΟΡΑΣ downwards: border of dots.	ΑΓΑΘΟΚΛΕΟΣ (in ex.) Similar.
			(C) Fine work; struck at Syracuse.	
388	265·5	AR 1·	Similar; behind, ΚΟΡΑΣ upwards.	ΑΓΑΘΟΚΛΕΟΣ (in ex.) Similar type; in field r., triquetra; in field l., ΑΙ.
			COPPER.	
389		Æ ·85	ΣΥΡΑΚΟΣΙΩΝ Young male head r., (Herakles?) wearing tainia: border of dots.	Lion advancing r.; above, club r.: border of dots.
390		Æ ·9	Similar; behind, strung bow.	Similar.
391		Æ ·9	Similar.	Similar; in ex., arrow r.
392		Æ ·9	Similar.	Similar.
393		AR ·75	Similar.	Similar; in e[illegible] [illegible]b, flami[illegible]
394		Æ ·85	Similar.	Simil[illegible]

No.	Wt.	Metal. Size.	Obverse.	Reverse.
395		Æ ·85	Similar; behind, cornucopiæ.	Similar.
396		Æ ·85	Similar.	Similar; in ex., ΤΣ and pine-torch flaming.
397		Æ ·85	Similar.	Similar; ex. plain.
398		Æ ·8	Similar; behind, tripod.	Similar; in ex., pine-torch flaming: border of dots.
399		Æ ·95	[ΣΥΡΑ]Κ[ΟΣΙΩΝ] Similar type l.	Similar; in ex., arrow r.
400		Æ ·8	ΣΥΡΑΚΟΣΙΩΝ Similar: border of dots.	Similar; in ex., pine-torch flaming.
401		Æ ·85	Similar.	Similar; in ex., ΣΤΡ.
402		Æ ·85	Similar; behind, star of eight rays.	Similar; in ex., pine-torch flaming: border of dots.
			[Head. Pl. IX. 3.]	
403		Æ ·9	Similar; behind, star of six rays.	Similar; ex. plain.
404		Æ ·85	Similar; behind, tripod.	Similar; in ex., pine-torch flaming: plain border.
405		Æ ·85	Bust of Artemis r., wearing earring and necklace; hair in knot behind; quiver over shoulder; in front, ΣΩΤΕΙΡΑ: border of dots.	ΣΥΡΑΚ ΟΣΙΩΝ Winged thunderbolt: plain border.
			[Head. Pl. IX. 4.]	
406		Æ ·8	Similar.	Similar.
407		Æ ·85	Similar.	Similar.
408		Æ ·6	Same type l. and legend.	Similar.
			[Head. Pl. IX. 5.]	
409		Æ 8	ΣΥΡΑΚΟΣΙ Head of Pallas r., wearing earring, necklace, and crested Corinthian helmet without neck-piece or covering for the ear.	Horseman r., wearing Phrygian helmet, cuirass, and chlamys; holding spear couched in r.; horse prancing.
			[Head. Pl. IX. 6.]	

No.	Wt.	Metal. Size.	Obverse.	Reverse.
410		Æ ·35	[ΣΥΡΑΚΟΣΙ]ΩΝ Similar; helmet adorned with running griffin.	Similar.
411		Æ ·65	Similar; behind, owl r.: border of dots.	Similar; beneath, Φ.
			[Head. Pl. IX. 8.]	
412		Æ ·85	ΣΥΡΑΚΟΣΙΩΝ Head of Pallas r., wearing earring, necklace, and crested Corinthian helmet without neck-piece or covering for the ear, adorned with running griffin; behind, trophy.	Pegasos flying l., both wings visible; beneath, trident l.: plain border.
			[Head. Pl. IX. 7.]	
413		Æ ·55	Head of Pallas r., wearing ear-ring, necklace, and crested Corinthian helmet.	[ΣΥΡΑΚ] ΟΣΙΩΝ Winged thunder-bolt.
			[Head. Pl. IX. 9.]	
414		Æ ·55	Same type l.: border of dots.	[ΣΥ]ΡΑΚ ΟΣΙΩΝ Winged thunderbolt: plain border.
415		Æ ·5	Similar.	Similar.

3rd coinage B.C. circ. 306–289.

With title ΒΑΣΙΛΕΥΣ.

GOLD.

No.	Wt.	Metal. Size.	Obverse.	Reverse.
416	87·8	AV ·65	Head of Pallas r., wearing ear-ring, necklace, and crested Corinthian helmet without neckpiece or covering for the ear, adorned with running griffin.	ΑΓΑΘΟΚΛΕΟΣ ΒΑΣΙΛΕΟΣ Winged thunderbolt; beneath, Ρ.

No.	Wt.	Metal. Size.	Obverse.	Reverse.
417	87·5	AV ·65	Similar: border of dots.	Similar; beneath, Φ.
418	88·1	AV ·6	Similar: no border.	Similar.
419	88·1	AV ·65	Similar.	Similar; beneath, .
420	88·3	AV ·65	Similar.	Same. (Same die.)
421	87·2	AV ·65	Similar.	Similar; no mon. beneath; above, .

SILVER.

For the silver staters of the third Syracusan issue, as described below, reduced to the weight of 8 litræ, see Colonies of Corinth.

No.	Wt.	Metal. Size.	Obverse.	Reverse.
	108· full wt.	AR ·8	No inscr. Head of Pallas, r. or l., wearing earring, necklace, and Corinthian helmet having neckpiece, but without crest or covering for the ear.	Pegasos flying l.; beneath, triquetra.

[Head. Pl. IX. 11.]

No.	Wt.	Metal. Size.	Obverse.	Reverse.
	108· full wt.	AR ·8	No inscr. Similar type r.; helmet without neckpiece; behind, owl r.	Similar; no triquetra; above, star of eight rays.

[Head. Pl. IX. 12.]

COPPER.

No.	Wt.	Metal. Size.	Obverse.	Reverse.
422		Æ ·85	Bust of Artemis r., wearing earring and necklace; hair in knot behind; quiver over shoulder; in front, ΣΩΤΕΙΡΑ: border of dots.	[Α]ΓΑΘοΚΛΕοΣ ΒΑΣΙΛΕοΣ Winged thunderbolt: plain border.

[Head. Pl. IX. 13.]

No.	Wt.	Metal. Size.	Obverse.	Reverse.
423		Æ ·9	Similar.	Similar.
424		Æ ·85	Similar.	Similar.
425		Æ ·8	Similar.	Similar.

No.	Wt.	Metal. Size.	Obverse.	Reverse.
			Democracy, B.C. 289–287.	
			COPPER.	
426		Æ ·85	Bust of Artemis l., wearing earring and necklace; hair in knot behind; quiver over shoulder; in front, ΣΩΤΕΙΡΑ: border of dots.	ΔΙΟΣ ΕΛΕΥ ΘΕΡΙΟΥ Winged t derbolt: plain border.
			[Head. Pl. IX. 14.]	
427		Æ ·8	Similar.	Similar.
428		Æ ·85	[ΔΙΟΣ ΕΛΕΥ]ΘΕ·Ρ·Ι·Ο·Υ Head of Zeus Eleutherios l., laur.; hair in three curls behind.	ΣΥΡΑΚ ΟΣΙΩΝ Winged thun bolt: plain border.
429		Æ ·8	Similar.	Similar.
			Hiketas, B.C. 287–278.	
			GOLD.	
430	65·7	AV ·65	ΣΥΡΑΚΟΣΙΩΝ Head of Persephone l., wearing earring and necklace; hair rolled and bound with wreath of barley behind, bee; beneath, traces of letter: border of dots.	ΕΠΙ ΙΚΕΤΑ (in ex.) l r., driven by Nike, l draped, holding goad reins; horses pranci above, Ϭ; beneath ho Θ.

No.	Wt.	Metal. Size.	Obverse.	Reverse.
431	65·4	AV ·65	Similar; behind, poppy-head; beneath, ΘΕ.	Similar.
			[Head. Pl. X. 2.]	
432	65·9	AV ·6	Same inscr., type, and border; behind, long torch flaming.	Similar.
433	66·3	AV 6	Similar; behind, cornucopiæ.	Similar.
434	65·5	AV ·6	Same. (Same die.)	Same inscr. and type; above, star of eight rays; beneath horses, ear of barley l.
435	66·5	AV ·65	Same. (Same die.)	Similar; above, thunderbolt; beneath horses, Σ.
			SILVER.	
436	201·1	AR 1·	Head of Persephone l., wearing earring and necklace; hair long and bound with wreath of barley; behind, bee: border of dots.	ΣΥΡΑΚΟΣΙΩΝ (in ex.) Quadriga l., driven by Nike, wearing long chiton, and holding goad and reins; horses in high action; above, star of eight rays.
			[Head. Pl. X. 3.]	
437	197·4	AR 1·	Same. (Same die.)	Similar.
438	195·5	AR ·95	Similar; behind, amphora.	Similar.
439	191·1	AR 1·	Similar; behind, bucranium.	Similar.
440	190·4	AR ·95	Similar; behind, X.	Similar. (Same die as no. 438.)
			[Head. Pl. X. 4.]	
			COPPER.	
			B.C. 287–282.	
441		Æ ·9	ΣΥΡΑΚΟΣΙΩΝ Head of Persephone l., wearing earring and necklace; hair long and bound with wreath of barley: border of dots.	Biga r., driven by charioteer, wearing long chiton, and holding goad and reins; horses cantering; above, star of eight rays.
			[Head. Pl. X. 5.]	
442		Æ ·9	Similar; behind, stalk of barley.	Similar.
443		Æ ·9	Similar.	Similar: plain border.

No.	Wt.	Metal. Size.	Obverse.	Reverse.
444		Æ ·85	Similar.	Similar.
445		Æ ·85	Similar.	Similar.
446		Æ ·9	Similar.	Similar; in ex., Ā.
447		Æ ·95	Similar.	Similar; beneath horses, N; in ex., ΨΕ.
448		Æ ·85	Similar.	Similar; in ex., Π.
449		Æ ·95	Similar.	Similar; beneath horses, N; in ex., Π.
450		Æ ·9	Similar. (Same die as no. 442.)	Similar; in ex., ξ.
451		Æ ·9	Similar.	Similar; in ex., ΣΩ: plain border.
452		Æ ·9	Same. (Same die.)	Similar; beneath horses, N; in ex., ΣΩ.
453		Æ ·95	Similar.	Similar; above horses, T; in ex., ΣΩ.
454		Æ 1·	ΣΥΡΑΚΟΣΙΩΝ Similar type r., without necklace; behind head, flaming torch: border of dots.	Similar; no letters.
455		Æ ·95	Similar; without earring.	Similar; in ex., ΨΕ Χ: plain border.
456		Æ ·9	Similar; with earring.	Similar; above, thunderbolt; beneath horses, Ā; in ex., K.
457		Æ ·95	Similar.	Similar; above, star of eight rays; in ex., ΨΙ Χ.

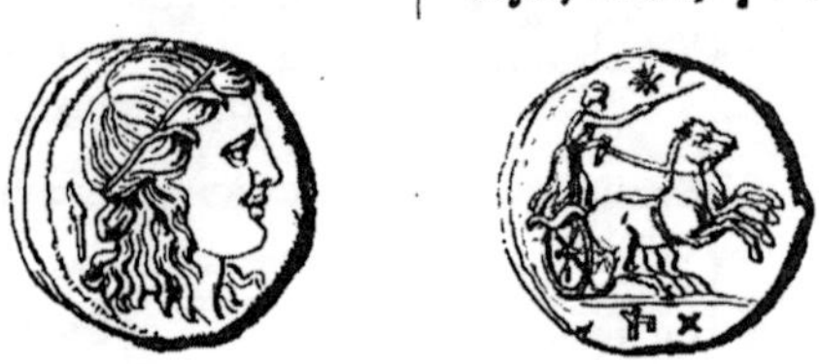

No.	Wt.	Metal. Size.	Obverse.	Reverse.
458		Æ ·95	Similar.	Similar; in ex., Ψι? X.
459		Æ ·9	Σ[ΥΡΑΚ] ИΩΙƐΟ Similar.	Similar; in ex., ΨΕ X.
460		Æ ·95	ΣΥΡΑΚ ИΩΙƐΟ Similar; without symbol.	Similar; in ex., ΠΟ Υ.
461		Æ ·85	ΣΥΡΑΚΟΣΙΩΝ Similar type l., with earring and necklace; behind, poppy-head and A: border of dots.	Similar type; above, thunderbolt: plain border.
462		Æ ·85	Similar.	Similar; above horses, T.
463		Æ ·9	Similar; no letter behind.	Similar; no letter above horses; beneath them, A̅.
464		Æ ·75	Similar.	Similar; horses galloping; no symbol; beneath horses, Φ: plain border.

No.	Wt.	Metal. Size.	Obverse.	Reverse.
465		Æ ·8	Similar; no symbol.	Similar; horses cantering; no letter.
466		Æ ·8	Similar.	Similar; in ex., A.
467		Æ ·8	Similar.	Similar; ex. plain.

(A restruck coin?)

COPPER.

B.C. 282–278.

(Cf. Copper of the Mamertini.)

No.	Wt.	Metal. Size.	Obverse.	Reverse.
468		Æ ·95	ΔΙΟΣ ΕΛΛΑΝΙΟΥ Head of Zeus Hellenios l., beardless and laur.; behind, thunderbolt: border of dots.	ΣΥΡΑΚ Ο ΣΙΩΝ Eagle l., on thunderbolt, wings open: plain border.
			[Head. Pl. X. 7.]	
469		Æ ·95	Similar.	Similar.
470		Æ ·9	Similar.	ΣΥΡΑΚΟΣΙΩΝ Similar.
471		Æ ·9	Similar; behind, bucranium.	ΣΥΡΑΚ ΟΣΙΩΝ Similar.
472		Æ ·9	Similar.	Similar; in field l., Α over star of eight rays.
473		Æ ·9	Similar; behind, trophy.	ΣΥΡΑΚ ΟΣΙΩΝ Similar; in field l., star of eight rays.
474		Æ ·9	Similar.	ΣΥΡΑΚ [ΟΣ]ΙΩΝ Similar; in field l., Α.
475		Æ ·9	Similar.	ΣΥΡΑΚΟΣΙΩΝ Similar.
476		Æ ·95	Similar; no symbol.	ΣΥΡΑΚ ΟΣΙΩΝ Similar.
			[Struck over previous type. Obv., Head of Persephone l. ℞, Biga r.]	
477		Æ ·85	Similar.	Similar; in field l., Α.
478		Æ ·95	Similar.	Similar; in field l., ΦΣ.
479		Æ ·75	Similar.	ΣΥΡΑΚ [ΟΣΙΩΝ] Similar type.
480		Æ ·9	ΑΛΛΛƎ ƸΟΙΔ Similar.	ΣΥΡΑΚΟΣΙΩΝ Similar type; in field l., uncertain object: plain border.

No.	Wt.	Metal. Size.	Obverse.	Reverse.
481		Æ ·9	ΔΙΟΣ ΕΛΛΑΝΙΟΥ Similar type r.; behind, trophy: border of dots.	ΣΥΡΑ ΚΟΣΙΩΝ Similar; in field l., star of eight rays: plain border.
482		Æ ·9	Similar.	ΣΥΡΑΚ ΟΣΙΩΝ Similar.
			[Head. Pl. X. 8.]	
483		Æ 1·	Similar; behind, club upwards.	ΣΥΡΑΚ ΟΣΙΩΝ Similar; in field l., Α over star of eight rays.
484		Æ ·95	Similar; behind, bucranium?	ΣΥΡΑΚΟΣΙΩΝ Similar.
485		Æ ·85	Similar; no symbol.	ΣΥΡΑΚ ΟΣΙΩΝ Similar.
			[These three coins are restruck upon Æ of Agathokles. Obv., Head of Artemis r.; ℞, ΑΓΑΘΟΚΛΕΟΣ ΒΑΣΙΛΕΟΣ Thunderbolt. On the first two are vestiges of both sides; on the third, of the reverse only.]	
486		Æ ·9	Similar.	ΣΥΡΑΚΟΣΙΩΝ Similar.
487		Æ ·9	Similar.	Similar; in field l., Α.
488		Æ ·85	Similar.	[ΣΥΡΑΚ] ΟΣΙΩΝ Similar; in field l., star of eight rays.
			[Restruck upon Æ of Agathokles, as before. Vestiges of both Obv. and ℞. types visible.]	
489		Æ 1·	Similar.	ΣΥ[ΡΑΚ] ΟΣΙΩΝ Similar; no symbol.
			[Restruck upon Æ of previous type. Obv. Head of Persephone. ℞, Biga r. The wheels of the biga and legs of the horses visible on the reverse.]	
490		Æ ·85	Similar.	Similar.

No.	Wt.	Metal. Size.	Obverse.	Reverse.
			Rule of Pyrrhos, B.C. 278–276.	
			Note.—The coins of Pyrrhos with ΒΑΣΙΛΕΩΣ ΠΥΡΡΟΥ, though mostly struck in Sicily, will be described under Epirus.	
			GOLD.	
491	66·4	AV ·65	Head of Persephone l., wearing earring and necklace; hair long and bound with wreath of barley; behind, pine-torch flaming: border of dots.	ΣΥΡΑΚΟΣΙΩΝ (in ex.) Biga r., driven by Nike, holding goad and reins; horses prancing: border of dots.
			[Head. Pl. X. 9.]	
			COPPER.	
492		Æ 1·	ΣΥΡΑΚΟΣΙΩΝ Head of Persephone l., wearing earring and necklace; hair long and bound with wreath of barley; behind, stalk of barley: border of dots.	Within oak-wreath, long torch flaming.
			[Head. Pl. X. 10.]	
493		Æ ·9	ΣΥΡΑΚΟΣΙΩΝ Head of young Herakles l., wearing lion's skin: border of dots.	Pallas Promachos r., wearing long chiton with diploïdion, and chlamys over shoulders; she holds spear in raised r., and shield on outstretched l. arm; in field l., wreath: plain border.
			[Head. Pl. X. 11.]	
494		Æ ·95	Similar.	Similar.
			[Restruck: outside border on rev. traces of previous inscr.]	
495		Æ ·85	Similar.	Similar; in field l., thunderbolt.
496		Æ ·85	Similar.	Similar; Pallas holds a thunderbolt in r.
497		Æ ·9	Similar.	Similar type; in field l., head of trident r.

No.	Wt.	Metal. Size.	Obverse.	Reverse.
498		Æ ·95	Similar.	Similar; in field r., owl r.
499		Æ ·9	Similar.	Similar.
500		Æ ·95	Similar.	Similar.
			[Restruck upon Æ of Agathokles. Obv., Head of Artemis r. ℞, ΑΓΑΘΟΚΛΕΟΣ ΒΑΣΙΛΕΟΣ Thunderbolt. Vestiges of both types visible.]	
501		Æ 1·	Similar.	Similar; in field l., trident upwards.
502		Æ ·95	Similar.	Similar.
503		Æ ·9	No inscr. Similar.	ΣΥΡΑ ΚΟΣΙΩΝ Similar type.

504		Æ ·85	Similar.	Similar.
505		Æ ·85	Similar.	Similar; in field r., owl r.
			Note.—The object wielded by Pallas on this and the preceding coin is doubtful, and may be either a thunderbolt or a spear.	
506		Æ ·8	Similar type r.: same border.	ΣΥΡΑΚΟΣΙ ΩΝ Similar type; no symbol.

Period of Decline; late.

Hieron II. B.C. 275–216.

GOLD.

No.	Wt	Metal. Size.		Obverse.	Reverse.
507	65·5	AV	·6	Head of Persephone l., wearing earring and necklace; hair long and bound with wreath of barley; behind, stalk of barley: border of dots.	ΙΕΡΩΝΟΣ Biga r., driven by female charioteer, wearing long chiton, and holding goad and reins; horses prancing; in front, ΚΙ: plain border.
508	68·6	AV	·6	Similar; behind, cornucopiæ.	Similar; no letters in front.
509	65·5	AV	·65	Similar; behind, palm bound with fillet.	Similar.
510	65·9	AV	·6	Similar; behind, poppy-head.	Similar.
				[Head. Pl. XI. 1.]	
511	65·7	AV	·6	Similar.	ΙΕΡΩΝΟΣ Similar type l.; above, ΑΡ : plain border.
512	65·8	AV	·65	Similar; behind, wing.	Similar; no letters above; beneath, Α.
513	65·8	AV	·6	Similar; behind, long torch flaming.	Similar.
514	65·8	AV	·65	Similar; behind, sea-horse upwards r.	Similar; beneath, Α or Α ?
515	65·8	AV	·65	Similar; behind, crescent, horns r.	Similar; beneath, Α: border of dots.
516	61·1	AV	·6	Similar; behind, wreath.	Similar; beneath, Α.
517	65·8	AV	·65	Similar; behind, cornucopiæ.	Similar.
518	65·8	AV	·65	Similar; behind, bucranium.	Similar.
519	64·8	AV	·6	Similar; behind, star of sixteen rays.	Similar; beneath, Ε.

No.	Wt.	Metal. Size.	Obverse.	Reverse.
520	65·	AV ·6	Similar; behind, earring?	Similar: plain border.
521	65·8	AV ·6	Similar; behind, poppy-head.	Similar; Nike winged, as charioteer.

SILVER.

Class A, with ΙΕΡΩΝΟΣ.

No.	Wt.	Metal. Size.	Obverse.	Reverse.
522	86·3	AR ·75	Head of Pallas l., wearing earring, necklace, and crested Corinthian helmet without neck-piece or ear-covering, adorned with serpent; behind, wing: border of dots.	ΙΕΡΩΝΟΣ Pegasos flying r.; beneath, Π: plain border.

[Head. Pl. XI. 2.]

No.	Wt.	Metal. Size.	Obverse.	Reverse.
523	85·5	AR ·85	Similar.	Same inscr. Similar type l.

Class B, with ΒΑΣΙΛΕΟΣ ΙΕΡΩΝΟΣ and portrait.

No.	Wt.	Metal. Size.	Obverse.	Reverse.
524	432·2	AR 1·4	Beardless male head l. (Hieron?) wearing diadem; behind, stalk of barley: border of dots.	ΒΑΣΙΛΕΟΣ ΙΕΡΩΝΟΣ Quadriga r., driven by winged Nike, half-draped, holding goad and reins; horses prancing; beneath, Ε: plain border.

No.	Wt.	Metal. Size.	Obverse.	Reverse.
525	428·4	Æ 1·35	Similar; behind, star of eight rays; beneath, Φ: border of dots.	Same inscr. Quadriga r., driven by Nike, half-draped, holding reins in both hands, no goad; horses in high action; above, star of twelve rays; beneath horses, K.

Class C, with name of Gelon and portrait.

No.	Wt.	Metal. Size.	Obverse.	Reverse.
526	106·	Æ ·85	Beardless male head l. (Gelon ?) wearing diadem: border of dots.	ΣΥΡΑΚΟΣΙΟΙ ΓΕΛΩΝΟΣ Biga r., driven by winged Nike, wearing long chiton and holding reins in both hands; horses trotting; beneath fore-leg of farther horse, A: plain border.
527	103·1	Æ ·75	Similar.	ΣΥΡΑΚΟΣΙΟΙ ΓΕΛΩΝΟΣ Biga r., driven by winged Nike, half-draped, holding reins in both hands; horses prancing; in front, BA and K: plain border.

No.	Wt.	Metal. Size.	Obverse.	Reverse.
528	103·7	Æ ·8	Similar; behind, strung bow.	Similar; Nike holds goad as well as reins; beneath hors[illegible] and Γ

No.	Wt.	Metal. Size.	Obverse.	Reverse.
529	98·3	AR ·8	Same. (Same die.)	Similar; no goad. [Inscr., letters, &c. obscure.]
530	105·7	AR ·85	Similar type r.; behind, stalk of barley; beneath, Φ.	Similar inscr. and type: plain border.
531	107·2	AR ·8	Similar; no symbol.	Similar; beneath horses' fore-legs, Σ.
532	103·	AR ·8	Similar type l.: border of dots.	Same inscr. Biga r., driven by winged Nike, wearing long chiton and holding reins in both hands; horses walking; above, ΑΦ; in front, ΒΑ: plain border.
533	105·	AR ·8	Similar.	Similar; above, ΒΑ; in front, ΜΙ.
534	52·	AR ·65	Similar type: border of dots.	ΣΥΡΑΚΟΣΙΟΙ ΓΕΛΩΝΟΣ Eagle, with closed wings, standing r. on thunderbolt; behind, Ε; in front, ΒΑ: plain border.
			[Head. Pl. XI. 5.]	
535	48·	AR ·65	Similar.	Similar; behind, Κ; in front, ΒΑ.
536	48·5	AR ·6	Similar.	Similar; behind, ΒΑ; in front, Κ.
537	50·4	AR ·65	Similar.	Similar; behind, ΒΑ; in front, Φ.

No.	Wt.	Metal. Size.	Obverse.	Reverse.
			Class D, with name of Philistis and portrait.	
538	404·3	Lead 1·15	Head of Philistis l., diademed and veiled.	ΒΑΣΙΛΙΣΣΑΣ ΦΙΛΙΣΤΙΔΟΣ Quadriga r., driven by winged Nike, wearing long chiton and holding reins in both hands; horses walking; above, Φ, to l. of which, crescent, horns l.
			[Probably a proof of a medallion of 32 litræ.]	
539	239·3	AR 1·1	Head of Philistis l., diademed and veiled; behind, stalk of barley.	ΒΑΣΙΛΙΣΣΑΣ [Φ]ΙΛΙΣΤΙ[ΔΟΣ] Quadriga r., driven by winged Nike, half-draped, holding reins in both hands; horses galloping; beneath them, ΣΜ; behind Nike, Φ.

No.	Wt.	Metal. Size.	Obverse.	Reverse.
540	214·8	AR 1·1	Similar; behind, Σ and palm bound with fillet.	ΒΑΣΙΛΙΣΣΑΣ ΦΙΛΙΣΤΙΔΟΣ Quadriga r., driven by winged Nike, wearing long chiton, holding reins in both hands and palm in r. over shoulder; horses trotting; beneath fore-leg of farthest horse, A: plain border.
			[Head. Pl. XI. 8.]	

No.	Wt.	Metal. Size.	Obverse.	Reverse.
541	214·5	Æ 1·	Similar; behind, Ϟ ? and cornucopiæ.	Similar; Nike without palm; in front, K.
542	215·2	Æ 1·	Similar; behind, Ϟ and wreath.	Similar; in front, Φ.
543	212·7	Æ 1·05	Similar; behind, Ϟ and leaf. (parsley ?)	[B]ΑΣΙΛΙΣ[ΣΑΣ] ΦΙΛΙΣΤΙΔΟΣ Quadriga r., driven by winged Nike, half-draped, and holding reins in both hands; horses prancing in step; beneath their fore-legs, E: plain border.
544	207·1	Æ 1·	Similar; behind, vase.	Similar; horses in high action.
545	216·1	Æ 1·1	Similar; behind, palm: border of dots.	Similar.
546	202·4	Æ 1·05	Similar; behind, long torch flaming.	Similar.
547	203·6	Æ 1·1	Similar; behind, star of eight rays.	Similar; above, star of eight rays; beneath horses' fore-legs, K.
548	205·7	Æ ·95	Similar; behind, stalk of barley.	Similar; above, KI; beneath horses' fore-legs, stalk of barley r.
549	207·7	Æ 1·05	Similar.	Similar; above, crescent upwards; in front, KI; beneath horses' fore-legs, stalk of barley r.
550	208·5	Æ 1·05	Similar; behind, star of eight rays.	Similar.
551	208·8	Æ 1·1	Similar type r.; behind, stalk of barley: border of dots.	Similar; beneath horses' fore-legs, Ϟ
552	207·8	Æ 1·	Similar type l.; behind, long torch flaming.	Same inscr. and similar type l.; Nike wears chiton; beneath horses' fore-legs, E: plain border.

[Head. Pl. XI. 7.]

No.	Wt.	Metal. Size.	Obverse.	Reverse.
553	209·5	AR 1·05	Similar; behind, thyrsos with fillet: border of dots.	Same inscr. Quadriga r., driven by winged Nike, wearing long chiton, holding reins in both hands; horses walking; in front, **A**.

No.	Wt.	Metal. Size.	Obverse.	Reverse.
554	208·2	AR 1·05	Similar.	Similar; above, crescent, horns r.; in front, **A**.
555	208·6	AR 1·05	Similar; behind, star of eight rays.	Similar; above, star of eight rays; in front, **K**: plain border.
556	203·	AR 1·05	Similar; behind, spear-head?	Similar; above, **MI**.
557	218·6	AR 1·05	Similar; behind, wreath.	Similar; in front, **Φ**.
558	207·6	AR 1·05	Similar.	Similar; above, **Φ**.
559	67·7	AR ·7	Head of Philistis l., diademed and veiled; behind, palm: border of dots.	**ΒΑΣΙΛΙΣΣΑΣ ΦΙΛΙΣΤΙΔΟΣ** Biga r., driven by winged Nike, half-draped, holding reins in both hands; horses prancing; in front, **E**: plain border. [Head. Pl. XI. 10.]
560	68·	AR ·7	Similar; behind, star of eight rays?	Similar; in front, **K**.

No.	Wt.	Metal. Size.	Obverse.	Reverse.
561	60·5	AR ·7	Similar; behind, leaf?	Same inscr. Biga r., driven by winged Nike, wearing long chiton, and holding reins in both hands; horses walking; in front, K: plain border.
562	69·	AR ·75	Similar; behind, wreath.	Similar; above, MI.

Class E, with ΣΙΚΕΛΙΩΤΑΝ.

No.	Wt.	Metal. Size.	Obverse.	Reverse.
563	104·3	AR ·95	Head of Demeter l., wearing wreath of barley and veiled; behind, serrated leaf: border of dots.	ΣΙΚΕΛΙΩΤΑΝ (in ex.) Quadriga r., driven by winged Nike, wearing long chiton, and holding goad in r. hand, reins in both; horses prancing; above, ΙΣ: plain border.

No.	Wt.	Metal. Size.	Obverse.	Reverse.
564	101·3	AR ·9	Same. (Same die.)	Same. (Same die.)

[Head. Pl. XI. 11.]

COPPER.

Class *a*, with ΙΕΡΩΝΟΣ and portrait.

No.	Wt.	Metal. Size.	Obverse.	Reverse.
565		Æ 1·05	Head of Hieron? l., laur.; behind, jaw-bone of boar: border of dots.	ΙΕΡΩΝΟΣ (in ex.) Horseman r., wearing helmet, cuirass, and chlamys, and holding couched spear in r.; horse prancing: plain border.
566		Æ 1·	Similar; behind, pileus.	Similar.

No.	Wt.	Metal. Size.	Obverse.	Reverse.
567		Æ 1·	Similar; behind, rhyton ending in fore-part of horse l.	Similar.
568		Æ 1·	Similar; behind, owl flying?	Similar; beneath horse, Ā.
569		Æ 1·05	Similar; behind, trophy?	Similar; beneath, AI.
570		Æ 1·05	Similar; behind, bee.	Similar; beneath, R.
571		Æ 1·1	Similar; behind, pedum?	Similar.
			[Head. Pl. XII. 1.]	
572		Æ 1·05	Similar; behind, capricorn r.	Similar; beneath, O.
573		Æ 1·	Similar; behind, plough r.	Similar; beneath, T.
574		Æ 1·	Similar; behind, wing.	Similar; beneath, Φ.
575		Æ 1·05	Similar; behind, pedum?	Similar.
576		Æ 1·05	Same; behind, term?	Similar.
577		Æ 1·05	Same; behind, Bœotian shield.	Similar; same letter?
578		Æ 1·35	Head of Hieron? l., wearing diadem: border of dots.	ΙΕΡΩΝΟΣ (in ex.) Biga r., driven by winged Nike, half-draped, holding reins in both hands; horses galloping; beneath, ξ

No.	Wt.	Metal. Size.	Obverse.	Reverse.
579		Æ 1·	Similar.	ΙΕΡΩΝΟΣ (in ex.) Horseman r., wearing helmet, cuirass, and chlamys, and holding couched spear in r.; horse prancing: plain border.
580		Æ 1·05	Similar; behind, cornucopiæ.	Similar.
581		Æ 1·1	Similar; no symbol.	Similar; beneath horse, A.
582		Æ 1·05	Similar; behind, thunderbolt.	Similar; beneath, A.
583		Æ 1·05	Similar; no symbol; beneath, Y.	Similar; beneath, E.
			[Head. Pl. XII. 2.]	
584		Æ 1·15	Similar; no symbol or letter.	Similar; beneath, Ι.
585		Æ 1·05	Similar.	Similar; beneath, Λ.
586		Æ 1·05	Similar.	Similar; beneath, ΛΥ.
587		Æ 1·05	Similar.	Similar; beneath, ΜΙ.
588		Æ 1·	Similar.	Similar; beneath, Ν.
589		Æ 1·05	Similar; behind, cornucopiæ.	Similar.
590		Æ 1·05	Similar; no symbol.	Similar; beneath, ΝΚ.
591		Æ 1·05	Similar.	Similar; ΝΚ.
592		Æ 1·	Similar.	Similar; beneath, ΣΩ.
593		Æ 1·05	Similar.	Similar; ΣΩ.
594		Æ 1·05	Similar; behind, dolphin l., downwards.	Similar; beneath, ΤΙ.
595		Æ 1·05	Similar; no symbol.	Similar; beneath, Φ.
596		Æ 1·05	Similar; behind, altar.	Similar.
597		Æ 1·05	Similar; behind, poppy-head.	Similar.

No.	Wt.	Metal. Size.	Obverse.	Reverse.
			Class β, with ΙΕΡΩΝΟΣ or ΙΕ, but without portrait.	
598		Æ ·95	Head of Poseidon l., wearing tainia: border of dots.	ΙΕΡ ΩΝΟΣ Ornamented trident, on either side of which a dolphin downwards; in field l., ⚹: plain border.
599		Æ ·85	Similar.	Similar; in field l., Ι.
600		Æ ·95	Similar.	Similar; in field l., Ϯ.
			[Head. Pl. XII. 4.]	
601		Æ ·8	Similar.	Similar; in field l., Μ.
602		Æ ·85	Similar.	Similar; in field l., Ν.
603		Æ ·85	Similar.	Similar; in field l., Ο.
604		Æ ·85	Similar.	Similar; in field l., Σ?
605		Æ ·75	Similar type.	Similar; in field r., Α.
606		Æ ·7	Similar.	Similar; in field r., ΑΠ.
607		Æ ·75	Similar.	Similar; in field r., ΔΑ.
608		Æ ·7	Similar.	Similar; in field r., ΛΥ.
609		Æ ·7	Similar.	Similar; beneath inscr., on either side, Ο Φ.
610		Æ ·75	Similar.	Similar; in field r., ΣΩ.
611		Æ ·7	Similar.	Similar; beneath inscr., on either side, Φ Ο.
612		Æ ·75	Similar; behind, owl r.	Similar; no letter.
613		Æ ·9	Head of Persephone l., bound with wreath of barley: border of dots.	ΙΕΡΩΝΟΣ Pegasos flying r.; beneath, Σ.
			[Head. Pl. XII. 5.]	

No.	Wt.	Metal. Size.	Obverse.	Reverse.
614		Æ ·6	Female head l., wearing ear-ring, necklace, and sphendone; behind, poppy-head: border of dots.	ΙΕΡΩΝΟΣ Pegasos flying l.
615		Æ ·6	Same. (Same die.)	Same. (Same die.)
			[Head. Pl. XII. 8.]	
616		Æ ·7	ΣΥΡΑΚΟΣΙΩΝ Head of Persephone l., wearing ear-ring and necklace; hair rolled, and bound with wreath of barley; behind, poppy-head: border of dots.	ΙΕ (in ex.) Bull butting l., above which, club l.; beneath club, ΑΓ: plain border.
617		Æ ·75	Similar; behind, bunch of grapes.	Similar; ΑΓ.
618		Æ ·75	Similar; no symbol.	Similar; Δ.
			[Head. Pl. XII. 6.]	
619		Æ ·75	Similar; behind, kantharos.	Similar; ΔΙ.
620		Æ ·75	Similar; behind, poppy-head.	Similar; Ξ.
621		Æ ·75	Similar; behind, kantharos.	Similar; Η.
622		Æ ·75	Similar; behind, bunch of grapes.	Similar; ΘΕ.
623		Æ ·75	Similar. (Symbol not visible.)	Similar; Ι.
624		Æ ·75	Similar; behind, poppy-head.	Similar; ΙΑ.
625		Æ ·75	Similar; no symbol.	Similar; Μ.
626		Æ ·8	Similar.	Similar; Ο.
627		Æ ·8	Similar. (Symbol not visible.)	Similar
628		Æ ·75	Similar; behind, poppy-head.	Simi

No.	Wt.	Metal. Size.	Obverse.	Reverse.
629		Æ ·65	Similar; no symbol: border of dots.	Similar; Ʀ.
630		Æ ·6	Similar.	Similar; ΛΥ.
631		Æ ·6	Similar.	Similar; Ν.
632		Æ ·65	Similar.	Similar; Σ.
633		Æ ·65	Similar.	Same inscr. Similar type and symbol, both r.; above, ΛΥ: plain border.
634		Æ ·65	Traces of inscr.? Head of Apollo l., laur.; hair long; behind, lyre.	ΙΕΡΩΝΟΣ Free horse prancing r.; above, ΛΥ.
635		Æ ·65	Similar; no symbol.	Same inscr. (in ex.) Similar.

[Head. Pl. XII. 7.]

Hieronymos. B.C. 216–215.

GOLD.

No.	Wt.	Metal. Size.	Obverse.	Reverse.
636	32·6	AV ·45	Head of Persephone l., wearing earring and necklace; hair bound with wreath of barley: border of dots.	ΒΑΣΙΛΕ•Σ ΙΕΡΩΝΥΜ•Υ Winged thunderbolt; above, ΚΙ.

[Head. Pl. XII. 9.]

SILVER.

No.	Wt.	Metal. Size.	Obverse.	Reverse.
637	291·4	AR 1·2	Head of Hieronymos l., diademed; behind, cornucopiæ: border of dots.	ΒΑΣΙΛΕΟΣ ΙΕΡΩΝΥΜΟΥ Winged thunderbolt; above, ΑΦ.

No.	Wt.	Metal. Size.	Obverse.	Reverse.
638	313·6	AR 1·2	Same. (Same die.)	Similar; above, **MI**.

No.	Wt.	Metal. Size.	Obverse.	Reverse.
639	130·3	AR ·9	Similar type and border.	Same inscr. and similar type; above, **ΑΦ**: plain border.

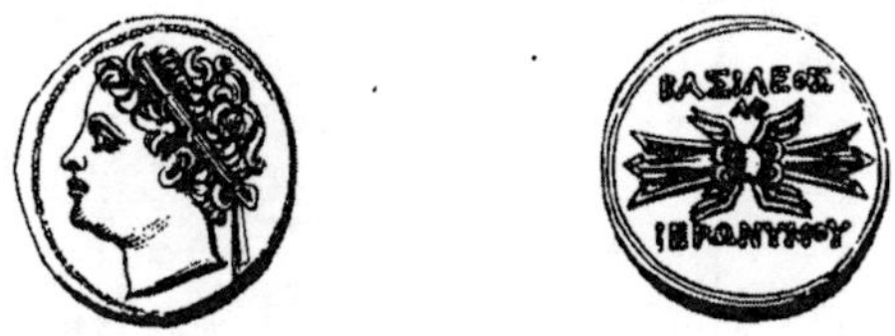

No.	Wt.	Metal. Size.	Obverse.	Reverse.
640	130·6	AR ·9	Similar; behind head, **ꓘ**.	Similar; above, **KI**.
			[Head. Pl. XII. 11.]	
641	125·5	AR ·9	Similar; no letter.	Similar; above, **MI**.
642	130·	AR ·9	Similar.	Similar; above, **ΣΩ**. (Thunderbolt varied.)
643	125·7	AR ·85	Similar.	Similar; above, **ΦΙ**.
644	65·6	AR ·7	Similar type and border.	Same inscr. and similar type; above, **KI**: plain border.
			[Head. Pl. XII. 12.]	
			COPPER.	
645		Æ ·85	Head of Hieronymos l., diademed: border of dots.	**ΒΑΣΙΛΕΟΣ ΙΕΡΩΝΥΜΟΥ** Winged thunderbolt; above, **ΑΠ**.
646		Æ ·85	Similar.	Similar; above and below, **Τ** **Α**.
647		Æ ·85	Similar.	Similar; but **Φ** **Ο**.
648		Æ ·85	Similar.	Similar. (Thunderbolt varied.)
			[Head. Pl. XII. 13.	

Autonomous. After B.C. 215.

GOLD.

No.	Wt.	Metal. Size.	Obverse.	Reverse.
649	42·	AV ·5	Head of Pallas l., wearing necklace and crested Corinthian helmet.	ΣΥΡΑΚΟΣΙΩΝ Artemis standing l., wearing endromides and short chiton with diploïdion, which has slipped from her shoulders, leaving them bare; she discharges an arrow from her bow; behind her back hangs a quiver; at her feet is a hound, running l.; in field l., ΣΩ.

SILVER.

No.	Wt.	Metal. Size.	Obverse.	Reverse.
650	210·4	AR 1·	Head of Zeus l., laur.: border of dots.	ΣΥΡΑΚΟΣΙΩΝ Quadriga r., driven by winged Nike, wearing long chiton, and holding goad in r. hand, reins in both; horses in high action; beneath them, Σ Λ; in ex., ΥΑ.

No.	Wt.	Metal. Size.	Obverse.	Reverse.
651	156·8	AR ·9	Head of Pallas l., wearing earring, necklace, crested Corinthian helmet, and ægis tied round throat with snakes; behind, Ⲁ: border of dots.	ΣΥΡΑΚΟΣΙΩΝ Artemis standing l., wearing endromides, short chiton with diploïdion, and quiver slung over her shoulder; she discharges an arrow from her bow; at her feet a hound, ΣΩ:

No.	Wt.	Metal. Size.	Obverse.	Reverse.
652	158·3	AR ·9	Similar; no mon.	Similar; in field l., ΥΑ ΣΛ
653	156·6	AR ·95	Similar; no earring or ægis; helmet adorned with serpent.	Similar; in field l., ΧΑΡ.
			[Head. Pl. XIII. 3.]	
654	102·	AR ·85	Head of Pallas l., wearing earring, necklace, crested Corinthian helmet, and ægis fastened round throat with snakes: border of dots.	ΣΥΡΑΚΟΣΙΩΝ Winged thunderbolt; beneath, ΞΑ.
655	104·4	AR ·85	Similar; behind head, [monogram].	Similar, ΣΩ.
656	104·6	AR ·85	Similar; helmet adorned with flying griffin; on back of helmet, Α.	Similar, ΥΑ Σ: plain border.
			[Head. Pl. XIII. 4.]	
657	103·7	AR 85	Same. (Same die.)	Similar; but ΥΑ ΣΛ.
658	108·	AR ·85	Head of Persephone l., wearing earring and necklace; hair rolled and curly, bound with wreath of barley; behind neck, owl l.	ΣΥΡΑΚΟΣΙΩΝ (in ex.) Quadriga r., driven by winged Nike, wearing long chiton, and holding goad and reins; horses prancing; above, [monogram]; beneath horses' fore-legs, ΑΙ; the quadriga rests on a narrow base inscribed ΛΥ: plain border.
			[Head. Pl. XIII. 5]	
659	78.6	AR ·75	Head of bearded Herakles l., wearing lion's skin, the ends tied beneath his chin: border of dots.	ΣΥΡΑΚΟΣΙΩΝ (in ex.) Biga r., driven by winged Nike, half-draped, holding goad in r. hand, reins in both; horses prancing; beneath their fore-le[illegible]: plain border.
			[Head. Pl. XIII. 6.]	

No.	Wt.	Metal. Size.	Obverse.	Reverse.
660	51·9	Æ ·75	Head of Apollo l., laur.; hair long: border of dots.	ΣΥΡΑΚΟΣΙΩΝ Winged Nike, half-draped, walking l., carrying palm in raised r. and trophy on l. arm; in field r., ΧΑΡ: plain border.

[Restruck upon coin of Hieron II., with name of Gelon.]

[Head. Pl. XIII. 7.]

No.	Wt.	Metal. Size.	Obverse.	Reverse.
661	130·7	Æ ·95	Head of Persephone l., wearing earring and necklace; hair long and bound with wreath of barley; behind, long torch, flaming: border of dots.	ΣΥΡΑΚΟΣΙΩΝ Zeus, laur., wearing himation, standing facing, and looking r.; with his r. he leans upon a sceptre; in field l., eagle flying r., above which, ΧΑΡ.

No.	Wt.	Metal. Size.	Obverse.	Reverse.
662	32·7	Æ ·55	Head of Apollo l., laur.; hair long: border of dots.	ΣΥΡΑΚΟΣΙΟΙ Female figure, standing towards l., with upturned face and flowing hair, wearing long chiton with diploïdion and inflated veil; she holds in r. a half-unfolded scroll, and in l. a branch, bound with fillet; in field r., Α: plain border.
663	33·2	Æ ·55	Similar.	Similar; in field l., Κ.
664	32·9	Æ ·55	Similar.	Similar; in field l., Φ.

[Head. Pl. XIII. 9.]

No.	Wt.	Metal. Size.	Obverse.	Reverse.
665	16·1	Æ ·45	Head of Artemis r., wearing earring and necklace; hair in knot behind; over shoulder, quiver: border of dots.	ΣΥΡΑΚΟΣΙΟΙ Owl r., on bar; in field l., Α: plain border.
666	16·1	Æ ·45	Similar.	Similar, Κ.

No.	Wt.	Metal. Size.	Obverse.	Reverse.
667	15·5	AR ·45	Similar.	Similar, Φ.
			[Head. Pl. XIII. 10.]	
668	11·3	AR ·35	Head of Pallas l., wearing crested Corinthian helmet: border of dots.	ΣΥΡΑΚΟΣΙΟΙ :XIII; beneath which, ΑΦ.
669	12·2	AR ·35	Similar.	Similar; beneath, Κ: plain border.
			[Head. Pl. XIII. 11.]	
			COPPER.	
670		Æ ·85	Head of Poseidon l., bound with tainia: border of dots.	ΣΥΡΑ ΚΟΣΙΩΝ Ornamented trident, on either side of which, a dolphin downwards; in field beneath, Α Γ: plain border.
671		Æ ·75	Similar.	Similar; in field, Ο Φ.
			[Head. Pl. XIII. 12.]	
672		Æ ·5	Similar type: same border.	ΣΥΡΑ ΚΟΣΙ Ω Ν Similar type.
673		Æ ·5	Similar.	ΣΥΡ ΑΚΟ ΣΙ ΩΝ Similar.
674		Æ ·5	Similar; behind, star.	Similar.
675		Æ ·5	Similar type r.; behind, crescent, horns upwards: border of dots.	Similar.
676		Æ ·5	Similar.	Similar: plain border.
677		Æ ·55	Similar; no symbol.	ΣΥ ΡΑΚ Ornamented trident: border of dots.
678		Æ ·85	Head of Apollo l., laur.; hair long: border of dots.	ΣΥΡΑΚΟΣΙΩ[Ν] (in ex.) The Dioscuri on horseback r.; r. arms raised; above the head of each, a star; horses cantering; beneath them, ΑΓ: plain border.
			[Head. Pl. XIII. 13.]	

Q Q

No.	Wt.	Metal. Size.	Obverse.	Reverse.
679		Æ ·9	Similar type.	Similar; beneath, ΟΦ.
680		Æ ·85	Similar.	Similar; beneath, Φ.
681		Æ ·45	Head of Apollo l., laur.; hair long; behind, cornucopiæ: border of dots.	ΣΥΡΑΚΟ ΣΙΩΝ Tripod-lebes with neck and three handles: plain border.
			[Head. Pl XIII. 14.]	
682		Æ ·45	Young head r., wearing tainia; hair long; behind, leaf?	ΣΥΡΑΚ ΟΣΙΩΝ Similar type.
683		Æ ·4	Similar type; behind, crescent, horns upwards.	ΣΥΡΑΚ ΟΣΙΩΝ Similar.

Under the Romans. After B.C. 212.

COPPER.

No.	Wt.	Metal. Size.	Obverse.	Reverse.
684		Æ 1·05	Head of Zeus r., laur.: border of dots.	ΣΥΡΑΚΟ ΣΙΩΝ Agalma of divinity, in triumphal quadriga r., holding flaming torch; horses walking: border of dots.
685		Æ 1·05	Similar.	Similar.
			[Head. Pl. XIV. 1.]	
686		Æ ·95	Similar.	Similar.
687		Æ ·95	Similar.	Similar.
688		Æ ·85	Head of Zeus r., laur.: border of dots.	ΣΥΡΑΚΟ ΣΙΩΝ Tyche, (of Syracuse?) standing l., wearing mural crown, holding rudder and leaning on sceptre: plain border.
689		Æ ·75	Similar.	Similar.
			[Head. Pl. XIV. 2.]	
690		Æ ·8	Head of Zeus r., laur.: border of dots.	ΣΥΡΑΚΟ ΣΙΩΝ Eagle, with wings open, on thunderbolt r.: border of dots.

No.	Wt.	Metal. Size.	Obverse.	Reverse.
691		Æ ·95	Head of Zeus l., laur.: border of dots.	ΣΥΡΑΚΟΣΙΩΝ (in ex.) Biga r., driven by winged Nike, holding whip and reins; horses galloping; above, crescent, horns upwards: plain border.
692		Æ ·8	Similar.	Similar.
693		Æ ·8	Head of Zeus l., laur.; behind, Macedonian helmet r.: border of dots.	Same inscr.; similar type l.: plain border.
694		Æ ·8	Similar.	Similar.
695		Æ ·8	Head of Zeus l., laur.	ΣΥΡΑΚΟΣΙΩΝ (in ex.) Biga l., driven by winged Nike; horses cantering; above, star: plain border.
696		Æ ·75	Head of Zeus r., laur.: border of dots.	Σ ΥΡΑ ΚΟΣΙ ΩΝ Biga r., driven by winged Nike; horses cantering: border of dots.
			[Head. Pl. XIV. 3.]	
697		Æ ·75	Similar.	ΣΥΡΑΚΟΣΙ Similar.
698		Æ ·8	Head of Pallas r., wearing crested Corinthian helmet: border of dots.	ΣΥ ΡΑ ΚΟΣ ΙΩΝ Nike facing, with wings spread, wearing long chiton; she kneels with l. knee upon the back of a prostrate bull r., which she is about to sacrifice with a sword, held in her r.: plain border.
			[Head. Pl. XIV. 4.]	
699		Æ ·8	Similar.	ΣΥΡΑ Κ Ο Σ ΙΩ[Ν] Similar type.
700		Æ ·8	Similar.	[ΣΥ]ΡΑ . . ΣΙ ΩΝ Similar type: border of dots.
701		Æ ·75	Head of Sarapis r., wearing tainia and head-dress of horns, globe, and plumes: border of dots.	ΣΥΡΑΚ Ο CΙΩΝ Isis l., wearing head-dress of globe and horns, holding sistrum and leaning upon sceptre: border of dots.

No.	Wt.	Metal. Size.	Obverse.	Reverse.
702		Æ ·8	Similar.	Similar.
703		Æ ·8	Similar.	Similar, without head-dress.
			[Head. Pl. XIV. 5.]	
704		Æ ·7	Head of Isis r., with long hair, bound with wreath of barley, surmounted by head-dress of horns, globe, and plumes; behind, : border of dots.	ΣΥΡΑ ΚΟ ΣΙΩΝ Head-dress of Isis, consisting of horns surmounted by globe and plumes, behind which, two ears of barley placed crossed: plain border.
			[Head. Pl. XIV. 7.]	
705		Æ ·75	Similar type: same border.	Similar.
706		Æ ·75	Head of Persephone r., hair rolled and bound with wreath of barley.	[ΣΥΡ]ΑΚ Ο ΣΙΩΝ Demeter l., veiled, and wearing long chiton and peplos, holding torch and sceptre.
707		Æ ·75	Similar.	Similar.
			[Head. Pl. XIV. 6.]	
708		Æ ·85	Similar.	Similar: border of dots.
709		Æ ·6	Head of Persephone l., wearing earring and wreath of barley; behind, cornucopiæ: border of dots.	ΣΥΡΑ ΚΟΣΙ ΩΝ within wreath of barley.
710		Æ ·55	Head of Persephone r., bound with wreath of barley.	Similar.
			[Head. Pl. XIV. 9.]	
711		Æ ·65	Head of Demeter r., veiled, and wearing wreath of barley.	ΣΥ ΡΑΚ [ΟΣ]Ι ΩΝ Two long flaming torches, crossed: border of dots.
			[Head. Pl. XIV. 8.]	
712		Æ ·75	Similar: border of dots.	ΣΥΡΑ ΚΟ ΣΙΩ Ν Similar.
713		Æ ·6	Head of Apollo l., laur.: (from archaic statue?) border of dots.	ΣΥΡ ΑΚΟ ΣΙ ΩΝ Long torch: border of dots.
			[Head. Pl. XIV. 10.]	

No.	Wt.	Metal. Size.	Obverse.	Reverse.
714		Æ ·55	Similar.	Similar.
715		Æ ·4	Head of Asklepios ? r., laur.	ΣΥΡ[Α] ΚΟΣΙ Tripod-lebes with neck and three handles.
716		Æ ·65	Head of Apollo r., laur.: border of dots.	ΣΥΡΑ Σ ΙΩΝ Sacrificial cap (galerus); in field r., Q: plain border.
			[Head. Pl. XIV. 12.]	
717		Æ ·5	Similar.	Similar.
718		Æ ·6	Bust of Demeter ? r., veiled and diademed: border of dots.	ΣΥΡ ΚΟ ΣΙΩΝ (*sic*) Quiver with strap, strung bow, and arrow, crossed: border of dots.
719		Æ ·75	Bust of Helios, radiate, r.; over shoulder, strung bow and quiver: border of dots.	ΣΥΡΑΚΟ ΣΙΩΝ Naked male figure of Egyptian style, (Osiris ?) advancing r., wearing modius, and holding wreath ? and branch: plain border.
			[Head. Pl. XIV. 11.]	
720		Æ ·7	Similar.	ΣΥΡΑΚΟ ΣΙ ΩΝ Similar figure, surmounted by crescent: plain border.
721		Æ ·8	Similar.	Similar.
722		Æ ·6	Head of Janus, bearded, and wearing wreath: border of dots.	ΣΥΡΑΚΟ ΣΙΩΝ Object resembling a quiver, with a circular radiate top and two fillets attached to rings on each side: border of dots.
			[Head. Pl. XIV. 13.]	
723		Æ ·5	Head of Asklepios r., laur.: border of dots.	Σ..ΑΚ ΟΣΙΩΝ Serpent entwined round staff: border of dots.

TAUROMENIUM.

GOLD.

Period of Decline; late.

No.	Wt.	Metal. Size.	Obverse.	Reverse.
1	17·	AV ·4	Head of Apollo r., laur.; behind, star of six rays: border of dots.	[T]AY P[OME] NITAN Tripod-lebes with neck and three handles: plain border.
2	16·5	AV ·35	Similar; behind, bee.	TAYPOME NITAN Similar type; in field r., uncertain symbol.
3	16·3	AV ·4	Same. (Same die.)	TAYPOME Similar type: plain border.
4	16·	AV ·4	Similar type l.; behind, cicada: border of dots.	TAYPOME NITAN Similar; in field l., AI.
5	16·5	AV ·45	Similar; behind, club.	TAYPOME NITAN Similar; in field r., EY.
6	16·5	AV ·4	Similar; behind, altar?	Similar; in field r., A.

SILVER.

Period of Decline; early.

No.	Wt.	Metal. Size.	Obverse.	Reverse.
7	13·2	AR ·4	Bull's head, facing: border of dots.	TAY POM Bunch of grapes.
8	13·3	AR ·35	Same. (Same die.)	Same: plain border visible. (Same die.)

Period of Decline; late.

No.	Wt.	Metal. Size.	Obverse.	Reverse.
9	76·9	AR ·85	Head of Pallas l., wearing earring, necklace, and crested Corinthian helmet adorned with griffin; no neckpiece; behind, H: border of dots.	T A YP OM A N Pegasos flying l.; beneath, star of eight rays.
10	48·3	AR ·7	Head of Apollo r., laur.; behind, star of ten rays: border of dots.	TAYPOME NITAN Tripod-lebes with neck and three handles: plain border.
11	50·9	AR ·65	Similar; star of eight rays.	Similar; in field l., AI.

No.	Wt.	Metal. Size.	Obverse.	Reverse.
			COPPER.	
			Period of Decline; early.	
12		Æ ·6	ΙΩΔϘΑΣ Female head l., wearing earring, necklace, and stephanos: border of dots.	Bunch of grapes with two leaves: plain border.
13		Æ ·55	Similar. (Inscr. obscure.)	Similar.
14		Æ ·5	Similar type.	Bunch of grapes with leaf and tendril: plain border.
15		Æ ·9	Head of Apollo Archegetes l., laur.; in front, ΑΡΧΑΓΕΤΑΣ: border of dots.	ΜΕΝΙΤΑΝ Bull walking l.
16		Æ 1·05	Similar.	ΤΑΥΡΟΜΕ Man-headed bull walking l.
17		Æ 1·	Similar.	ΤΑΥΡΟΜ ΕΝΙΤ ΑΝ Similar type: border of dots.
18		Æ 1·	Similar; beneath, Α.	ΤΑΥΡ ΙΤΑΝ Similar type; in front, bunch of grapes.
19		Æ ·75	Similar, without letter.	ΤΑΥΡΟ ΜΕΝ ΙΤΑΝ Bull butting l.
20		Æ ·8	Similar; beneath, Α.	ΤΑΥΡΟΜΕ ΝΙΤ ΑΝ Similar type; in ex., bunch of grapes: border of dots.
21		Æ ·8	Similar, without letter.	ΤΑΥΡΟΜΕΝΙΤΑΝ Similar type; in ex., uncertain monogram: plain border.
22		Æ ·85	Similar.	Similar; beneath, Σ.
23		Æ ·9	Similar.	Similar; in ex., ΝΣ.
24		Æ ·7	Similar.	ΜΕΝ ΤΑΝ Similar type.

No.	Wt.	Metal. Size.	Obverse.	Reverse.
25		Æ ·65	Similar type ; around, ΑΡΧΑΓΕ ΤΑϟ : border of dots.	ΤΑΥΡΟΜ ΕΝΙΤ ΑΝ Fore-part of butting bull l. : border of dots.
26		Æ ·85	Head of Apollo l., laur.; in front, ΑΡΧΑΕΕΤΑ (*sic*) : border of dots.	ΤΑΥΡΟΜ ΕΝΙΤΑΝ Lyre of seven strings ; above, bunch of grapes : border of dots.
27		Æ ·85	Similar. (Inscr. obscure.)	Similar.
28		Æ ·75	Head of Apollo r., laur. : border of dots.	ΤΑΥΡΟΜΕ ΝΙΤΑΝ Similar type : same border.
29		Æ ·85	Head of Apollo l., laur.; in front, ΑΡΧΑΓ ΤΑϟ (*sic*) : border of dots.	ΤΑΥΡΟΜ ΕΝΙΤΑΝ Tripod-lebes with neck and three handles : plain border.
30		Æ ·75	Similar.	Similar.
31		Æ ·5	Similar type ; in front, ΑΡΧΑΓΕΤΑ : same border.	ΤΑΥΡΟΜ ΕΝΙΤΑΝ Bunch of grapes on stalk.
32		Æ ·6	Similar type : same border.	ΤΑΥΡΟΜΕ ΝΙΤΑΝ Similar type : plain border.
			Period of Decline ; late.	
33		Æ 1·	Head of bearded Herakles r., bound with tainia ; behind, ⋟Ε : border of dots.	ΤΑΥ ΡΟΜΕΝΙΤΑΝ Bull butting r. : plain border.
34		Æ ·9	Similar.	ΤΑΥΡΟΜΕΝΙΤΑΝ Similar.
35		Æ ·8	Similar ; behind, Υ ?	ΤΑΥΡΟΜΕ Similar.
36		Æ ·8	Head of Apollo l., laur. ; behind, ⋟Ε : border of dots.	ΤΑΥΡΟ ΜΕΝΙΤΑΝ Tripod-lebes with neck and three handles : plain border.
37		Æ ·8	ΤΑΥΡΟΜΕΝΙΤΑΝ Head of young Dionysos l., crowned with ivy : border of dots.	ΑΠΟΛ ΛΩΝΟΣ Similar type : border of dots.

No.	Wt.	Metal. Size.	Obverse.	Reverse.
38		Æ ·85	Similar.	Similar.
39		Æ ·8	Head of Apollo r., laur.: border of dots.	TAYPOME NITAN Similar type: plain border.
40		Æ ·9	Head of Pallas l., wearing necklace and crested Corinthian helmet; behind, owl l.: border of dots.	TAYPOMEN I TAN Pegasos l., prancing: plain border.
41		Æ ·9	Similar.	TAYPOMENI TAN Pegasos l., galloping: plain border.
42		Æ ·9	Similar.	Similar. (Restruck coin.)
43		Æ ·7	Head of Pallas r., wearing earring, necklace, and crested Corinthian helmet: border of dots.	TAYPOMENI TAN Pegasos r., prancing: plain border.
44		Æ ·65	Similar.	NITAN Similar.
45		Æ ·7	Similar type; behind, M.	TAY P Similar type: plain border.
46		Æ ·9	Head of Apollo l., laur.; behind, bee.	TAYPO MENITAN Tripod-lebes with neck and three handles: border of dots.
47		Æ ·9	Similar; no symbol visible.	Similar.
48		Æ ·8	Similar type; behind, bee: border of dots.	TA MENITAN Bull butting r.
49		Æ ·75	Similar.	TAYPA MENITAN (*sic*) Similar type: plain border.

No.	Wt.	Metal. Size.	Obverse.	Reverse.
50		Æ ·6	Similar type r.	TAYPO NITA Similar type.
51		Æ ·6	Similar type: border of dots.	TAYPOME Similar type: plain border.
52		Æ ·6	Dionysiac head r., crowned with ivy; in front, owl l.	TAYPOM NITAN Bull standing r.
53		Æ ·75	Head of Pallas r., wearing earring, necklace, and crested Corinthian helmet: border of dots.	TAYPOME NI Owl r., standing on amphora r.: border of dots.
54		Æ ·7	Similar.	TAYPOME NITAN Similar.
55		Æ ·9	Head of young Dionysos r., crowned with ivy: border of dots.	TAY PO MENITAN Mainad l., clad in short chiton, holding in r. fruit, in l. thyrsos; at her feet, panther l.: border of dots.
56		Æ ·85	Similar.	Similar.

No.	Wt.	Metal. Size.	Obverse.	Reverse.
			TYNDARIS.	
			COPPER.	
			Period of Finest Art.	
1		Æ ·85	ΤΥΝ ΔΑΡΙΣ Head of Tyndaris (Helen?) l., wearing earring and stephane; behind, star of eight rays: border of dots.	One of the Dioscuri r., on horseback, wearing hat and chlamys; over l. shoulder, palm; horse cantering: border of dots.

2		Æ ·65	ΤΥΝΔΑΡ Ι ΤΑΝ Head of Apollo r., laur.: border of dots.	Horse's head l., bridled: border of dots.
3		Æ ·65	ИΑΤ ΙΡΑΔИΥΤ Similar type l.: same border.	Similar type r.: same border.
4		Æ ·65	ΤΥΝΔΑΡΙΤΑΝ Similar type r.: same border.	Cock r.; in front, grasshopper; behind, star of eight rays: border of dots.
5		Æ ·6	Τ Δ Τ ΑΝ Similar.	Similar.
			Period of Decline; early.	
6		Æ ·8	[Τ]ΥΝΔΑΡΙΤΑΝ Head of Persephone l., wearing wreath of corn; hair flowing: border of dots.	The Dioscuri l., on horseback, wearing chlamydes; horses galloping; above, ΣΩ Τ Η Ρ[Ε Σ].
7		Æ ·85	Similar type.	Similar type; above, ΣΩΤΗΡΕΣ.

No.	Wt.	Metal. Size.	Obverse.	Reverse.
			Period of Decline; late.	
8		Æ ·8	Female head r., (Tyndaris ?) veiled, and wearing earring and stephane; behind, star of eight rays: border of dots.	TYNΔA PITAN The Dioscuri, wearing pilei and chlamydes, charging r. on horseback, lances couched: border of dots.
9		Æ ·85	Head of Zeus r., laur.: border of dots.	TYNΔAPITAN (in ex.) The Dioscuri standing, facing, each holding by the bridle a horse, l. and r.
10		Æ ·7	Similar.	TY ITAN The Dioscuri standing l.; each holds in l. a spear and extends r. hand: plain border.
11		Æ ·7	Similar type; behind, star of eight rays: same border.	TY NΔA PITAN Eagle r., standing on thunderbolt, wings open: border of dots.
12		Æ ·65	Head of Poseidon r., wearing tainia: border of dots.	[T]YNΔA PITAN Ornamented trident: border of dots.
13		Æ ·65	Similar.	Similar.
14		Æ ·7	Bust of Pallas r., wearing crested Corinthian helmet: border of dots.	TYNΔAPITAN Winged caduceus between olive-branch and stalk of barley: border of dots.
15		Æ ·7	Similar.	TY NΔA PITAN Hermes l., wearing winged petasos, chlamys, and cothurni; he holds in r. patera? in l. caduceus: plain border.
16		Æ ·65	Female head r., veiled and laur.: border of dots.	YNΔAPIT The pilei of the Dioscuri, surmounted by stars.
17		Æ ·65	Similar.	ꟿ

No.	Wt.	Metal. Size.	Obverse.	Reverse.

UNCERTAIN OF SICILY.

With monogram K [KAM]

Period of Decline; early.

SILVER.

No.	Wt.	Metal. Size.	Obverse.	Reverse.
1	8·5	AR ·4	Free horse r., galloping.	K within olive-wreath r.

COPPER.

No.	Wt.	Metal. Size.	Obverse.	Reverse.
2		Æ 1·3	Ѧ Bull l., butting: plain border.	Star of sixteen rays, the alternate ones longer: plain border.

No.	Wt.	Metal. Size.	Obverse.	Reverse.
3		Æ 1·35	Similar.	Similar.

(The above two coins restruck on coins of Syracuse: Obv. Head of Pallas l. Rev., Star-fish between dolphins.)

No.	Wt.	Metal. Size.	Obverse.	Reverse.
4		Æ ·55	Campanian helmet r., with cheek-piece and neck-piece.	K within olive-wreath r.

(The above coins may have been struck by the Campanians in Sicily.)

With inscr. TYPPH.

Period of Decline; early.

COPPER.

No.	Wt.	Metal. Size.	Obverse.	Reverse.
1		Æ 1·2	TYPPH Head of Pallas r., wearing crested close helmet with neck-piece: plain border.	Pallas l., armed, holding in r spear, in l. shield, which rests on the ground: plain border.
2		Æ 1·15	Similar.	Similar; in field r., M.

(These coins restruck on coins of Syracuse: Obv., Head of Pallas l. Rev., Star-fish between dolphins. They may have been issued by Tyrrhenian mercenaries in Sicily.)

HERBESSUS ?

Period of Decline; early.

COPPER.

No.	Wt.	Metal. Size.	Obverse.	Reverse.
1		Æ 1·15	Female head r., wearing myrtle-wreath; hair rolled.	Eagle, with closed wings, standing r., looking back, holding in beak coiled serpent.

(Restruck on a coin of Syracuse: Obv., Head of Zeus Eleutherios l. Rev., Free horse l. Attributed by Dr. Imhoof-Blumer to Herbessus; cf. F. e L. Landolina Paternò, Illustrazione storiche sulle monete della antica Sicilia, Tav. IX. 2.)

HIMERA ?

Period of Finest Art?

COPPER.

No.	Wt.	Metal. Size.	Obverse.	Reverse.
1		Æ ·6	Draped female figure, standing l., sacrificing with patera at altar; around, several globules.	Boar running r.; beneath, ivy-leaf: border of dots.

(Cf. Berliner Blätter für Münz-Siegel-und-Wappenkunde, Bd. V., p. 50.)

HIPANA.

Period of Archaic Art.

SILVER.

No.	Wt.	Metal. Size.	Obverse.	Reverse.
1	11·3	AR ·5	ΑΝΑ ΤΑΜ ⅂ Ι Eagle, with closed wings, standing l. on Ionic capital, holding in beak uncertain object: plain border.	Dolphin l.; beneath, scallop.

(This attribution may be considered certain; as a town called Hipana, not far from Panormus, is mentioned by Polybius, I. 24.)

SILERAE ?

Period of Decline; early.

COPPER.

No.	Wt.	Metal. Size.	Obverse.	Reverse.
1		Æ 1·1	Inscr. obscure. Fore-part of man-headed bull, swimming l.	Warrior, wearing crested helmet, charging r., with spear and shield.

(Restruck on a coin of Syracuse: Obv., Head of Pallas l. Rev., Star-fish between dolphins. Dr. Imhoof-Blumer reads ИΩΙΑϘƎΛΙƸ on a similar coin.)

THERMAE HIMERAEAE.

Period of Finest Art.

COPPER.

No.	Wt.	Metal. Size.	Obverse.	Reverse.
1		Æ ·8	**IMEPA** ? Female head l., with short horns, bound with reeds.	Traces of inscr. (**MEPA MITAN** ?) Paniskos, horned and with goat's feet, facing, playing on double flute and dancing with crossed legs; behind him, three simulacra, bottle-shaped, the bodies ornamented, and the heads surmounted by modii.

UNATTRIBUTED.

No.	Wt.	Metal. Size.	Obverse.	Reverse.
1		Æ ·85	**M A PM N** Forepart of man-headed bull, swimming l.: border of dots.	Nike, wearing chiton with peplos, flying l., holding in r. aplustre bound with fillet, and in l. her chiton.
2		Æ ·7	Female head r., wearing earring and necklace; hair tied behind with a fillet, having falling ends.	Ram walking r.; in front, barleycorn.
3		Æ ·6	Female head r.; hair rolled.	Ram standing r.; in front, barleycorn.

ROMAN COINS PROBABLY STRUCK IN SICILY.

COPPER.

No.	Wt.	Metal. Size.	Obverse.	Reverse.
1		Æ ·65	Head of Apollo l., laur.; hair in formal curls behind: border of dots.	Q Two ears of corn growing on one stem: border of dots.
2		Æ ·7	Similar.	Similar.
3		Æ ·8	Female head r., wearing ear-ring, necklace, and stephane: border of dots.	Laurel-wreath with berries: border of dots.
4		Æ ·75	Similar.	Similar.
5		Æ ·75	Female head l., wearing stephane and veil: border of dots.	Similar wreath: same border.
6		Æ ·6	Dolphin r.	Laurel-wreath: border of dots.
7		Æ ·55	Similar.	Similar.

No.	Wt.	Metal. Size.	Obverse.	Reverse.
			SICULO-PUNIC COINS.	
			SOLUS.	
			Period of Finest Art.	
			SILVER.	
1	10·3	AR ·4	Cock l.: border of dots.	|𐤀𐤓 𐤐𐤊 Fish l.
			COPPER.	
			With marks of value.	
			Hemilitron.	
2	116·	Æ ·8	Head of bearded Herakles r., wearing lion's skin: plain border.	𐤊𐤐𐤓𐤀 Cray-fish r., upside-down, between ●●● ●●●.
3	114·	Æ ·8	Similar.	𐤊𐤐𐤓𐤀 Similar.
			Trias.	
4	69·	Æ ·7	ΣΟΛΟΝΤΙΝΟΝ Similar.	𐤊𐤐𐤓𐤀 Cray-fish r., between ●●●.
			Without marks of value.	
5		Æ ·55	Head of Pallas, three-quarter-face towards r., wearing Athenian helmet with three crests.	𐤊𐤐𐤓𐤀 Naked archer, wearing pilos, kneeling r., discharging an arrow; slung at his side, bow-case.
			Period of Decline; early.	
6		Æ 1·	Head of Persephone l., wearing wreath of corn and earring; around, dolphins (two visible).	Man-headed bull advancing r.
7		Æ ·8	Head of Persephone l., wearing wreath of corn, earring, and necklace.	𐤊𐤐𐤓𐤀 (in ex.) Similar type l.

MOTYA.

Period of Transition.

SILVER.

No.	Wt.	Metal. Size.	Obverse.	Reverse.
1	264·6	Æ 1·05	Eagle r.: border of dots.	Crab.

2	265·1	Æ 1·05	Similar.	Similar type; beneath, fish r.

3	124·5	Æ ·9	Female head r., wearing diadem almost covered by hair, rolled over it and turned up behind; behind, ivy-leaf.	Hound r., gnawing stag's head; above, head r.

4	127·4	Æ ·9	Same. (Same die.)	Same. (Same die.)
5	129·9	Æ ·95	Similar.	Hound r., head raised; beneath him, plant.

No.	Wt.	Metal. Size.	Obverse.	Reverse.
6	133·1	AR ·85	Same. (Same die.)	Similar type, tail raised; no symbol: border of dots.
7	5·3	AR ·35	Fore-part of swimming man-headed bull r.	[Phoenician inscription] Female head r.

Period of Finest Art.

No.	Wt.	Metal. Size.	Obverse.	Reverse.
8	130·6	AR ·85	Head of water-nymph, three-quarter-face towards r., wearing necklace and ampyx; around, six dolphins: plain border.	[Phoenician inscription] Crab; above, fish r.: plain border.

No.	Wt.	Metal. Size.	Obverse.	Reverse.
9	9·6	AR ·45	Similar head: same border.	Same inscr. type and symbol l.
10	10·8	AR ·5	Head of water-nymph, three-quarter-face towards r.: border of dots.	[Phoenician inscription] Date-palm, without fruit.
11	10·9	AR ·45	Head of Gorgon: border of dots.	[Phoenician inscription] Similar type.
12	9·3	AR ·5	Similar.	[Phoenician inscription] Similar type.
13	10·	AR ·45	Similar; hair in short curls.	Similar.
14	10·3	AR ·5	Similar; hair close.	Same inscr. Date-palm, with fruit.
15	11·3	AR ·5	Similar type; hair wavy.	[Phoenician inscription] . . . Date-palm, without fruit.

No.	Wt.	Metal. Size.	Obverse.	Reverse.
			COPPER.	
			With marks of value.	
			Trias.	
16	96·	Æ ·8	Head of Gorgon; beneath, ●●● : plain border.	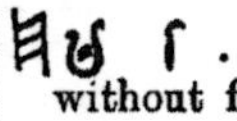 Date-palm, without fruit.
			Without marks of value.	
17		Æ ·4	Fore-part of running horse r.	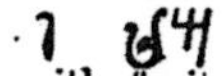 Date-palm, with fruit.
			MOTYA?	
18		Æ ·5	Head of water-nymph, three-quarter-face towards r., wearing ampyx: plain border.	Young male head r.
19		Æ ·5	Similar.	Similar.
20		Æ ·5	Similar.	Similar type l.

PANORMUS?

Period of Transition.

SILVER.

No.	Wt.	Metal. Size.	Obverse.	Reverse.
1	11·3	Æ ·4	Poseidon, naked to waist, seated r. on rock, holding trident in left, and extending r. towards dolphin r. downwards: border of dots.	[illegible] Naked youth, seated sideways on man-headed bull galloping r., holding caduceus in r. hand, l. extended.
2	9·5	Æ ·45	Female head r., wearing necklace, hair bound with broad diadem ornamented with mæander pattern, the back hair turned up under diadem and protruding in a bunch above; around, four dolphins r.: border of dots.	Poseidon, naked to waist, seated r. on rock, holding trident in l., and extending r. towards dolphin r. downwards.

No.	Wt.	Metal. Size.	Obverse.	Reverse.
3	9·5	Æ ·45	Similar.	Same. (Same die.)
4	8·1	Æ ·4	Similar.	Similar type l.

Period of Finest Art.

SILVER.

No.	Wt.	Metal. Size.	Obverse.	Reverse.
5	260·8	Æ 1·	[illegible] Female head r., wearing broad ornamented ampyx and necklace; around, two dolphins.	Quadriga r., driven by charioteer holding reins and goad, about to pass meta in form of fluted column; horses cantering; above, Nike flying l. crowning charioteer; in ex., cray-fish r., behind which, uncertain letter?

No.	Wt.	Metal. Size.	Obverse.	Reverse.
6	268·8	Æ 1·	Female head r., wearing necklace and broad diadem, round which the hair is rolled; in front and behind, a dolphin; above, a long fish r.	𐤑𐤉𐤑 (in ex.) Quadriga l.; (charioteer obscure;) horses cantering; in ex., on r., muscle - shell: border of dots.

7	264·4	Æ 1·	Similar type; diadem double; around, three dolphins.	Similar type; charioteer holding goad and reins; above, Nike flying r., about to crown him; ex. obscure.
8	264·6	Æ 1·1	Female head l., wearing broad ornamented diadem, earring, and necklace; around, three dolphins.	𐤑𐤉𐤑 (in ex.) Quadriga r., driven by charioteer holding reins and goad; horses cantering; above, Nike flying l., crowning charioteer; in ex., wingless sea-horse r.: border of dots. (Double-struck.)

9	259·5	Æ 1·05	Similar.	Similar.
10	269·	Æ ·95	Female head l., wearing earring; hair curly; in front, two dolphins.	𐤑𐤉𐤑 (in ex.) Quadriga l., driven by charioteer holding goad and reins; horses in high action; above, Nike flying r., about to crown charioteer: plain border.

No.	Wt.	Metal. Size.	Obverse.	Reverse.
11	256·7	Æ 1·05	Head of Persephone l., crowned with corn, wearing earring and necklace; around, four dolphins: border of dots.	Same inscr. Similar type; in ex., two dolphins meeting on either side of inscr. (Double-struck.)
12	252·8	Æ 1·	Similar.	Same. (Same die.)

13	258·9	Æ ·95	Similar; behind, [illegible].	Same inscr. Similar type; above horses' heads, star of eight rays; no dolphins in ex.
14	255·	Æ ·9	Similar; no symbol.	Same: border of dots. (Same die.)
15	261·1	Æ ·95	Similar.	Same. (Same die.)
16	268·1	Æ 1·	Similar.	Same. (Same die.)
17	265·6	Æ ·95	Similar. (Three dolphins visible.)	Similar; no symbol.
18	123·5	Æ ·85	Female head r., wearing earring, necklace, and sphendone ornamented behind with stars.	Hound r., looking back; above, murex.
19	127·7	Æ ·8	Similar.	Same inscr. Hound r.: plain border.
20	124·7	Æ ·8	Young male head r.; around, three dolphins.	Free horse r., prancing: border of dots.

With marks of value.

No.	Wt.	Metal. Size.	Obverse.	Reverse.
21	13·6	Æ ·55	Dolphin r.; beneath, cockle: above, ●●●●: border of dots. (Some marks of value are perhaps effaced.)	Eagle r., devouring hare.

No.	Wt.	Metal. Size.	Obverse.	Reverse.
			Without marks of value.	
22	9·7	AR ·45	Female head r., wearing sphendone and necklace; behind, .	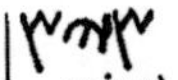 Fore-part of swimming man-headed bull r.; beneath, muscle.
23	9·8	AR ·45	Similar.	Similar.
24	10·3	AR ·5	Head of young river-god l., with short horn: plain border.	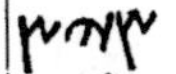 Fore-part of swimming man-headed bull r.
25	8·4	AR ·45	Similar type.	Similar.
26	10·6	AR ·35	Young male head r., bound with reeds?	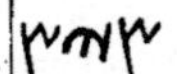 Man-headed bull, running r.
27	8·4	AR ·45	Young male head l.: border of dots.	 Man-headed bull l., head facing: plain border.
28	10·4	AR ·4	Similar.	Similar.
29	13·6	AR ·4	Similar type; behind, : border of dots.	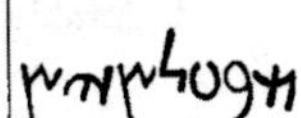 Similar.
30	10·6	AR ·35	Similar; behind, dolphin.	Similar.
31	7·5	AR ·35	Similar; no symbol.	Same inscr. (in ex.) Similar.
			COPPER.	
			With marks of value.	
			Hemilitron.	
32	190·	Æ ·95	Cock r.: (inscr. effaced:) border of dots.	
33	161·	Æ ·9	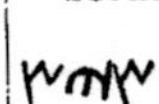 Similar.	Similar.
			Trias.	
34	151·	Æ ·75	Same inscr. Similar type.	
35	143·	Æ ·8	Similar: border of dots.	Similar.
			Hexas.	
36	40·	Æ ·6	Similar type.	

No.	Wt.	Metal. Size.	Obverse.	Reverse.
			Without marks of value.	
37		Æ ·65	 ? Boar running l.	Man-headed bull l.
			Period of Decline ; early.	
38		Æ ·85	Head of Hera l., crowned with stephanos, wearing earring and necklace.	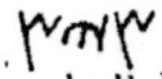 (in ex.) Man-headed bull l., head facing ; above, globe surrounded by rays.
			[Restruck on Æ of Syracuse. Obv. Head of Persephone l. Rev. Pegasos flying l.]	
39		Æ ·7	Head of Apollo l., laur. ; in front, uncertain letter ? behind, dolphin.	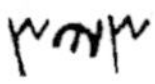 Pegasos flying l.
40		Æ ·75	Similar.	Similar.
41		Æ ·75	Similar.	Similar.
42		Æ ·75	Similar : border of dots.	Similar type.
43		Æ ·55	Head of Apollo l., laur. ; behind, dolphin : border of dots.	Pegasos flying r. : plain border.

HERACLEA MINOA.

SILVER.

Period of Finest Art.

No.	Wt.	Metal. Size.	Obverse.	Reverse.
1	252·	Æ 1·	Bearded head r., wearing laurel-wreath with two branches.	[Punic inscription] (in ex.) Quadriga l., driven by charioteer, holding goad and reins; horses in high action; above, caduceus l.: border of dots.
2	262·6	Æ 1·	Female head l., wearing earring, necklace, and sphendone tied above and ornamented with stars behind; around, three dolphins: border of dots.	[Punic inscription] (in ex.) Quadriga l., driven by charioteer, holding goad and reins; horses cantering; above, Nike flying r., about to crown charioteer.
3	257·4	Æ ·95	Head of Persephone r., wearing wreath of corn, earring, and necklace; around, three dolphins.	[Punic inscription] (in ex.) Similar type: border of dots.
4	266·7	Æ ·9	Similar: border of dots.	Same. (Same die.)
5	255·	Æ 1·	Head of Persephone l., wearing wreath of barley, earring, and necklace; around, three dolphins: border of dots.	[Punic inscription] (in ex.) Similar type.
6	264·4	Æ 1·	Head of Persephone r., wearing wreath of corn, earring, and necklace; around, four dolphins: border of dots.	Same inscr. Similar type r.; horses in high action: border of dots.

No.	Wt.	Metal. Size.	Obverse.	Reverse.
7	266·	Æ 1·	Same. (Same die.)	Same inscr. Similar type; horses prancing.
8	265·5	Æ 1·1	Similar.	Same inscr. Similar type; horses in high action: border of dots.
9	265·	Æ 1·05	Same. (Same die.)	Same. (Same die.)
10	267·5	Æ 1·	Similar type; around, four dolphins.	Same inscr. Similar type; horses galloping.
11	266·	Æ 1·	Similar type; around, four dolphins: border of dots.	Same inscr. Similar type; horses in high action: border of dots.
12	263·1	Æ 1·05	Same. (Same die.)	Same. (Same die.)
13	263·	Æ ·95	Similar. (Three dolphins visible.)	Inscr. obscure. Similar type; charioteer holds reins and goad.
14	260·	Æ ·9	Similar type; around, four dolphins.	Same inscr. Similar type l.; charioteer holds goad and reins.
15	264·4	Æ 1·05	Similar type; around, three dolphins.	Similar type r.; horses cantering. (Ex. off coin.)
16	265·1	Æ ·95	Head of Persephone l., wearing wreath of corn, earring, and necklace; around, three dolphins.	Inscr. obscure. Similar type l.; horses in high action.
17	252·6	Æ ·95	Similar. (Two dolphins v ble.)	type; and

No.	Wt.	Metal. Size.	Obverse.	Reverse.
18	259·4	AR 1·	Female head l., wearing earring and necklace; hair rolled; around, three dolphins: border of dots.	Same inscr. Quadriga l., driven by charioteer, holding goad and reins; horses cantering; above, Nike flying r., about to crown charioteer.
19	263·5	AR 1·	Similar type r.; around, three dolphins: border of dots.	Inscr. obscure. Similar type; horses in high action.
20	263·9	AR 1·	Female head r., wearing broad diadem, earring, and necklace; hair rolled; on either side, dolphin: border of dots.	Same inscr. Similar type r.; charioteer holds reins and goad; horses prancing.
21	262·9	AR 1·05	Similar type; in front, two dolphins; behind, barley-corn: border of dots.	 (in ex.) Quadriga l., driven by charioteer, holding goad in l. hand, r. extended; horses cantering; above, Nike flying r., about to crown charioteer; in front of horses, upright caduceus.

No.	Wt.	Metal. Size.	Obverse.	Reverse.

SICULO-PUNIC.

UNCERTAIN.

Period of Finest Art.

SILVER.

With letter 𐤌.

No.	Wt.	Metal. Size.	Obverse.	Reverse.
1	264·9	Æ ·95	Head of Persephone r., wearing wreath of corn and earring; in front, two dolphins.	𐤌 (in ex.) Quadriga r., driven by charioteer, holding goad and reins; horses in high action; above, Nike flying l., about to crown charioteer.

Without inscription.

No.	Wt.	Metal. Size.	Obverse.	Reverse.
1	266·6	Æ 1·05	Female head l., wearing earring and necklace; hair in net; around, three dolphins.	Quadriga l., driven by charioteer, wearing Phrygian cap, holding goad and reins; horses in high action; above, Nike flying r., about to crown charioteer; in ex., cista.
2	271·1	Æ 1·	Same. (Same die.)	Same. (Same die.)

COPPER.

With inscription 𐤑 𐤌.

No.	Wt.	Metal. Size.	Obverse.	Reverse.
1		Æ ·8	𐤑 𐤌 Female head l., wearing earring and Phry[illegible] helmet adorned with [illegible] at side: border of dot[illegible]	Free horse r., [illegible] on [illegible] side of u[illegible] [illegible]s: [illegible] borde[illegible]

No.	Wt.	Metal. Size.	Obverse.	Reverse.
			Without inscription.	
1		Æ ·7	Head of Persephone l., wearing earring and wreath of barley.	Free horse prancing r.
2		Æ ·55	Similar. Countermarked with star of eight rays.	Similar: plain border.
3		Æ ·65	Similar; no countermark.	Similar.
4		Æ ·6	Similar type: plain border.	Similar.
5		Æ ·6	Similar.	Similar.
6		Æ ·55	Bust of Artemis? l., wearing earring and necklace; hair in knot behind.	Free horse standing l., right fore-leg raised: plain border.
7		Æ ·65	Head of Persephone l., wearing wreath of barley, earring, and necklace: plain border.	Free horse prancing r.: plain border.
8		Æ ·6	Similar: no border.	Similar: no border.
9		Æ ·5	Similar type: plain border.	Similar type: plain border.

ISLANDS OF SICILY.

LIPARA.

Class I.

COPPER.

Hemilitron.

No.	Wt.	Metal. Size.	Obverse.	Reverse.
1	798·	Æ 1·5	Head of bearded Hephaistos r., wearing pilos: border of dots.	ИOIAꟼ A ΠIΛ Stern of ship going l.; above which, ●●● ●●● : border of dots.

No.	Wt.	Metal. Size.	Obverse.	Reverse.
2	773·	Æ 1·45	Similar.	Same.
3	706·	Æ 1·45	Similar.	ΛΙΠΑΡ ΑΙΟΝ Similar type r.: same marks of value and border.
4	619·	Æ 1·55	Similar type.	ΛΙΠΑ Similar type? same marks of value, small: same border.
5	551·	Æ 1·45	Similar.	ΛΙΠΑΡΑ Ι ΟИ Same type as no. 3, l., above and below which, ●●● (vertical) and ●●●: same border.

No.	Wt.	Metal. Size.	Obverse.	Reverse.
				Trias.
6	397·	Æ 1·2	Head of bearded Hephaistos r., wearing pilos: border of dots.	ИOIAΡAΠIΛ round ●●● .
7	394·	Æ 1·25	Similar.	ΛΙΠΑΡΑΙΟИ Same marks of value: border of dots.
8	369·	Æ 1·15	Similar.	Similar.
9	363·	Æ 1·2	Similar.	Similar; marks of value inverted.
				Hexas.
10	275·	Æ 1·05	Head of bearded Hephaistos r., wearing pilos.	ΛΙΠ, above and below which, ●● : border of dots.
			[Restruck upon an older coin apparently not of Lipara.]	
11	265·	Æ ·9	Similar.	Similar.
12	250·	Æ ·9	Similar type: border of dots.	ΛΙΠ Similar.
13	221·	Æ 1·1	Similar.	ΛΙΠ Similar, I connecting ●●.
				Uncia.
14	171·	Æ ·85	Head of bearded Hephaistos r., wearing pilos: border of dots.	Λ I, between which, ●: border of dots.
15	129·	Æ ·9	Similar.	I Λ Similar.

No.	Wt.	Metal. Size.	Obverse.	Reverse.
			Class II. Litra.	
16	457·	Æ 1·2	Female head r.	Dolphin r., beneath which, three large waves.
17	391·	Æ 1·25	Young Hephaistos, naked, seated r. on four-legged stool, holding [hammer] in lowered r. hand, which rests on stool, and [vase on l. or by handle].	[ΛΙ] Π [ΑΡΑΙΟΝ] Dolphin l.
18	241·	Æ 1·	Similar type? kantharos on hand.	ΛΙΠΑΡ ΑΙΟΝ Similar type: border of dots.
19	222·	Æ 1·	Similar.	Π ΑΡ Dolphin r. above waves.
20	245·	Æ 1·05	Similar type; kantharos held by handle: border of dots.	ΛΙΠΑ ΡΑΙΟΝ Dolphin r.: border of dots.

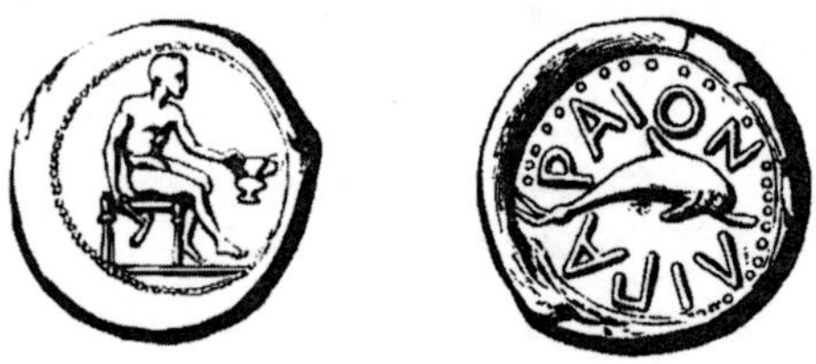

No.	Wt.	Metal. Size.	Obverse.	Reverse.
21	78·	Æ ·9	Similar type? (vase obscure.)	Same inscr. Similar type.
22	133·	Æ ·9	Similar type? (vase obscure.)	ΛΙΠ ΑΡΑΙ ΩΝ Similar type.
23	94·	Æ ·9	Similar type to no. 20.	Similar.
24	114·	Æ ·95	Similar type?	ΛΙΠΑΡΑ ΙΩΝ Similar type.
25	113·	Æ ·85	Similar type; Hephaistos holds by handle kantharos, which rests on stand; in field r., bunch of grapes: border of dots.	ΛΙΠΑΡΑΙ ΩΝ Dolphin l. above waves.
26	113·	Æ ·75	Similar.	Similar

No.	Wt.	Metal. Size.	Obverse.	Reverse.
27	103·	Æ ·85	Similar type, varied; in field l., star of eight rays.	Similar.
28	81·	Æ ·8	Similar type? border of dots.	ΡΑΙΩΙ Similar type.
29	95·	Æ ·8	Similar type and border to no. 25; in field r., large star of eight rays.	ΛΙ Similar type.
30	120·	Æ ·9	Similar type; in field r. and l., star of six rays: same border.	ΛΙΠΑΡΑΙ ΩΝ Similar type.
31	95·	Æ ·9	Similar type?	Similar.
			Hemilitron.	
32	134·	Æ ·85	Young Hephaistos, naked, seated r. on four-legged stool, holding hammer in lowered r. hand, which rests on stool, and kantharos on l.: border of dots.	VOIAꟼAΠIΛ around ●●● ●●●: border of dots.
33	120·	Æ ·85	Similar type.	ΛΙΠΑΡΑΙΟΝ around ●●●●●●: border of dots.
34	89·	Æ ·85	Similar.	Same inscr. around ●●●●●●: same border.
35	71·	Æ ·85	Similar type?	Traces of inscr. around ●●●●●●.
36	129·	Æ ·85	Similar type to no. 32: border of dots.	ΛΙΠΑΡΑΙΟΝ around ●●● ●●●: border of dots.
37	76·	Æ ·85	Similar.	Similar.
38	23·	Æ ·6	Similar.	Similar.

No.	Wt.	Metal. Size.	Obverse.	Reverse.
39	65·	Æ ·7	Similar type. Hephaistos holds by handle kantharos resting on stand.	[Λ] ΙΠΑΡΑΙ [ΩΝ] around ●● ●● ●●: plain border.
40	52·	Æ ·7	Similar.	Similar.
41	50·	Æ ·65	Similar type: border of dots.	Similar.
42	40·	Æ ·6	Similar type. Hephaistos wears pilos? no vase-stand: border of dots.	Similar: border of dots.
			Trias.	
43	94·	Æ ·7	Young Hephaistos, naked, seated r. on four-legged stool, holding mallet in lowered r. hand, extended behind, and small vase on l.	ΛΙΠΑΡΑΙΟΝ around ●●●: border of dots.
44	49·	Æ ·65	Young Hephaistos, naked, seated r., on four-legged stool, holding mallet in lowered r. hand, which rests on stool, and kantharos on l.	Similar inscr. and type.
45	40·	Æ ·6	Similar type: plain border.	ΛΙΠΑΡΑΙΟΝ Similar.
46	29·	Æ ·5	Similar type. Hephaistos holds by handle kantharos, which rests on stand.	ΛΙΠΑΡΑΙΩΝ around ●●●: border of dots.
47	23·	Æ ·45	Similar.	Similar.
48	23·	Æ ·5	Similar type: border of dots.	Similar.
			Hexas.	
49	55·	Æ ·6	Young Hephaistos, naked, seated r., on four-legged stool, holding mallet in lowered r. hand, which rests on stool, and kantharos on l.: border of dots.	ΛΙΠ; above and below which, ●, ●, connected by Ι: border of dots.

No.	Wt.	Metal. Size.	Obverse.	Reverse.
50	25·	Æ ·55	Similar type; vase obscure.	Similar.
51	26·	Æ ·55	Similar.	Similar.
52	21·	Æ ·55	Similar type; vase of uncertain form on l. hand: border of dots.	Similar.
53	19·	Æ ·45	Similar type; vase of uncertain form rests on stand: border of dots.	Similar.
54	15·	Æ ·45	Similar.	Similar.
55	13·	Æ ·45	Similar type; vase-stand not visible: border of dots.	Similar.
			Uncia.	
56	50·	Æ ·6	Young Hephaistos, naked, seated r. on four-legged stool, holding hammer in lowered r. hand extended behind, and vase on l.: border of dots.	Λ I between which ●: border of dots.
57	59·	Æ ·55	Young Hephaistos, naked, seated r. on four-legged stool, holding hammer in lowered r. hand, which rests on stool, vase on l.: border of dots.	Similar.
58	22·	Æ ·5	Similar.	Similar.
59	18·	Æ ·45	Similar type, obscure in details.	Similar.
60	17·	Æ ·4	Similar type, obscure in details; Hephaistos holds kantharos by handle: border of dots.	Similar.

No.	Wt.	Metal. Size.	Obverse.	Reverse.
			Class III.	
61		Æ ·8	Head of young Ares? l., laur.: border of dots.	ΛΙΠΑ ΡΑΙΩΝ Ornamented trident: plain border.

No.	Wt.	Metal. Size.	Obverse.	Reverse.
62		Æ ·8	Similar.	Similar inscr. and type.
63		Æ ·9	Similar.	Similar: plain border.
64		Æ ·85	Similar.	Similar.
65		Æ ·8	Similar.	Similar.
66		Æ ·6	Bust of Ares l., bearded, and wearing helmet with low crest.	ΛΙΠΑ ΡΑΙΩΝ Trident.
67		Æ ·65	Head of Poseidon? r., laur.: border of dots.	Similar.
68		Æ ·4	Similar type?	Traces of inscr. Ornamented trident.
			Class IV.	
69		Æ ·45	Pilos: border of dots.	Young Hephaistos, naked, seated r. on four-legged stool, holding hammer in lowered r. hand, which rests on stool, vase on stand? with l.
70		Æ ·65	Prow l.	ΛΙΠΑ / ΡΑ Dolphin l.: plain border.
71		Æ ·4	Lituus, head l.: border of dots.	Dolphin r.: plain border.
72		Æ ·4	Bunch of grapes: plain border.	Dolphin r.: border of dots.

Class V.

No.	Wt.	Metal. Size.	Obverse.	Reverse.
73		Æ ·75	Head of Poseidon? l., laureate: border of dots.	ΛΙΠΑΡΑΙΩΝ Young Hephaistos l., naked, holding tongs [and sceptre]: border of dots.
74		Æ ·8	Similar type.	Same inscr. Similar type.
75		Æ ·8	Similar type: border of dots.	Traces of inscr. Similar type: border of dots.
76		Æ ·7	Similar type.	Similar type: same border.
77		Æ ·7	Head of young Hephaistos r., wearing laureate pilos; behind, tongs.	ΛΙΠΑΡΑΙΩΝ Young Hephaistos l., holding tongs and sceptre.
78		Æ ·8	Head of bearded Hephaistos r., wearing pilos; behind, tongs.	Traces of letters. Young Hephaistos, running r., holding [hammer] in raised r., tongs in l.: border of dots.
79		Æ ·7	Head of young Hephaistos r., wearing laureate pilos; behind, tongs: border of dots.	ΛΙΠΑΡΑΙΩΝ Young Hephaistos, naked, wearing pilos, running r., holding hammer in raised r., tongs in l.: border of dots.

No.	Wt.	Metal. Size.	Obverse.	Reverse.
80		Æ ·6	Hephaistos, bearded? wearing pilos, running r., holding hammer in raised r., tongs? in l.: border of dots.	ΛΙΠΑ ΡΑΙΩ. Tongs l.: border of dots.

No.	Wt.	Metal. Size.	Obverse.	Reverse.
			Class VI.	
81		Æ ·7	ΛΙΠΑΡΑΙΩΝ Head of young Hephaistos l., wearing laureate pilos.	ΓΛΡΚΙΟ • Γ•ΧΣΩΝΕΥ. ΔΥΟΝΔ Tongs r.
82		Æ ·7	Similar.	Similar.
83		Æ ·8	Similar; on pilos, uncertain countermark.	ΛΡΚΙΟΣΛΕ (Λ doubtful) ΓΧΣΩΝΕΥΣ ΔΥΟΝΔ Similar.
84		Æ ·8	Similar; countermarked in same manner.	Same inscr.? Similar type.
85		Æ ·65	Head of Poseidon? r., laur: border of dots.	ΛΙΠΑΡΑΙΩΝ Military figure l., wearing crested helmet, lorica, and parazonium, holding spear and resting l. on hip: border of dots.
86		Æ ·7	Head of Poseidon? r., laur?	ΛΙΠΑ ΡΑΙ Female figure l., holding [patera] and long staff with two parallel cross-pieces at top: border of dots.
87		Æ ·7	Similar.	ΡΑΙ ΩΝ Similar.
88		Æ ·65	Similar type: border of dots.	ΛΙΠΑ ΡΑΙ Similar.

SARDINIA.

COPPER.

No.	Wt.	Metal. Size.	Obverse.	Reverse.
1		Æ ·9	M•ATIVS BALBVS • PR Young male head l.	SARD• P ATER Head of bearded warrior r., with head-dress resembling the crest of a helmet; behind neck, spear.
2		Æ ·95	Similar.	Similar.
3		Æ ·85	Similar.	Similar.
4		Æ ·85	Similar.	ꓷЯAƧ Similar type.

INDEX I.

GEOGRAPHICAL.

INDEX II.

TYPES.

F.

G.

H.

M.

N.

O.

P.

Q.

INDEX III.

REMARKABLE SYMBOLS.

INDEX IV. A.

KINGS, QUEENS, TYRANTS, &c.

INDEX IV. B.

MAGISTRATES' NAMES.

INDEX V.

ROMAN MAGISTRATES' NAMES.

R.

SEX · RVFO IIVIR, (so, rather than **REO**) Agrigentum, 22.

L· SEIO PROCOS, Panormus ? 128.

SEPT · EIBA · D · IIVIR, Panormus ? 128.

S.

SALASSO II VIR, Agrigentum, 22.

T.

P· TE, Panormus ? 127.

TRI, Panormus ? 128.

INDEX VI.

ENGRAVERS' NAMES.

INDEX VII.

REMARKABLE INSCRIPTIONS AND LEGENDS.

1. *Greek.*

K.

Λ.

Μ.

Ν.

Π.

Σ.

Τ.

Υ.

Φ.

2. *Latin.*

A.

ARC, Alaesa, 28.

C.

C · PAN, Panormus, 126.
COMITIAE, Agrigentum, 22.
CRYSAS, Assorus, 31.

D.

D · D, Panormus? 128 *seq.*
IIVIR, Agrigentum, 22; Alaesa, 28; Enna, 59; Panormus, 125, 128.

M.

MVN · HENNAE, Enna, 59.

P.

POR? Panormus, 124.
PROCOS, Agrigentum, 22; Panormus, 125; Panormus? 128.

Q.

Q, Panormus? 126; Uncertain, 241.

S.

SARD PATER, Sardinia, 265.

X.

X · L, Calacte, 32.

TABLE
OF
THE RELATIVE WEIGHTS OF ENGLISH GRAINS AND FRENCH GRAMMES.

Grains.	Grammes.	Grains.	Grammes.	Grains.	Grammes.	Grains.	Grammes.
1	·064	41	2·656	81	5·248	121	7·840
2	·129	42	2·720	82	5·312	122	7·905
3	·194	43	2·785	83	5·378	123	7·970
4	·259	44	2·850	84	5·442	124	8·035
5	·324	45	2·915	85	5·508	125	8·100
6	·388	46	2·980	86	5·572	126	8·164
7	·453	47	3·045	87	5·637	127	8·229
8	·518	48	3·110	88	5·702	128	8·294
9	·583	49	3·175	89	5·767	129	8·359
10	·648	50	3·240	90	5·832	130	8·424
11	·712	51	3·304	91	5·896	131	8·488
12	·777	52	3·368	92	5·961	132	8·553
13	·842	53	3·434	93	6·026	133	8·618
14	·907	54	3·498	94	6·091	134	8·682
15	·972	55	3·564	95	6·156	135	8·747
16	1·036	56	3·628	96	6·220	136	8·812
17	1·101	57	3·693	97	6·285	137	8·877
18	1·166	58	3·758	98	6·350	138	8·942
19	1·231	59	3·823	99	6·415	139	9·007
20	1·296	60	3·888	100	6·480	140	9·072
21	1·360	61	3·952	101	6·544	141	9·136
22	1·425	62	4·017	102	6·609	142	9·200
23	1·490	63	4·082	103	6·674	143	9·265
24	1·555	64	4·146	104	6·739	144	9·330
25	1·620	65	4·211	105	6·804	145	9·395
26	1·684	66	4·276	106	6·868	146	9·460
27	1·749	67	4·341	107	6·933	147	9·525
28	1·814	68	4·406	108	6·998	148	9·590
29	1·879	69	4·471	109	7·063	149	9·655
30	1·944	70	4·536	110	7·128	150	9·720
31	2·008	71	4·600	111	7·192	151	9·784
32	2·073	72	4·665	112	7·257	152	9·848
33	2·138	73	4·729	113	7·322	153	9·914
34	2·202	74	4·794	114	7·387	154	9·978
35	2·267	75	4·859	115	7·452	155	10·044
36	2·332	76	4·924	116	7·516	156	10·108
37	2·397	77	4·989	117	7·581	157	10·173
38	2·462	78	5·054	118	7·646	158	10·238
39	2·527	79	5·119	119	7·711	159	10·303
40	2·592	80	5·184	120	7·776	160	10·368

TABLE
OF
THE RELATIVE WEIGHTS OF ENGLISH GRAINS AND FRENCH GRAMMES.

Grains.	Grammes.	Grains.	Grammes.	Grains.	Grammes.	Grains.	Grammes.
161	10·432	201	13·024	241	15·616	290	18·79
162	10·497	202	13·089	242	15·680	300	19·44
163	10·562	203	13·154	243	15·745	310	20·08
164	10·626	204	13·219	244	15·810	320	20·73
165	10·691	205	13·284	245	15·875	330	21·38
166	10·756	206	13·348	246	15·940	340	22·02
167	10·821	207	13·413	247	16·005	350	22·67
168	10·886	208	13·478	248	16·070	360	23·32
169	10·951	209	13·543	249	16·135	370	23·97
170	11·016	210	13·608	250	16·200	380	24·62
171	11·080	211	13·672	251	16·264	390	25·27
172	11·145	212	13·737	252	16·328	400	25·92
173	11·209	213	13·802	253	16·394	410	26·56
174	11·274	214	13·867	254	16·458	420	27·20
175	11·339	215	13·932	255	16·524	430	27·85
176	11·404	216	13·996	256	16·588	440	28·50
177	11·469	217	14·061	257	16·653	450	29·15
178	11·534	218	14·126	258	16·718	460	29·80
179	11·599	219	14·191	259	16·783	470	30·45
180	11·664	220	14·256	260	16·848	480	31·10
181	11·728	221	14·320	261	16·912	490	31·75
182	11·792	222	14·385	262	16·977	500	32·40
183	11·858	223	14·450	263	17·042	510	33·04
184	11·922	224	14·515	264	17·106	520	33·68
185	11·988	225	14·580	265	17·171	530	34·34
186	12·052	226	14·644	266	17·236	540	34·98
187	12·117	227	14·709	267	17·301	550	35·64
188	12·182	228	14·774	268	17·366	560	36·28
189	12·247	229	14·839	269	17·431	570	36·93
190	12·312	230	14·904	270	17·496	580	37·58
191	12·376	231	14·968	271	17·560	590	38·23
192	12·441	232	15·033	272	17·625	600	38·88
193	12·506	233	15·098	273	17·689	700	45·36
194	12·571	234	15·162	274	17·754	800	51·84
195	12·636	235	15·227	275	17·819	900	58·32
196	12·700	236	15·292	276	17·884	1000	64·80
197	12·765	237	15·357	277	17·949	2000	129·60
198	12·830	238	15·422	278	18·014	3000	194·40
199	12·895	239	15·487	279	18·079	4000	259·20
200	12·960	240	15·552	280	18·144	5000	324·00

TABLE

FOR

CONVERTING ENGLISH INCHES INTO MILLIMÈTRES AND THE MEASURES OF MIONNET'S SCALE.

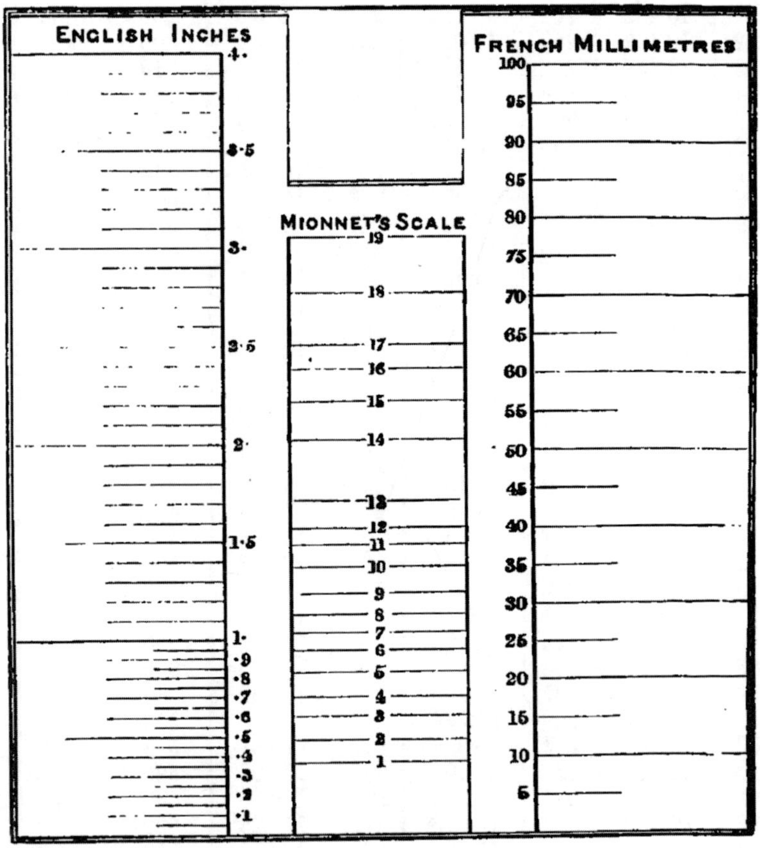

Woodfall & Kinder, Printers, Milford Lane, Strand, London, W.C.

Published by

Facsimile Publisher
Ashok Vihar, Delhi-110052 (India)
Website: www.facsimilepublisher.com

Distributed by

Gyan Books Pvt. Ltd.
5, Ansari Road, Daryaganj, New Delhi-110002 (India)
E-mail: books@gyanbooks.com, Website: www.gyanbooks.com

9 789333 017213